Managing in the Modern Corporation

In recent years, widespread organisational change in large corporations has almost invariably led to work intensification and increased stress for managers. *Managing in the Modern Corporation* explains how and why large companies have changed their organisational structures and philosophies, focusing in particular on how these changes affect the careers of middle managers. Based on in-depth interviews with over 200 middle and senior managers working in large corporations in the USA, the UK and Japan, it shows how the working lives of managers have been subjected to major disruption, involving work intensification and reduced opportunities for career progression. Furthermore, it argues that such widespread overwork and poor treatment of highly skilled and highly motivated staff has created a major international problem that must be addressed. The book discusses a range of solutions to this significant problem, suggesting that there are possibilities for saner, less brutal organisational environments.

JOHN HASSARD is Professor of Organisational Analysis at Manchester Business School, University of Manchester, and Fellow in Management Learning at the Judge Business School, University of Cambridge. Professor Hassard has published thirteen books, over a hundred research articles and received a large number of awards from UK research councils. He is currently a council member of the Society for the Advancement of Management Studies.

LEO MCCANN is Lecturer in International and Comparative Management at Manchester Business School, University of Manchester. He has conducted qualitative research in many large firms across several countries, from transitional to highly developed economies. He has published a number of articles on the subject of white-collar work in journals such as *Human Relations, Journal of Management Studies* and *Organization Studies*.

JONATHAN MORRIS is Professor of Organisational Analysis and Head of the Human Resource Management Section at Cardiff Business School, Cardiff University. He has written a number of books on human resource management and employment studies and regularly publishes in journals such as *Organization Studies, Journal of Management Studies, Public Administration* and *Human Relations*.

Managing in the Modern Corporation

The Intensification of Managerial Work in the USA, UK and Japan

JOHN HASSARD,

LEO McCANN

AND

JONATHAN MORRIS

CAMBRIDGE
UNIVERSITY PRESS

CAMBRIDGE UNIVERSITY PRESS
Cambridge, New York, Melbourne, Madrid, Cape Town, Singapore, São Paulo, Delhi

Cambridge University Press
The Edinburgh Building, Cambridge CB2 8RU, UK

Published in the United States of America by Cambridge University Press, New York

www.cambridge.org
Information on this title: www.cambridge.org/9780521845823

First published 2009

Printed in the United Kingdom at the University Press, Cambridge

A catalog record for this publication is available from the British Library

ISBN 978-0-521-84582-3 hardback

For Roisin, Kate and Catherine

Contents

Acknowledgements

We would like to thank the 251 executives, managers and supervisors in private and public sector organisations in Japan, the UK and the USA who volunteered to be interviewed in the course of this study. Without their help and cooperation this research would not have been possible. We would also like to thank the Economic and Social Research Council of the UK for funding the first three years of research. The research was entitled 'Management and New Organizational Forms: Middle Management in the UK, USA and Japan', (R000239288). Without this funding we would not have been able to complete the fieldwork in large-scale organisations on which this book is largely based. Our sincere thanks also go to Ms Seiko Kubo of the Japan Local Government Center for arranging access to several of our case study organisations in Japan. We would also like to thank Professor Yuji Yamasaki of the University of Kitakyushu and Professor Hirokuni Tabata of the University of Tokyo for their advice on the subject of Japanese organisational change and for the assistance they gave us with access to companies. Finally we would like to thank Sue Haffner of the Manchester Business School, University of Manchester, for her assistance in assembling the final manuscript.

About the cover

In seeking a suitable cover graphic for the book, we scanned literally hundreds of images on various websites; in the end we picked a simple paper-chain. As some readers may have guessed, this was chosen to resonate with the book that provides much of the inspiration for our study, Harry Braverman's *Labor and Monopoly Capital: The Degradation of Work in the Twentieth Century* (1974/1998), the cover of which features a similar paper-chain design. However, whereas Braverman's paper-chain from the 1970s is continuous and strong, ours of the new century is divided and weak: in contrast to Braverman's intact and united workforce, ours has been downsized and restructured.

1 | Going under the knife: Downsizing and de-layering the modern corporation

I think this will make us simpler, nimbler and quicker.

(Mark Hurd, CEO, Hewlett-Packard)[1]

One could be forgiven for thinking that the large, publicly listed corporations – for decades the economic cornerstones of modern developed societies – are now in crisis. Business change consultants regularly denounce them as organisational dinosaurs, collapsing under their own bureaucratic dead weight. In today's era of hyper-competition, so the argument goes, the management systems and organisational structures of large firms have become redundant, along with thousands of their employees. Firms are arguably obliged, under the pressures of globalisation and the logic of shareholder value, to become flatter, leaner and faster to react to changing conditions. As international competitive pressures grow in their intensity, those corporations that fail to restructure face stagnation or collapse.

This view, of the urgent requirement for corporations to change, has become widespread and influential since the 1990s. Media stories appear regularly of large blue-chip companies making significant job cuts, adding to the sense of corporate crisis. While job losses have always been a harsh fact of life under capitalism, white-collar workers were traditionally insulated from the risk of redundancy. Now their careers are more precarious. For example, in just three weeks in July 2005, Kodak, Sanyo, Hewlett-Packard and Asda all announced deep employment cuts to the British media, referring in their press releases to 'unnecessary' white-collar management and 'back office' staff.[2] The Ford Motor Company stated its plan to shed 14,000 salaried staff,

---

[1] 'New HP boss plans 14,500 job cuts', *The Guardian*, 20 July 2005.

[2] 'Asda cuts 1,400 managers in fight to stay No. 2 grocer', *The Guardian*, 6 July 2005; 'New HP boss plans 14,500 job cuts', *The Guardian*, 20 July 2005; 'Kodak cuts 10,000 more jobs as its film division weakens', *The Guardian*, 21 July 2005; 'Sanyo looks to shed 14,000 workers', *The Japan Times*, 6 July 2005.

one-third of the total, in September 2006.[3] Citibank announced its intention to shed 17,000 staff in April 2007, 'removing certain layers of management and eliminating some corporate offices'.[4] Indeed, since the onset of the 2008 global economic downturn similar announcements have become even more commonplace.

Such restructuring notices, however, are not restricted to the most open, flexible and liberalised market economies of the USA and the UK. High-profile, household-name companies based in all societies, even in Japan and Germany – until recently the standard-bearers for long-term employment and durable, committed capital – have undergone similar restructurings, including, for example, Sony, Siemens and Volkswagen.[5] No company, no matter how large, no matter how well regarded, appears immune from pressures to reform. Mainstays of the motor industry such as Ford, GM, Volkswagen and Mitsubishi repeatedly announce job cuts to the stock markets, citing reasons such as fierce competition, increased raw material costs and (particularly in US companies) rising healthcare and pensions liabilities. In a real sign of the times the UK's last remaining volume car manufacturer, MG Rover, finally collapsed in April 2005 after years of intense struggle, and what future it may have left lies in the hands of China's Nanjing Automobile Corporation. This collapse symbolises the apparent weakness of large-scale manufacturing in established Western countries, as the locus of production shifts ever eastwards.

The corporate squeeze is by no means restricted to the manufacturing sector. Just as manufacturers of consumer goods have subcontracted production to low-cost Asian firms, or opened greenfield plants in these countries, financial services companies have increasingly offshored jobs to English-speaking low-wage countries such as India and Sri Lanka. Again, the motivation for change is pressure to reduce costs, with this tending to exert more influence on the minds of senior executives than other pressures, such as customer service and the domestic retention of jobs and skills.

Amid the whirlwind of corporate change there is one group, however, that emerges unambiguously as 'winners' – a small cadre of elite

---

[3] 'Job cuts and sales slump could put Ford $9bn in red', *The Guardian*, 16 September 2006.
[4] 'Citigroup plans 17,000 job cuts', BBC News, 11 April 2007.
[5] 'VW may axe 30,000 jobs', *The Guardian*, 13 September 2005; 'Sony fights losses with 10,000 job cuts', *The Guardian*, 23 September 2005.

managers that has benefited from huge rises in salaries and stock options. Nevertheless, other stakeholders in the firm have not been so fortunate. Dramatic increases in executive compensation have frequently occurred hand-in-hand with job cuts and pay freezes for staff further down the organisational hierarchy (Erturk *et al.* 2004). Alongside such growing income inequalities in modern corporations there have also been concerns about gender and ethnic inequalities. Women and ethnic minorities are still under-represented in the higher echelons of corporate life (Hite 2007; Watts 2009). In other words, transformations in some areas of the corporation have been radical, but elsewhere change is slow. All kinds of organisational traditions (for good or ill) persist despite rounds of corporate change. So what exactly is happening to large-scale modern corporations?

Media stories about job loss and poor corporate performance have been commonplace for some time as companies have struggled to stay competitive in what is widely perceived as an increasingly turbulent and unpredictable world environment. This situation took a dramatic turn for the worse from October 2007 onwards when the full scale of what became known as the 'sub-prime mortgage crisis' started to emerge. The crisis originated in the USA, but it has made a heavy impact on all OECD economies; it demonstrated just how far these financial markets had exposed themselves to risk in their bids to achieve higher returns. All manner of companies and institutions displayed a cavalier attitude towards debt, ignored concerns about trading highly complex and vaguely understood new financial instruments, and rashly rewarded risk-taking employees with lavish bonuses. Supposedly arm's-length institutions, such as the UK's Financial Services Authority or the USA's Securities and Exchange Commission, which were supposed to regulate the finance industry, were exposed as weak and complacent, ceding the banks' excessive freedom of action following liberalisation and so-called 'soft touch' regulation. Rating agencies were guilty of providing falsely boosted ratings for all kinds of investment products as there were few incentives to provide lower, more realistic appraisals. Taken together, these effects generated the largest economic bubble since the Wall Street Crash of 1929.[6]

The ensuing bankruptcy of the venerable US brokerage Lehman Brothers and the hasty sale of Merrill Lynch in September 2008 were

---

[6] For an early academic assessment of the crisis and the possibilities for recovery, see Shiller (2008).

among the most dramatic examples of corporate failure in modern economic history. Their sudden demise triggered further market fallout across the world as investors panicked at the extent to which they had become exposed to sub-prime-related investment products which had collapsed in value. In an effort to prevent further bank failures, US Congress authorised the largest financial bailout package of all time, the $700 billion Troubled Asset Relief Programme (TARP), which provided capital injections to dozens of US banks. Similar relief packages were developed in other OECD nations (most notably in the UK) to bail out and partly nationalise their banks. Governments in Europe, Japan and the USA announced a series of fiscal stimulus packages of tax cuts and public works programmes in desperate attempts to reflate their economies.

It did not take long for large firms in other sectors to suffer following the investment banking collapses. Ford, GM and Chrysler requested financial bailouts from US Congress in their bids to avoid bankruptcy.[7] Citigroup announced a plan to make an astonishing 52,000 job cuts in late 2008, the largest announcement of cuts since those at IBM in 1993. Citigroup was eventually partly nationalised by the US government.[8] In the UK, BT expressed its intent to cut 10,000 posts, and Rolls-Royce 2,000.[9] All of the above took place in just one week in November 2008. That particular month saw a total of 533,000 job losses reported in the USA, the worst monthly figures since 1974.[10] Job losses also hit Japan. Its major carmakers experienced collapses in sales and cut thousands of temporary jobs in response. Sony announced the loss of another 8,000 posts in December 2008.[11]

Large workplaces have therefore experienced significant processes of change in recent times. Amid the stories of crisis and stagnation, most large firms hold massive financial assets. Some of them have annual revenues that dwarf the GDP of developing countries. Nevertheless, they are facing considerably tougher times than they did in the 1980s

---

[7] 'Big 3 automakers make bailout case to the public', *Washington Post*, 20 November 2008.

[8] '52,000 jobs to be cut at Citigroup', *USA Today*, 17 November 2008.

[9] '10,000 jobs to go as BT joins rush to cut workforce', *The Guardian*, 14 November 2008; 'Rolls-Royce plans 2,000 job cuts', BBC News, 20 November 2008.

[10] 'America isn't working: jobless total grows by most for 34 years', *The Guardian*, 6 December 2008.

[11] 'Sony to cut plants and 8,000 jobs', BBC News, 9 December 2008.

and early to mid-1990s. Corporations face increased levels of competition from domestic and foreign competitors. The logic of 'shareholder value' (although often misunderstood and overstated) is almost certain to exert more pressure on costs than in previous economic eras. In short, many powerful, household-name firms, headquartered in a range of countries, have been jolted out of their relatively stable existence and into a more complex and challenging era. This has had very serious implications for the livelihoods of their employees. The impacts of restructuring have been felt at many levels of the corporation. Traditionally it has been workers on the lowest rungs of the organisational ladder who have suffered most, through pay freezes, redundancies and the removal of fringe benefits. However, since the early 1990s, the burden of change has fallen increasingly on a hitherto rather better protected and better rewarded group of people – salaried white-collar middle managers.

This book is about the changing employment fortunes of managers in large corporations in America, Britain and Japan. It is based primarily on in-depth, life-history interviews with middle managers and strategy-focused consultations with senior human resource executives. Wherever possible, we have attempted to gain an 'inside' view of corporate restructuring. By this we mean making a detailed examination of both formal company structures and employees' subjective interpretations of changing working conditions. During times of change hitherto more secure conceptions of working life become subject to difficult transformations. What is meant by fair remuneration when reward levels differ so greatly? What is meant by loyalty when jobs are being cut? What is my real career position when hierarchies are being flattened? What am I worth when pay scales are being regraded?

In recent times middle managers in large corporations have been castigated from several directions. They have been most heavily attacked by the business 'gurus' and consultants who regularly condemn them as surplus to requirements in the new 'digital networked economy'. The widespread use of ICT has seemingly eliminated the need for many of the traditional roles of middle managers, such as monitoring the performance of front-line employees and conducting horizontal and vertical communication. Besides, the 'gurus' argue that tougher times call for tougher measures: that one cannot mourn the passing of 'cradle to grave' employment systems or shed a tear for the death of the kinds of privileges and stability that bureaucratic hierarchy brings. Out go long-service awards and retirement trophies, with these being replaced by performance monitoring and short-term financial bonuses. Organisational hierarchies are flattened as 'de-layering' policies strip out levels of management. Pay systems are transformed from tall 'scales' to broad 'bands'. Corporate headquarters are redesigned; boundaries between office and shop floor are (supposedly) removed as managers are encouraged to 'muck in' with the mundane work and 'buy in' to new corporate cultures. Welsh-born Sir Howard Stringer, Chief Executive of Sony, summed up this new order with a very Japanese turn of phrase: 'We must be Sony United, and fight like the Sony warriors we are.'[12] In short, ours is a leaner, tougher age in which all forms of corporate tradition are subject to revision or erasure. Just as large firms have faced up to increased competitive pressures in recent years, white-collar salaried personnel in many developed economies are confronting increasingly severe pressures in their working and personal lives.

In adopting a more local, personal perspective, and taking seriously the accounts of people on the receiving end of corporate transformation, this book attempts to cut through some of the hyperbole surrounding organisational change in order to provide a more 'grounded' analysis of the realities of restructuring than presented in, for example, excited press stories of 'corporate crisis', the 'death of the middle manager' and the 'slashing of jobs'. Rather than assert the widespread destruction of bureaucracy and the white-collar managerial class, our study suggests that while thousands of middle managers have indeed been eliminated from large corporations, many thousands more remain in gainful employment. Far from being redundant pen-pushers and time-servers, their roles have increased massively in scope and scale. The middle managers in this study almost universally described substantial changes to their work tasks, a major growth in their responsibilities and volume of work, but with significant shrinking of promotion prospects. These changes have important implications for middle managers' quality of life, morale, productivity and willingness to make continual sacrifices for the benefit of the firm. Interestingly, despite some clear differences in corporate governance across countries, and differences in the ways in which changes were executed across firms, seemingly the same organisational pressures are being felt by middle managers in all three countries studied, suggesting a surprising degree of *convergence* as regards

---

[12] 'Sony fights losses with 10,000 job cuts', *The Guardian*, 23 September 2005.

the changing role of middle management. Moreover, rather than accepting, at face value, current accounts of the trend towards 'organisational networks' and 'flows of digital information' – accounts that have become dominant in mainstream academic explanations of the modern corporation – our analysis suggests that bureaucracy and traditional top-down control, not to mention authoritarianism, are alive and well.

Some readers might regard our use of the phrase 'modern corporation' outdated given the recent discussions about 'postmodern', 'networked' or 'fluid' forms of organisation. We decided to use the more classical terminology as it reflects a long and distinguished history of discussion about the power and influence of large firms, and especially the relationship of that power to the broader society. The classic work of Berle and Means (1933) is still a critical reference point for these debates. It is perhaps more relevant than ever, given the continued accretion of corporate power since their day. The first edition was published during the Great Depression which was triggered by the dramatic Wall Street Crash of 1929, so further echoes to 2007–8 are obvious.

Berle and Means argued that the larger, more powerful and more influential the modern corporation grows, the more potential it has to cause social disruption when crises occur. Berle and Means were quite forceful in their original argument, suggesting that new forms of social and political power need to be developed to regulate and counteract the power of publicly traded corporations:

> Such a great concentration of power and such a diversity of interest raise the long-fought issue of power and its regulation – of interest and its protection. A constant warfare has existed between the individuals wielding power, in whatever form, and the subjects of that power. Just as there is a continuous drive for power, so also is there a continuous desire to make that power the servant of the bulk of the individuals it affects. (Berle and Means 1933: 353)

This phrase was highly prescient: Berle and Means could not possibly have imagined in the 1930s quite how powerful and potentially disruptive these firms, and the wider financial architecture into which they are embedded, would become. The need for a rebalance of social and corporate interests is precisely what is being discussed in the aftermath of the bank failures brought on by the sub-prime crisis. Their argument was recalled in more recent work on corporate governance by Smith and Walter (2006: 61–2, 271), who refer to Berle and Means' pertinent identification of the key issue of rebalancing social interests against corporate interests. Smith and Walters' very thorough and thoughtful study predates the sub-prime mortgage crisis, which is unfortunate timing. Perhaps in light of recent events they could have been even more forthright in their criticisms of recent practices that have led to the collapse.

While these debates are highly relevant to our discussions, the analysis we offer in this book differs somewhat from the above in that it describes the modern corporation from within; discussing how the corporation functions by an analysis of the daily working world of its white-collar managerial employees.

In the remainder of this chapter, we discuss the extent to which large organisations have engaged in major restructuring. We take an historical approach to this question, observing the changing nature of firms themselves and the shifting philosophies surrounding issues of management, hierarchy, authority, work, loyalty and career. We delve into the sociological 'classics' of the US corporation and its white-collar staff dating back to the 1950s (e.g. Drucker 1947, 1964; Mills 1953; Whyte 1960) to demonstrate that in a bygone era, issues of collegiality, stability, loyalty and mutual gain were given a much higher profile, in the minds of both management and staff. We suggest that recent disruptions to traditional career structures, while possibly leading to increased worker involvement and larger financial rewards (Barley and Kunda 2004), have also been accompanied by reduced employee security, widespread job losses, heightened performance pressures and increased stress levels. Although the cutting of jobs and entitlements has been less severe in Japan than in Western countries (Jacoby 2005; Matanle 2003; Robinson and Shimizu 2006; Iida and Morris 2008), the flattening of managerial levels, diminution of loyalty and collegiality, and the intensification of labour result from very similar organisational restructuring measures taken by top management.

How much corporate change?

As the previous section indicates, structural changes to large corporations have been substantial since the 1980s. In response to renewed competitive threats, firms have attempted to cut 'unnecessary' ranks of management (often dismissed as 'bureaucracy') and subjected themselves to the tenets of 'lean' thinking, ending the 'entitlement culture' of the firm and making significant reductions in headcount. In the last thirty years large firms across the world have engaged in making major cuts to their employment levels. Burke and Nelson (1997: 325) state that more than 43 million US jobs were eliminated between 1979 and 1996, and that 90 per cent of the firms in a Canadian survey no longer offer job security to employees (1997: 326). Cameron *et al.* (1991: 58) state that more than 85 per cent of the *Fortune* 1000 firms downsized their white-collar workforce between 1987 and 1991, affecting more than five million jobs, and that '[a]lmost a million American managers with salaries exceeding $40,000 lost their jobs' in 1990. Many other studies provide similar evidence of widespread cuts, reduction of employee entitlements and collapsing morale (Heckscher 1996; Gowing *et al.* 1998; McGovern *et al.* 1998; Burchill *et al.* 1999).

However, it would be wrong to assert that the era of restructuring in large firms has meant universal downsizing and employment cuts. Under certain circumstances the headcount figures for large corporations have grown. This is what Littler and Innes (2004: 1160–3) call the 'paradox' of managerial downsizing; i.e. despite widespread reports of redundancies and corporate shrinkage, macro numbers of managers have often increased through, for example, mergers and acquisitions, movements into new markets, or simply through the retitling of staff as 'managers'.[13] Froud *et al.* (2006: 16) reveal that the total numbers of employees in large firms in the UK and the USA have been surprisingly stable in recent times. In 1983 the average FTSE 100 firm employed 36,548 staff. This number rose to 48,185 in 1990 before declining to 44,741 in 2002. In the USA, there is even less change. The average S&P 500 firm employed 36,421 in 1983, a figure that crept to 44,517 in 2002. A similar picture is painted by Matanle's research on levels of corporate growth in Japan (2003: 88–9). Data on job tenure in the UK also shows limited change (Doogan 2001), with several analysts noting in recent years that the widely held view of increasing job insecurity is a myth, based on unsubstantiated 'nightmare' scenarios that posit a radical new environment of flexibility and constant change (as popularised by high-profile commentators such as Anthony Giddens and

---

[13] One senior HR manager we interviewed in the US Hospital case study disparagingly referred to this latter phenomenon as 'title creep'.

Richard Sennett: see Fevre 2007).[14] White *et al.* (2004) suggest that the flattening of UK firms was 'short-lived' (2004: 61), and that expansion of employment grades is now the norm as internal labour markets and career jobs make a comeback. Our study also suggests that significant de-layering now seems to have largely halted, although firms still threaten staff with further employment cutbacks on a regular basis.

So the commonly held view of post-1990 corporate life being associated with widespread downsizing and the slashing of employee entitlements is one that requires moderating. While there certainly have been major cuts and restructuring exercises, firms have not necessarily been getting smaller, as job reductions at one time are offset by endogenous growth and merger and acquisition activity at others. Baumol *et al.* (2003: 259–61) argue that downsizing has only really taken place in manufacturing, a sector of the economy that of course has been contracting since the late 1960s. Contrary to the popular view, the majority of firms in Baumol *et al.*'s sample (large US companies making regular press announcements of redundancies) actually grew their labour forces by at least 10 per cent during the period of their survey.

On the other hand, at the day-to-day level of individual business units and workplaces, the managers in our study (and in other studies, such as Worrall *et al.* 2000; Grimshaw *et al.* 2001; Beynon *et al.* 2002: 140–4; White *et al.* 2004) categorically assured us that managerial job cuts have been made, and a multitude of white- and blue-collar staff have left their businesses in recent years. Moreover, they describe in detail how companies have reduced their dependence on traditional, open-ended employment contracts, increasing their deployment of part-time, contract, flexible and otherwise contingent labour. It was extremely common to hear that, following a corporate restructuring exercise, surviving managers were working longer hours and operating under greater pressure to 'perform' than they were previously.[15] As

---

[14] One explanation for the apparent stability of the macro labour market numbers is that such quantitative studies tell us little about the realities of life within large firms. Even though there may be significant degrees of employment security, there can be massive insecurity regarding an employee's role. Furthermore, the numbers tells us little about senior managers' motivations in making employment changes, and the feelings of insecurity created by frequent internal reorganisations.

[15] The increase in the volume of work for surviving managers is reported even in the more mainstream, managerialist literature which is otherwise relatively

for the flattening of managerial hierarchies, this was also widespread, having occurred in the vast majority of our UK, US and Japanese case corporations. Such changes (downsizing and de-layering) generally took place in numerous 'rounds' of restructuring since the mid-1990s, with the US firms usually embarking on both types of change earlier than their UK and Japanese counterparts. According to the literature and our own research, major changes in US corporations started to take place around 1987–8, with UK firms starting to follow suit around 1994–5. Similar changes in Japanese firms generally took place rather later, around 1999–2002, and their reforms have been less radical (Jacoby *et al.* 2005).

What have been the major impacts of these changes? Analysts have made some bold statements and uncovered significant evidence of change. According to Barley and Kunda (2006: 45) recent reforms are 'shaking the foundations' of employment in the United States. White *et al.* (2004: 178) describe 'tumultuous' change in Britain. And Japan has undergone a 'particularly dramatic environmental change', in the words of Robinson and Shimizu (2006: 44). Much of the mainstream literature that makes a 'business case' for change (Hammer and Champy 1993) is optimistic about such restructuring, and describes the results as making firms more flexible and responsive to customer demand and financial necessity. In a similar vein is the work of Arthur and Rousseau (1996) who argue that organisational restructuring can liberate managers from the corporate straightjacket, thus encouraging 'boundaryless' or 'portfolio' careers.

On the other hand, most of the critical academic (such as Beynon *et al.* 2002; McCann *et al.* 2004) and journalistic accounts (such as Fraser 2001; Bunting 2004) are highly pessimistic, describing large-scale job loss, widespread employee anxiety and unmanageable, even health-threatening, workloads (Green 2006). Noer (1998) and Cascio (1998) paint particularly depressing pictures. Noer (1998: 219) goes as far as to suggest that 'full-time, permanent employees are an endangered species. All employees are now in a sense temporary.'

It is easy, however, to get seduced by the drama of organisational change. Indeed, it is not uncommon for observers to overstate both the

enthusiastic about restructuring, e.g. 'As a result of downsizing, for example, fewer numbers of employees were left in the firm to do more work and, frequently, to do a more complex set of tasks than before. [...] Management burn-out was a common complaint' (Cameron *et al.* 1991: 53–4).

degree of change and its positive or negative results on employees and
their organisations. One of the most obvious examples of such exaggeration is Richard Sennett's *The Corrosion of Character* (1998), which
tells a story of social fragmentation and personal identity crisis brought
on by corporate change. Despite the fact that the book is based on
extremely sketchy and anecdotal evidence, this has not dented its popu-
larity, reputation or sales figures.

Serious analysts of organisational change, therefore, must address the
question of whether their assessments of the results of restructuring are
overly pessimistic. In a refreshingly honest passage, Barley and Kunda
(2004: 23) describe how their approach to studying contract IT specialists (many of whom had been 'restructured out' of large employers such
as IBM or Cisco Systems) had changed markedly as they listened to
workers' stories. Initially they were convinced by the view that:

[C]ontingent work was a clear and unambiguous social problem. Temps and
contractors were victims of systemic changes promulgated by exploitative
employers acting entirely in their self-interest without regard for the common
good. [...] As sociologists with a background in industrial relations and a taste
for left-of-centre politics, our initial response was to side with the institution-
alists and to treat the rhetoric of market freedom with a healthy dose of
disbelief, if not cynicism. (Barley and Kunda, 2004: 24–5)

However, their basic analytical orientation was to change when many
of the contractors they interviewed spoke glowingly about life outside
the giant corporations, describing themselves as 'free agents' in command of their own destiny, unshackled from managerial authority and
gaining larger incomes. Indeed, the pessimistic picture that is so often
painted by workplace analysts can be overblown. Away from the darker
sides of corporate restructuring may lie a more upbeat world, one in which
change has been positive for employees, even emancipatory. Several studies of workplace change describe committed employees, working on
more interesting and rewarding tasks, possibly earning higher pay, even
when they are overstretched and overworked (Thomas and Dunkerley
1999). A fairly upbeat appraisal is also provided by White *et al.* (2004) for
the UK, although they too express concerns about overwork and stress
(2004: 102).

Our analysis, based on over 200 interviews with middle managers
and approximately fifty interviews with senior HR managers/executives,
offers partial support for both positions, optimistic *and* pessimistic. We

uncovered a complex situation. There have been some improvements to the outward appearance of life in large companies: several managers spoke of more enlightened, less secretive and less authoritarian behaviour by their bosses. However, this took place alongside a steady and constant increase in performance pressure and work intensification, with a general lengthening of the working day and week. The focus on short-term results, motivated by firms' renewed attention to 'shareholder value', radically reduced the time-frame in which work was expected to be completed. Work spilled over into the home as the boundaries between the two became increasingly blurred; this being compounded both by access to new technologies (e.g. email, text, BlackBerry) and by the pressing burdens of what we call the 'new organisational ideology' (see McCann *et al.* 2004) – the set of ideas and precepts about what working life demands and requires that have emerged and become orthodox over the last fifteen to twenty years. For some middle managers, keeping in contact with work and colleagues bordered on the obsessional. Although not often admitted as such, fear appeared to play a major role in this 'work addiction' – fear of job loss, fear of poor appraisals (and loss of bonus pay), fear of being labelled a failure, fear of a crisis developing at work when absent and unable to rectify, and fear of being totally swamped by work at a later date if parts of the backlog are not tackled now. And if 'now' means evenings, weekends or even while on vacation, then so be it.

Understandably, we became concerned by the scope and scale of penetration of this ideology. It certainly does seem to contribute to a more stressful working life for white-collar managers. Although there was evidence of major revisions to corporate structures and organisational forms, there was however little to suggest a real shift towards 'post-bureaucracy' or the 'boundaryless organisation' as advocated by organisational theorists such as Ashkenas *et al.* (1995) and Heckscher and Donnellon (1994), or even a genuine devolvement of power. Our managers told us that authoritarianism and top-down rule were alive and well – although change has certainly taken place, it has not resulted in an end to bureaucracy or hierarchy. Working hours were long, and appeared to be lengthening. The demands of work could rarely be met, and middle managers fought ongoing battles to stay on top of their workloads.

The culture of the organisation rested on spoken and unspoken assumptions that employment in a large firm reflected, as Rapoport *et al.* (2002: 6) have suggested, a 'model of professional commitment and associated work devotion [...] underpinned by the concept of the ideal worker who has unlimited time available to spend at work'.[16] Louise Roth, in her study of the experiences of female traders on Wall Street, describes a similar work environment of 'around-the-clock devotion' (2007: 26–8). Our study of middle management in a variety of settings suggests that this culture of total commitment exists equally strongly in less rarefied settings. In many cases, the idea of the devoted worker rested on underlying gendered assumptions that women can be relied on to support male workers with the 'unspoken work' of family support (Hochschild 1997; Reis 2004; Roth 2007: 27), especially in Japan (Ogasawara 1998). This culture of total submersion in work created extreme difficulties for staff with family commitments, and especially for female middle managers. Unsurprisingly in this context, stress and anxiety were problems not just at middle management level, but throughout the corporation. Although the HR community and some enlightened elements of senior management were aware of the problem of middle management workload stress, seemingly little was being done to resolve the problem in a genuine fashion.

What struck us forcefully, despite the demanding and often fraught nature of the workplaces we studied, was the competence and dedication of the middle managers within. One of the major explanations for their heavy workloads was precisely that levels of responsibility had increased significantly. Despite such demanding work pressures, these managers nevertheless appeared highly able and committed to achieving both personal and corporate goals. Many spoke highly of their workplace and their colleagues. As such, the impression we formed was that the widely held stereotype of the middle manager as an obstacle or anachronism in the modern corporation should be re-evaluated.

We did begin to appreciate, however, why cutting middle management jobs is such a seductive proposition for senior management wishing to demonstrate its ability to deliver 'leaner', more agile and more profitable organisations. If middle managers are conceptualised as 'dead wood' then de-layering managerial ranks and cutting the white-collar payroll should almost by default accelerate decision-making, enhance performance and

---

[16] For example, the impact of highly demanding work on family time is captured well in Watts' (2009) study of female professionals in the civil construction industry, and in the more general study by Rapoport *et al.* (2002).

deliver better shareholder value. Nevertheless, as numerous studies have shown (Smith 1990; Heckscher 1996) middle managers have always been more than simple executors of downward decisions. They have frequently been in post longer than senior management and have a heightened sensitivity to matters 'on the ground'. Sacrificing white-collar staff on the altar of competitiveness means ridding the organisation of localised skills and experience. It can also mean severing senior management's link to others in the organisation. This can be highly dangerous (Huy 2001). Organisational change is difficult to implement, costly and risky. So why do firms insist on putting themselves through such a process on a regular basis?

Why restructure?

Despite the promise of substantial cost reductions and the possible acceleration of business processes, various studies have shown that restructuring brings with it hidden costs. Cascio's (1993; 1998) work in the USA shows that downsizing, in particular, is very risky. Back in 1993 he argued that the majority of radical restructuring exercises have not resulted in the gains hoped for by top management and market analysts. Instead, the common result is diminished morale, increased fear and lower productivity, particularly when downsizing is carried out 'indiscriminately' (1993: 101). Cascio (1998) later reported (in a study of 311 downsized firms) that employment reductions by themselves do not lead to financial improvements.

Elsewhere Fisher and White (2000) argue persuasively that downsizing can badly damage firms' capacities for learning and innovation, while Burke and Nelson (1997: 326) report findings from a survey in Canada in which 61 per cent of firms reported decreased morale. Burke and Nelson also argue that 'survivor syndrome' is a major problem for restructured corporations – denial, depression and distrust affect those 'fortunate' enough to escape the cutbacks (see also Noer 1993; 1998).

A survey by Burchill *et al.* (1999) of white-collar staff in twenty large British firms is particularly pessimistic. They provide a general picture of stress and insecurity, with one of Burchill *et al.*'s (1999: 8) senior executives stating bluntly that he requires '[a] workforce that can be picked up and put down whenever I need them'. Their findings as regards 'increasing stress' (1999: 46) and 'lack of trust' (1999: 36–7) were particularly concerning, with 44 per cent of staff claiming to trust management 'only a little or not at all'. Work intensification was also 'very significant' (1999: 30), with 64 per cent of respondents reporting an increase in the speed of work, and 61 per cent an increase in effort.

Concerns about life in the modern corporation are not only raised in academic debates. Mainstream literature, such as surveys commissioned by the consultancy Accenture, point to similar results in the USA. According to one of its studies, only 28 per cent of middle managers were positive about their prospects for advancement, and one-third of respondents described their organisations as 'mismanaged'.[17] Another Accenture study reported more of the same in nine countries across Europe, the United States and Asia.[18] Elsewhere, 85 per cent of the respondents to the HR consultancy Roffey Park's annual survey of UK employees claimed to work longer hours than they are paid for (Garrow and Stirling 2007: 43), and 85 per cent claimed to experience stress (Gifford *et al.* 2009: 7). Green's (2006) highly detailed analysis of social survey data (2006) suggests that although wages and affluence have generally increased in the OECD countries, and jobs are not nearly as insecure as many analysts claim, the *quality* of jobs has declined significantly, mostly because of increased managerial control over work processes and intensification of work demands.

If the surveys suggest that restructuring hurts employees so much, why are firms so keen to implement it, particularly given the ubiquity of 'employee empowerment' and related HR rhetoric? The key might lie in the realm of finance. A particularly important aspect of corporate life since the 1980s has been the degree of dependency of large firms on financial markets (Golding 2003: 228). As demonstrated by Froud *et al.* (2006: 39), corporate finance has moved away over time from debt and has increasingly relied on securitised assets. Financial markets are fickle, demanding and unforgiving; they are more and more unwilling to tolerate wastage and tardiness, and it is frequently employees who become squeezed in the often desperate attempts to cut costs and reduce time-frames. There are whole sectors (most notably industrials) that are

[17] 'US Middle Managers' Satisfaction with Employers Drops, Accenture Survey Finds', accenture.com website, story posted October 2005: http://accenture.tekgroup.com/article_display.cfm?article_id=4275
[18] 'Middle Managers Worldwide Are Unsatisfied', accenture.com website, story posted in January 2007: http://digitalforum.accenture.com/DigitalForum/Global/ViewByTopic/TechnologyCareers/0701_managers_ww_unsatisfied.htm

perennially lowly valued by stock markets, and others (such as basic materials extraction, oil and gas, pharmaceuticals and banking) that are highly (or over) valued. This is one of the reasons why the liberal market economies of the USA and the UK have wound down so much of their heavy manufacturing over the last twenty to thirty years, whereas the 'coordinated economies' of Germany and Japan – whose firms are comparatively less dependent on share capital (see Froud *et al.* 2006: 39–40; Vitols 2001) – have retained much more substantial industrial bases.

On the other hand, it is important not to get too carried away with the shareholder value logic arguments of Lazonick and O'Sullivan (2000), for as Froud *et al.* (2000: 80–7; 2006: 36) have convincingly argued, shareholder value is a 'loose rhetoric'. There are numerous kinds of shareholders with different objectives and motivations. Moreover, the performance of securities is clearly not the sole concern of corporate senior management. If delivering shareholder value was their sole *raison d'être* then Ford, for example, would possibly stop making cars and turn its attention to financial services. Although the expansion of credit facilities was a major focus of the former Ford CEO Jacques Nasser (Froud *et al.* 2006: 265–81), it would almost be inconceivable for Ford to exit the automotive industry for good. Therefore, alongside delivering improved returns to shareholders, to be successful firms must also, for example, improve product design, overhaul their marketing systems and offer better customer service. We must remember that large firm restructuring has been very widespread in countries such as Japan, France and Germany, where the capital markets are considerably less dominant, suggesting that shareholder value logic cannot be the sole factor driving firms in their recurrent attempts to streamline operations and ramp up performance.

It should also be noted that the variety and availability of different competitors' products are now so widespread that firms' offerings have to be highly competitive. Firms face a danger of losing sight of product competitiveness if they focus too hard on shareholder returns (Porter 1990: 730). Furthermore, and perhaps more importantly, firms frequently engage in what Littler (2006) calls 'false signalling', and so we should always be sceptical of the extent of restructuring actually carried through. Such announcements to the stock exchange (which are often later reported in alarmist newspaper articles) can serve not only to overstate a firm's intentions to reduce headcount, but also to create a short-term uplift in share prices (Baumol *et al.* 2003: 1, 28–62).[19] This signalling, then, is part of a longer-term 'narrative' of management performance (Froud *et al.* 2006) in which CEOs demonstrate their intent and ability to deliver sustained returns to investors, often by invoking rhetoric around 'harsh but necessary' restructuring. Once again, the complexity of the situation must be considered. Neither the mainstream view of the 'business case for change' or the critical interpretation of firms 'recklessly downsizing' should be taken at face value.

Aside from the underlying corporate motives, does restructuring actually yield better performance results? Again, opinion differs. There have been a number of analysts who have answered in the affirmative. The substantial, and largely unpredicted, recovery of the US economy from the mid-1990s led many to believe that corporate America had successfully responded to risky but urgent surgery. Michael Best (2001: xi) opened the preface to *The New Competitive Advantage* with the phrase 'What a difference a decade makes.' The change in tone from his highly pessimistic 1990 book was striking. He essentially argued that the prescriptions he made in 1990 for restructuring business processes and responding to the Japanese threat had now been achieved with admirable success. The highly respected and influential strategy author Michael Porter also gave a damning verdict on the USA in 1990 (Porter 1990: 723–33), but noted much-improved performance in the 2004–5 *Global Competitiveness Report*, in which the USA was once again ranked the most competitive economic environment in the world (Porter *et al.* 2005). Amid the general pessimism of Burke and Nelson's 1997 article, they also claimed that downsizing had improved productivity (1997: 326). For slightly different reasons, Barley and Kunda (2004; 2006) were also surprisingly sanguine about the results of organisational change, at least for highly skilled and entrepreneurially minded IT experts. In the UK meanwhile, White *et al.* (2004) provided an upbeat picture, and Porter *et al.* (2003) were also guardedly optimistic that large UK firms had understood the challenge of competitiveness and were roughly heading in the right direction: that of flexibility, heightened employee mobility and 'high skills'.

---

[19] Baumol *et al.* (2003: 1) in fact cite several econometric analyses that contradict the popular view that job-cut announcements have a temporary uplift effect on share prices.

Others, however, have been less positive. Froud *et al.* (2000a; 2000b; 2006) point to the very modest financial results of organisational restructuring, with senior management being the only obvious winners, not shareholders or customers. They suggest that 'serial restructuring is likely to be a negative process for labour that generates transitory benefits for capital' (Froud *et al.* 2000b: 771). Burke and Nelson's review of the literature in the 1990s agrees that 'the goals of such organisational changes were rarely, if ever, realised' (1997: 325). They go on to cite damning figures from the US Department of Labor that suggest 'a $1 investment in a portfolio of downsizing firms would yield $1.047 three years later. In comparison, the same investment in a portfolio of firms in the same industry that did not engage in downsizing would yield $1.343 in the third year.' (1997: 327). In what is probably the first in-depth study of the impact of downsizing in America by economists, Baumol and his colleagues (2003: 261–2) demonstrate that downsizing has not led to improvements in productivity or share values, although it has led to increased profits because of the squeeze on labour – the so-called 'dirty little secret of downsizing'. Cascio (1993; 2002a) has argued for many years that restructuring measures usually do not result in improved results, largely because of the hasty and ill thought-out methods of execution. Osterman *et al.* (2001) express deep concerns about how restructurings in the USA have meant substantially reduced conditions for the employees who have borne the brunt of these reform measures. This is a problem of particular concern when one considers how well rewarded senior executives have been during the same period. Ackroyd (2002: 259) is also somewhat pessimistic about the competitiveness of the UK economy, suggesting that it 'manufactures the wrong sorts of things (low value-added goods) in inefficient ways (undercapitalised plants which rely too heavily on contributions from labour which is not well educated or trained)'. He concludes that 'it is not at all clear that the interests of the British economy or the people of Britain are being well served' (2002: 262) by corporate restructuring that results in the reduction of employee entitlement alongside the enrichment of top executives (2002: 89–90).

Interestingly, during the time we were researching (2003–7), Japan, arguably, appeared to be coming out of its prolonged recession. Suddenly market analysts and fund managers were talking positively about the country once more. A major question, therefore, and one that relates to both Japan and to the USA and the UK, is whether the improved macroeconomic results during this period were due to the success of reform measures, however painful they may have seemed.

This is a tough question to answer. It is not obvious that one can make the analytical jump from assessing the impact of large-scale organisational change to passing verdict on the performance of national economies. Speaking to our senior HR executives and middle managers about this issue has led us to believe that company performance has improved somewhat compared to the 1980s, but that this has come at the expense of a severe harshening of the terms of employment for many employees, including the middle managers that we were observing. Although restructuring can lead to moderately better financial results, this rarely, if ever, culminates in a major turnaround of corporate performance, for the simple reason that restructuring is ubiquitous. All firms are engaged in a continuous process of rethinking their systems and strategies in order to improve their market share and stock prices, and the net result is that few companies surge ahead and that nobody can be complacent. Struggles over organisational restructuring never rescind, and the threat of change never fades.

Restructured firms probably are leaner, more internationalised and more responsive to customer demand than they once were. However, their financial results are typically far from encouraging, and the results as regards employee well-being are far worse. Our study repeatedly uncovered very concerning evidence of stress, overwork, low morale and insecurity, and we interpret this in terms of the new organisational ideology, rooted in capitalism's very nature. The incessant demands of the international economy are worked out at the level of employees in their firm, and nowhere is this struggle more visible than in the everyday exertions of white-collar professionals.

Our interpretation, therefore, shares ground with Braverman's (1974/1998) classic work on blue-collar workers. He famously asserted the 'degradation of work' as technological innovations and the profit motive drive down skill and autonomy levels of workers as progressively greater numbers of people, organisations and processes get drawn into the workings of an internationalising capitalism. While our evidence does not support Braverman's notion of 'de-skilling' – in fact our middle managers described increasing skill and responsibility levels – the overall picture of exploitation, strong labour control and work intensification of middle managers corresponded very closely with that described in *Labor and Monopoly Capital*.

Braverman's coverage of managerial labour is not particularly extensive, but he asserts that:

Management has become administration, which is a labor process conducted for the purpose of control within the corporation, and conducted moreover as a labor process exactly analogous to the process of production, although it produces no product other than the operation and coordination of the corporation. (Braverman 1974/1998: 267)

This is a contentious statement, and one that has been criticised by Armstrong (1989: 308) as overly simplistic and running counter to Braverman's main thesis. However, there is a large grain of truth here. Modern corporations are squeezing staff in their attempts to deliver enhanced performance and cut costs, and this includes managerial staff. Moreover, the single-minded insistence on cost reduction and work intensification does not always lead to improved results in terms of market share or shareholder value. We suggest that many large firms are still getting by on the goodwill of white-collar employees, and that this well is in danger of running dry, particularly as firms have for some time been providing only modest returns to shareholders and labour but large financial rewards to senior executives. However, given the pressures of international capital so vividly described by Braverman, such a rethink is unlikely. The next section reviews evidence of the impact of restructuring on white-collar managers.

Assessing the impacts of restructuring on middle managers

As the huge literature on company strategy, organisational change and workplace relations continues to grow and mature, the fortunes of middle management become linked with a progressively larger set of issues. This includes the logic of shareholder value (Froud *et al.* 2000a; Lazonick and O'Sullivan 2000; Williams 2000), the productivity of firms and nations (Best 1990; 2001; Porter 1990; Porter *et al.* 2005) and the technological capacity, skills and intellectual capital of firms as they attempt to emulate the 'high performance work systems' necessary for survival and prosperity in the highly competitive new global marketplace (Appelbaum and Batt 1994; Appelbaum *et al.* 2000). Other authors cover the impact of restructuring on employment and sectoral change and the decline of traditional manufacturing (Hirst and Zeitlin 1990) and the demise of a national industrial policy (Ackroyd

2002: 244–69). Our intention in this section is to review the literature on this issue in order to provide a backdrop to the findings we present in the later chapters. Again, there is a wide range of opinions on the matter. Many authors claim that corporate restructuring has had serious negative consequences for white-collar professionals, but others are far more positive.

Clearly the life of the middle manager has undergone major changes since its depiction by C. Wright Mills (1953). His description of the classical bureaucratic white-collar life does not sound especially attractive today. This is just the sort of existence rejected by Barley and Kunda's (2004) IT specialists. The tiresome rigidity and narrow scope associated with classical bureaucracies have been strongly challenged in recent years. Senior management has made considerable efforts to change the old-style top-down, command and control mentality, resulting in cost savings and, in some cases, a rejuvenation of the managerial labour process. A central concept of this change, clearly revealing the profound influence of Japanese-inspired 'lean' thinking (Womack *et al.* 1990), has been employee 'empowerment' and downward devolvement of decision-making. But such change can also have unpleasant side effects: expansion of role and responsibility is not always accompanied by expansion of pay, and when considered within the context of headcount reduction, surviving staff are often forced to take on the work of those who have left.

Downward devolvement of authority, while in principle a laudable concept carrying connotations of a more democratic workplace (which may indeed happen in some cases), is similarly described as 'a better way of doing things' than what went on before. Flat structures, flexibility, devolved decision-making and teamwork are staple concepts of MBA programmes and consultant prescriptions. Such ideas have even penetrated as far as the US military, as bureaucracy becomes a target for elimination:

The US military had come a long way since Vietnam [...]. The men directing the Iraqi campaign had come of age during the Vietnam conflict, when top brass tended to micromanage every firefight, robbing ground commanders of initiative and spontaneity. There was more willingness now to let officers in the field respond and adapt to fluid situations. (Zucchino, 2004: 129)

Alongside the shift of emphasis away from hierarchy is a process of individualisation. Instead of the collective we associate with classical understandings of large workplaces (Mills 1953; Whyte 1960), the individual is now championed, as performance-related bonuses and broad banding replace national payscales and collective bargaining, and corporate loyalty becomes widely regarded as a thing of the past. A weakened and simulated collectivity is promulgated by management (as exemplified by Wal-Mart's company songs) amid a harsher reality of cost-cutting and minimal wage growth. Although unpopular, bureaucracy is actually essential to the running of all large organisations (Hales 1999; du Gay 2000). Hales aptly describes not the fashionable concept of 'post-bureaucracy' but 'bureaucracy-lite', in which bureaucracy stays in place, but amid a new organisational ideology in which individuals must take on more responsibility, have wider spans of control and increased workloads.

The devolvement of authority must, therefore, be considered in the light of the reduction of staff that many firms have experienced. Although lower-ranked staff may in theory have more authority to run things 'on the ground' this is not decentralisation as traditionally understood (for example, the 'classical' decentralisation of GM under Sloan: see Chandler 1977; McCraw and Tedlow 1997: 285–8). Some literature emanating from the discipline of business strategy argues that middle managers can be important players in 'bending the ear' of senior executives and helping to shape firm strategy (Dutton and Ashford 1993; Dutton *et al.* 1997). Unfortunately we did not come across much evidence of this in our study. The kind of decentralisation we found involved devolvement of authority alongside cuts to employment numbers, which tended to mean a centralisation of core strategic goals and concepts and the re-establishment of top management prerogative. Senior management's core message in the 2000s is communicated down the hierarchy clearly and repetitively, similarly to how it was done in the time C. Wright Mills was writing. According to the managers spoken to in our study, so-called 'devolvement' in this context usually meant loading extra work onto the shoulders of staff. If there were greater numbers of colleagues among whom to share the workload, then perhaps the downward devolvement of authority would be more welcome. Downward devolution of authority and widening responsibilities are commendable concepts, but they rarely work out so well for employees in practice given the cost-cutting and job-reducing context in which such change tends to take place. Although one positive effect of restructuring reported by middle managers was that their work has become more interesting and rewarding, the downside was that it has certainly got tougher and more demanding.

Who are the middle managers? And why study them?

It is worth considering in more detail exactly who middle managers are. The study of the middle ranks of management has a long history, but it is one strewn with polemics and opinion-pieces. There is little theoretical development. In this section we briefly overview some classic pieces of literature and draw out common analytical themes.

The business and management literature has always had problems defining exactly who middle managers actually are (McCann *et al.* 2004: 30). Huy (2001: 73) usefully defines them as 'any managers two levels below the CEO and one level above line workers and professionals'. But this tells us little about who they are and what they do. In general, this is a problem throughout the literature: many analysts have a lot to say about middle managers, but few have ever developed cogent theoretical-analytical accounts of them.

Exemplified by C. Wright Mills' brilliant polemic *White Collar*, middle managers are often cast as pitiful, unromantic characters (Mills 1953: xii). This is not to say that they are unimportant. The white-collar everyman is described in a peculiar 'love-hate' fashion in much of the Western literature. He is pitied yet envied, puny yet powerful. Here Mills (1953: 88) describes the contradictory and multi-layered nature of middle management:

Seen from the middle ranks, management is one part people who give you the nod, one part system, one part yourself. White-collar people may be part management, like they say, but management is a lot of things, not all of them managing. You carry authority, but you are not its source. As one of the managed, you are on view from above, and perhaps you are seen as a threat; as one of the managers, you are seen from below, perhaps as a tool. You are the cog and the beltline of the bureaucratic machine itself; you are a link in the chains of commands, persuasions, notices, bills, which bind together men who make decisions and men who make things; without you the managerial demiurge could not be. But your authority is confined strictly within a prescribed orbit of occupational actions, and such power as you wield is a borrowed thing. Yours is the subordinate's mark, yours the canned talk. The money you handle is someone else's money; the papers you sort and shuffle already bear someone else's marks. You are the servant of decision, the assistant of authority, the minion of management. You are closer to management than the wage-workers, but yours is seldom the last decision.

William H. Whyte is even more unsympathetic to them, damning the massed ranks of bureaucrats as unthinking, quasi-socialist automatons. But even here there was still a grudging respect. Whyte (1960: 8) describes middle managers as 'dominant members of our society'. The Cold War rhetoric implicit in this kind of literature describes a fear that corporations and their armies of faceless managers have become too powerful, suppressing the rugged individualism, entrepreneurship and executive iron will that the United States was supposedly built on. During this post-Second World War period, both the size of the giant corporation and the numbers of middle managers were growing rapidly. From a more leftist position, Galbraith (1967) argued in *The New Industrial State* that large corporations and government agencies had grown so much in stature and influence that they disproved the classical economic doctrines of 'free' markets. Similar arguments were made by Chandler (1977): the growth of managerial power vested in large corporations amounted to a 'visible hand' that is the true driver of economics, not the abstract 'laws' of supply and demand.

Although their growing power is readily acknowledged, throughout the classic literature there is little sympathy for middle managers, a feeling that survives in much of today's literature (with the partial exception of Japan, where white-collar staffers have traditionally received more favourable treatment in media and popular culture; see Matanle 2003: 9). Middle managers are described as dependent creatures, currying favour from above and slavishly communicating top management's orders down to the bottom ranks. Compared to manual workers (such as the downtrodden toilers on car production lines: see Beynon 1986; Fine 2004) they have never been romanticised in academic or popular sources. There appears nothing heroic about attending meetings or shuffling papers. This has contributed to the generally depressing nature of the literature on middle managers. This gloomy portrayal pertains both to their widely perceived irrelevance and obstructive nature as depicted in the mainstream consulting or 'guru' literature, and to their insecurity, stress and overwork emphasised so strongly in the more sympathetic, industrial relations, sociology of work or labour-process analyses. There are few sources on middle management that provide a more upbeat picture, except possibly the small strand of strategic management literature that claims middle managers can and should influence top management strategy development (Dutton and Ashford 1993; Dutton *et al.* 1997; Balogun 2003). One exception is an article by Huy (2001) entitled 'In praise of middle managers', in which he argued that they are actually highly skilled, committed and knowledgeable workers who possess broader social networks within the firm than those of senior management. They are, therefore, best placed to communicate with, and appreciate the needs of, other stakeholders. While our evidence supports this sympathetic appraisal of middle managers' skills and unique position in the geography of the organisation, it does not, in general, back up the optimistic idea that they should, and do, influence top management decision-making. Rather, a labour process-inspired interpretation of middle management's role in the large firm appears more accurate: white-collar managers are just as much subject to top-down labour control as other members of the firm, even if this control often appears voluntary, and is rarely manifested in direct supervision and outright authoritarianism.

   The study of middle managers tends to proceed hand-in-hand with the study of the nature and performance of the large organisations that house them. Older, more technical, studies on white-collar life contain far fewer moral judgements about middle managers, although their value is somewhat limited by the straightjacket of functionalist sociology that dominated the era. One of the first 'scientific' approaches to studying large firms was March and Simon's *Organizations* (1958), in which the emphasis is firmly placed on routines and standardisation of procedure. In keeping with much of the literature of this era, it claimed that there was 'one best way' to manage firms and their staff, involving a kind of 'managerial Taylorism' (Taylor 1911), a strict division of tasks and the elimination of conflict and confusion. This was a highly stylised depiction of organisational life, devoid of the conflict and human realism that figure in later studies. Partly this could be explained by the 'scientific' tone of sociology of that era, and by the restrictive political environment of the age, when the logic of the Cold War and the threat of state socialism were highly influential. This limited the degree to which academic texts could speak with a critical voice, and resulted in rather apolitical, technical and de-humanised descriptions of large companies that downplayed the role of organisational conflict, notably that between management and labour. Hassard (1993), for example, offers a critical review of the literature which focuses on the structural-functionalist tendency underpinning much of the mainstream received wisdom of management studies. More historically oriented studies of corporate affairs were provided rather later by business and labour historians, such as Chandler (1977) and Jacoby (1997). And in 1961, Burns and Stalker published *The Management of Innovation* (reissued with a new preface in 1994) which further established the scientific-technical approach to studying the behaviour of firms. This approach framed the development of later works of industrial sociology and organisational administration by pre-eminent social scientists of the day such as Blau and Meyer (1987), Alfred Stinchcombe (1974) and Henry Mintzberg (1973). Stinchcombe's *Creating Efficient Industrial Administrations* (1974) exemplified the genre. For a detailed review of this literature, see Handel 2003: 5–16, 39–44; Hassard, 1993: 4–48).

The prescriptive tone of these classic works lives on in the 'managerialist' or 'guru' literature of today, a vast publishing industry devoted to popularising the ideas of star consultant/academics such as Michael Hammer, Charles Handy and Tom Peters. This industry really emerged in the early 1980s as the first signs of real struggle for the US economy emerged. A slow-growth economic climate ensured steady growth in the market for new management ideas. As writers such as Abegglen and Stalk (1988), Dore (1973), Rohlen (1974) and Vogel (1980) highlighted the strengths of the Japanese economy, concerns became widespread in the US business literature about the likelihood of being caught up and overtaken by Japanese firms and their sophisticated manufacturing and management techniques.

Amid the growing pessimism about US large firms, several high-profile books emerged in the 1970s and 1980s that contained more detail about the actual lives of managers, including the growing number of white-collar women (Kanter 1977). The afterword to the 1993 edition of Rosabeth Kanter's *Men and Women of the Corporation* tells a downbeat story of the state of US firms, and suggests a need for urgent change. Kanter's book is an excellent ethnography of 'Indsco', a classical US industrial behemoth that was essentially living in the past. She argues that firms such as Indsco are overly exclusionary and hierarchical, and that they need to share power and devolve it in order to improve staff morale and corporate performance. This idea is further developed in Kanter's *When Giants Learn to Dance* (1989a), a more general book about the parlous state of large US bureaucratic firms that mixes the close ethnography of *Men and Women* with more consultant-like prescriptions.[20] Many other influential books emerged around this time, symbolised by Peters and Waterman's best-selling *In Search of Excellence* (1987) and Hammer and Champy's *Re-engineering the Corporation* (1993), along with others putting forward the 'business case' for downsizing, de-layering and business process engineering in order to meet the demands of what Best (1990) called *The New Competition*.

At around the time the 'gurus' were sharpening their surgical tools, Robert Jackall's *Moral Mazes* (1988) provided a fascinating and uncompromising insight into the culture and ethics of corporate life in the 1980s. He paints a realistic and gritty picture of internal struggles, and documents the ruthlessness of some individuals in climbing the corporate ladder; his managers talk of a 'take the money and run' mentality (1988: 94–5). According to Jackall, the US corporation was characterised by aggression, secrecy and male dominance. His organisation is a monolith, a blunt instrument of scale and scope, in which there is no place for subtlety or flexibility, neither in terms of its business strategies nor of the behaviour of its managers. The US corporation appeared as an anachronism: a sclerotic, short-sighted juggernaut, staffed by ruthless, selfish bureaucrats. The organisation and its staff were unable to meet the challenge of the highly coordinated, flexible and lean Japanese firm and its highly skilled and loyal workforce. Similar findings appear in Starkey and McKinlay's (1994) article on managers at Ford, although here the need for change was at least acknowledged, if incompletely applied.

In the late 1980s to 1990s, work emanating from the disciplines of political science, comparative economics and industrial relations were also highly critical of the US or 'Anglo-Saxon' model. Authors who had researched the successes of the Japanese or German model, such as Dore (1973; 1987) and Vogel (1980), argued that the chronic dependence of US and UK firms on share capital made them averse to the long-term thinking that was the bedrock of Japanese and German success. The flagship firms of these countries, based on more 'patient' capital offered by long-term credit from closely aligned banks, were able to invest in

---

[20] Kanter's book, along with Peters and Waterman's *In Search of Excellence* (1987) has received some rough treatment from more critical academic analysts. It would be fair to point out, however, that Kanter is one of the few 'business case for change' authors who consistently draws attention to the dark side of restructuring, especially the increasing pressures it places on staff and their families (1989: 291–4).

new technologies and higher skills, providing higher value-added goods at competitive prices, and offering seniority-based employment that resulted in higher morale and better performance from loyal staff (Amable 2003: 1–2). According to this picture, the behaviour of top management of the Anglo-Saxon firms was not encouraging in meeting this challenge. Rather than adopt the successful principles of Japanese or German capitalism, they indulged in further short-termism, slashing costs through mass downsizing exercises in an attempt to impress financial markets.

By the end of the 1990s, therefore, discussions around middle management life had come full circle. The 'cold warriors' of the 1960s used to express concerns that organisations and their bureaucrats had become too powerful and had 'subjugated the many to the whims of the few' (Barley and Kunda 2004: 24). But in the globalising world of the twentieth and early twenty-first century, many observers of corporate change worry that both the corporation and its middle management staff have been emasculated (Smith 1990; Heckscher 1996), and that cuts to organisations have been unnecessarily damaging (Burke and Nelson 1997; Sennett 1998; Cascio 2002a, 2002b). As Pfeffer (1998) argues, corporate America's first reaction in a downturn – to cut costs and employee entitlements – is not always the best one. Therefore, instead of bemoaning the overbearing size and influence of large corporations, certain contemporary authors now advocate the defence, or reconstruction, of the traditional longer-term employment focus of the large firm.

Restructuring now occupies centre stage in most studies of management and organisation. The grudging respect of middle managers from the 1960s gave way to either criticism of their perceived uselessness (Peters 1992; Hammer and Champy 1993), or sympathy as to the new toughness of their plight (Sennett 1998). More recent works have built on the ethnographic tradition of Kanter (1977), Jackall (1988), Heckscher (1996) and Smith (1990), providing in-depth studies of white-collar work in a variety of settings, such as IT specialists in Silicon Valley (Barley and Kunda 2004), or life assurance sales staff in Tokyo (Graham 2003; 2005). These studies offer different kinds of evidence and arguments, but the themes of organisational change, the crisis of the monolithic firm and individualisation of work are very prominent.

Mills' classic description of the 'managerial demiurge' (1953: 77–111) was a damning one. His interpretation bears much in common with

Weber's 'iron cage' metaphor or Habermas' 'colonisation of the life-world' thesis – of organisational dystopias staffed by thousands of faceless bureaucrats subsumed into the system. However restricting this form of white-collar working life might have been (and the reader has to digest healthy servings of exaggeration in Mills' text), the paternalism and security of large firms in the classical period did possess several advantages that have gradually been destroyed in recent years. The onset of corporate change has meant that the system is being fragmented, and we essentially argue in this book that some of it should be saved. In particular we are concerned with defending the loyalty, reward, respect and longevity associated with secure employment. We are in favour of the protection from arbitrary treatment that can be provided by trade unions, and argue that greater wage equality, plus a more collegiate, cooperative environment that is less overwhelming of staff time, are praiseworthy concepts. Sustainable success is invariably built on firm employment foundations, including hiring, supporting and retaining core staff by treating them with dignity (Pfeffer 1995/2005). Despite the excited claims of much of the 'New Economy' and globalisation literature, economic life is not all about accelerating change, hyper-competition and fluid networks. Stability and discipline, and investments in loyal and trusted workforces, may be a better strategy for delivering high performance than constant change, an obsession with flexibility and radical innovation, and hiring celebrity CEOs. Even some of the best-selling 'guru' literature would support part of this argument (Collins 2001; Walker 2006: 121). In short there is a huge danger in overstating the need for change and the imperative for a radical rethink of bureaucratic structures and the kinds of employment systems they imply (but of course a 'no change' story neither sells books nor consultancy services!).

Over time the institutions of bureaucracy, the history of the firm (what a senior HR manager in our USBank2 case study described as a firm's 'DNA'; see Chapter 3) and trade union influence, have all served as brakes on senior management's ability to restructure and force through radical change. However, all over the USA and the UK (and to a lesser extent Japan), these brakes are being released. For new firms these brakes were, in fact, never installed. The disembedding of large firms from the traditions of the 'managerial demiurge' has meant a reasserting of senior management authority, leading to reduced security, senior executive wage inflation and ramped-up demands on all staff with little in the way of increased pay to compensate for work intensification.

The arguments in favour of high inequalities in incomes as a form of incentivisation likely to induce higher corporate performance are continually reinforced in the US business media and the more mainstream parts of business and management studies. It has come to something when some Japanese observers also agree. In a response to an article that praises US firms which have adopted Japanese-style wage compression, long-term employment and 'symbolic egalitarianism' (Pfeffer 1995/2005: 101), Toru Hatano, a consultant at Nomura, makes the counter-claim that Japanese firms should move to 'results/performance-based wages and broad banding systems' and eliminate '"bad" egalitarianism' (Hatano 1995/2005: 107). Dore (1996) also details the diminution of traditional Japanese wage equality. A more outspoken and simplistic attack on the egalitarianism of Japanese workplaces published by Japan's Research Institute of Economy and Trade and Industry argues:

Japan's income distribution is probably the most equitable among all the nations of the world, and a widening of the income gap would do the country more good than bad. There must be a change of mindset from equality of outcome to equality of opportunity, so that hard work is rewarded. (Kwan 2002)

This view is unfair on Japanese white-collar workers who, in our experience, were generally working hard and making sacrifices in trying times. Kwan (2002) and others, such as Kosai (2002) and Hatano (1995/2005), to a greater or lesser extent advocate the introduction of a US-style culture of performance-related bonuses, employment flexibility, a market for senior management talent and higher wages to 'best performers'.

Although some of these changes appear reasonable when the conformity, authoritarianism and lack of democracy of Japanese workplaces are considered, there are genuine grounds for concern associated with the destruction of employment security, the individualisation of the workplace culture and the increased likelihood of top management 'value-skimming'. Japanese firms would be well-advised to recognise that the wholesale introduction of US management concepts and tools, such as the highly lauded reforms of General Electric under Jack Welch (Froud *et al.* 2006: 299–368) may not necessarily be compatible with the ideology of Japanese organisational life. The most powerful finding of Froud *et al.*'s work is that all the painful and controversial financial and organisational re-engineering of Anglo-Saxon firms since the late 1970s have resulted in such modest results. If the critical analysis of Froud *et al.* were to be replicated across the multitude of firms found in the Japanese post-bubble recession, similar results might be found.[21]

The Japanese reformist view is backed by mainstream HRM thinking (itself mostly a North American creation), put forward by HR advocates such as Pfeffer (1995/2005: 101) who argues for both higher rewards for higher performance and symbolic egalitarianism – where executive carparks are abolished and 'everyone wears a blue smock'. Pfeffer's version is actually less individualistic than most – he defends long-term employment security and is critical of firms that engage in cutbacks and retrenchment as an automatic reaction to tough times – but the HR world is a peculiar mixture of US and Japanese influences. It is not easy to blend the (Japanese-influenced) ideas of few visible differences between management and labour, 'lean' thinking, employee empowerment, centralisation and long-term internal strong HR departments, with the (US-influenced) concepts of financialisation, shareholder value, boundaryless careers, decentralisation and relatively weak HR departments, but this is the organisational alchemy that so many current analysts attempt to pull off.

This review of some of the main contributions to the literature on middle management indicates that large private firms, at the time the classic works such as Whyte (1960) and Mills (1953) were published, were similar in many ways to public sector bureaucracies, featuring lifetime employment for workers, stable markets and minimal risk and uncertainty (Jacoby 1997). Indeed, this stability is still true in some sense today (see the JSteel case study, Chapter 5). But over the course of the 1980s and 1990s, large firms in the UK and the USA increased their levels of debt gearing and risk, and chased higher returns (Golding 2003: 73). In Japan, the recession of the 1990s brought about over a decade of soul-searching, some high-profile bankruptcies and a clamour for change. These long-term pressures on Anglo-Saxon

---

[21] We would like to thank Dr Peter Matanle of the University of Sheffield's School of East Asian Studies, for this point.

and Japanese capitalism have meant harsher performance pressures, job cuts and a move away from seniority reward systems alongside higher potential bonuses for high-performing survivors and for senior management.

In the process of interviewing middle managers and senior HR executives, we took the view there was no genuine prospect of a return to the traditional, long-term paternalistic Chandlerian firm, but that some of its features, notably its tendency towards more equal financial rewards and concern for long-term employee development were, and still are, laudable concepts. The extreme pace and pressure of modern corporations are not, in our view, particularly conducive to dignified working lives. We were concerned by the demands that restructuring placed on middle management through role expansion and widening spans of control, and particularly disturbed with how many middle managers responded to these pressures without much apparent resistance. To paraphrase Bunting (2004) and Fraser (2001) they appeared very much as 'willing slaves' in the 'white-collar sweatshop'. Senior management had very successfully inculcated this kind of regime in which major personal sacrifices were regularly made to the firm, and no alternatives were considered, either by senior management initiating change or by the middle managers at the receiving end.

To what extent then do senior management's imperatives for change and exhortations to greater effort actually 'filter down' to middle managers? Is there any scope for middle management resistance to top management restructuring drives? Much of the mainstream, managerialist literature claims recalcitrant middle management is one of the key stumbling blocks on the path to organisational renaissance. Perhaps surprisingly, our research did not reveal much direct resistance to the new organisational ideology. There was some evidence of middle managers refusing to get too heavily drawn into the overwork culture; a much more common feeling was resigned compliance. This is, however, to anticipate the analysis of the coming chapters, and this issue of resistance will be dealt with in more detail below. The penultimate section of this chapter discusses another element to our story – in researching large employers across the three countries, we also examined how far the new ideology of organisations has penetrated into other sectors of work and employment where there are far fewer direct connections to financialisation and globalisation: the public sector.

Restructuring public administration: Different roots, similar outcomes

The public sectors of all developed societies, despite their popular notion as sleepy environments, have actually been subjected to numerous efficiency drives as states (just like large firms) look to bring their cost structures under control. The Labour government in the UK has been heavily influenced by the US economist Robert Reich and his arguments as made famous in *The Work of Nations* (Reich 1991). As Bill Clinton's Secretary of Labor, Reich was instrumental in promoting radical new models for delivering public services. Bunting (2004: 132) also suggests that the influence of Osborne and Gaebler's *Reinventing Government* (1992) was substantial in the refashioning of the UK Labour Party before its election in May 1997. Reformist governments such as this were 'fascinated by a new model of public administration gaining credibility among American Democrats which might be able to achieve a better standard of services without costing the earth' (Bunting 2004: 132).

Our conversations with managers in the public sector in Japan, the USA and, especially, the UK, indicated that the imperatives for restructuring were felt to a substantial degree even in these environments. The new organisational ideology, therefore, is not just derived from the direct pressures of economic globalisation, but by the politics of restructuring – the fashions for organisational change, for 'lean' management principles, for cutting out wastage and bureaucracy and inculcating a 'performance culture' modelled on cutting-edge multinational corporations.

In our case research of city administrations in the three countries studied, the UK city council had undergone the most dramatic alterations, and it was here that the labour process of the middle managers was the toughest and most intensified, and where their employment was the least secure. This took place within a major policy initiative to cut costs and downsize many parts of the UK public sector infrastructure. An 'Independent Review of Public Sector Efficiency' published in 2004 under Sir Peter Gershon claimed that cost savings of £20 billion could be made by 2007–8, involving a profound cull of jobs. It specifically targeted the middle ranks of employment in an attempt to cut waste and redirect funds into front-line services. Gershon argued for the elimination of 80,000 posts in four years (Gershon 2004: 20). At the time of writing (late 2008), HM Revenue and Customs is nearing completion of its programme to remove 12,500 posts before 2009 (with a possible further 12,500 to come).[22]

Research into Japanese public sector work is sparse in the West, and little is known about the pressures for reform, other than brief news coverage of the privatisation and reform of Japan Post.[23] In our observations of a city council in West Japan, we uncovered substantial imperatives for change and significant restructuring. Perhaps ironically, it was the city council in north-western USA that had exhibited the least evidence of major change. Across all the city councils we found senior management attempts to flatten hierarchy and accelerate decision-making. There was some evidence of a devolvement of authority, and some very serious complaints of increased work pressures and workloads among public sector managers. Morale in the public sector is even more of a concern than in the private sector firms, because these public servants have not received the increased financial returns that have offset the deterioration of working conditions for so many private sector managers.

Our tentative findings on public sector white-collar life point to the conclusion that something more than the simple direct imposition of global market forces is at work. There is a new ideology to consider, of flatter, leaner and more responsive large organisations that pervades the mindset of senior managers, consultants and reformist politicians. We argue that this 'new organisational ideology' ought to be subjected to critical scrutiny if organisations are genuinely to consider the needs of their overstretched and under-pressure white-collar staff.

Conclusions

It has probably become clear by now that we share a concern with highlighting the less palatable sides of organisational restructuring. Having spoken to many committed yet under-pressure managers who were making sacrifices for the (assumed) good of their firms, we became sympathetic to their stories. In order to contextualise and understand the changes wrought on them we turned to the traditions of labour process theory. The classic insights of Harry Braverman (1974/1998),

---

[22] 'First fall in public-sector jobs for 8 years', *The Guardian*, 14 September 2006.
[23] 'Japan's postal shake-up approved', BBC News, 14 October 2005.

although much maligned in recent years, have an enormous contemporary relevance to our story of ratcheted pressures and reduced
entitlements. We acknowledge some of the weaknesses of Bravermanian
analysis – e.g. its dated insistence on class antagonisms and de-skilling
(Littler 1982; Littler and Salaman 1982; Penn and Scattergood 1985),
sparse coverage of agency and subjectivity (Armstrong 1989; O'Doherty
and Willmott 2001) and limited and simplistic discussion of the managerial labour process (Teulings 1986) – but are nevertheless strongly
attracted to its understanding of the rationalising principles of capitalism;
principles that are regularly translated into tougher conditions for workers, particularly labour intensification and the removal of security. These
last two features were strongly and repeatedly found in our research.
Throughout the following chapters we will make reference to the white-
collar labour process, and part of the book's aim is to develop a more
in-depth and realistic approach to studying the labour process of middle
managers, coverage of which was rather thin in Braverman (Armstrong
1989). We will return to this issue in the final chapter, offering some
possible ways forward for research in this area.

In developing this theoretical angle, we emphasise the role of social
structure and political economy. In recent times there has been a proliferation of new concepts and philosophies in the fields of management
and organisational studies. These have included post-structuralism,
post-modernism and a focus on symbolism, identity and culture in
organisations. While we welcome a plurality of approaches, we have
become concerned that the basic sociological story of modern work
organisations, involving a tangible and realistic explanation of the
tougher edges of the new capitalism, is not adequately accounted for
in these heterodox perspectives. What principally interests us in this
study is not only the internal, personal interpretations of changing work
lives by themselves, but understanding what are the economic and
organisational drivers behind these changed times; how the changing
structures of contemporary capitalism impact on the lives of working
people, for better or worse (see Mills 1953: xx).

Post-modernism perhaps 'overpsychologises' labour and organisation (Tinker 2002). Although we do attempt to do justice to people's
agency and their personal interpretations of events, we still insist that
social structures are real, and operate on a level that is often beyond the
control of individual actors. Structures (particularly those associated
with economic trends and market forces) have powerful roles in shaping

and influencing organisational forms and personal action. Counter to the obsession with discourse, identity formation and 'identity work', storytelling, language and textual analysis that dominates a great deal of recent work in management and organisation studies (including work on middle management – see Thomas and Linstead 2002; Sims 2003; Sveningsson and Alvesson 2003), we approach our subject with a greater sensitivity to the role of forces beyond the scope of individual agency. Middle managers' stories by themselves are only part of the story; a more complete picture is created when these narratives are linked into a broader discussion of the changing nature of contemporary capitalism. We sympathise, therefore, with the approach taken by Beynon and his colleagues, in arguing for 'a touch of realism' (Beynon *et al.* 2002: 34–6), and Reed (2005) when he calls for 'retroductive' analysis.

The motivation for this approach stems from our concern with the dangers of a subjectivist 'slide'. While we would not wish to deny the importance of individual subjectivity, storytelling and agency – for we base much of our analysis on qualitative life-history interviews after all – we do take issue with authors who deny or downplay the explanatory role of social structure. Instead we argue that the processes of organisational change – restructuring, financialisation, downsizing, de-layering and the removal of employee entitlements – are real, knowable processes. Organisational change is stimulated by the deliberate decision-making processes of senior managers as they react to developments in the wider political economy. Senior managers, therefore, are responsible for the decisions they take. Indeed, many have received enormous personal financial pay-offs from the changes wrought. During this time, lower level white-collar workers, on the other hand, have been subjected to duress.

Furthermore, senior management, despite the rhetoric of increasing competition and the imperatives of shareholder value, does have some degree of choice in how it goes about the task of organisational change. Although broader economic forces are clearly real and pressing, responding to them with downsizing and intensification of labour are not the only courses of action available. The ways in which restructuring has been carried out did differ between our case study companies, with some employers at least attempting to give consideration to ameliorating the harshest effects of change on affected staff (for example, see the Japanese firms' almost universal refusal to indulge in redundancies, and the seriousness with which some of the UK companies consulted and interacted with their trade unions – see below, Chapters 4 and 5).

In relation to this topic, one last point should be added before we move on to discuss the nature of our study. Organisational form is an important, but by no means the sole determinant of company success. The strong assumption in the 'business case for change' literature is that organisation reforms, especially those built around a charismatic CEO, based on a clear philosophy or narrative of performance improvement, and embedded in a recognisable set of metrics such as high-performance work systems (Appelbaum *et al.* 2000), or Six Sigma, are universal in both their appropriateness and (positive) effects on performance. Both assumptions are highly questionable, particularly in an international context. A substantial publishing industry has emerged over the last couple of decades arguing that what Jack Welch achieved at GE, for example (see Froud *et al.* 2006: 299–388), can be effectively copied and rolled out to other diverse firms operating in other sectors or countries. In the real world, this is far from likely. The worlds of commerce and industry are complex and difficult places, in which corporate 'success' or 'failure' (besides being rather relative and elastic concepts) depend on all kinds of complex – if not uncontrollable – factors. These factors include the shifting fortunes of product and financial markets, geographical position, customer whims and the availability of technology, skills and people. This book, therefore, will not make statements as to the success or failure of different case study firms' restructuring measures. What it aims to do instead is to offer a detailed and fair portrayal of the struggles of organisational life – i.e. in terms of senior management's attempts to elicit strong growth through 'effective' organisational forms and people management, and for white-collar managers' attempts to survive and even prosper after firm restructuring.

2 | Exploring corporate life: A realist view on management restructuring

[O]ne of the great tasks of social studies today [is] to describe the larger economic and political situation in terms of its meaning for the inner life and the external career of the individual.

(C. Wright Mills, 1953: xx)

Gaining access to large organisations to conduct research inquiries can be extremely difficult. When the topics of inquiry include such sensitive issues as job cuts, stress and employee dignity, the task can be made considerably tougher. Adding an international element to the mix complicates matters yet further, especially when one of the nations to be studied is Japan, a country renowned for complex trusted relationships, and where requests for information from outsiders are met with silence, or guarded responses shrouded in corporate *tatemae*.[1] These concerns were prominent in our minds as we embarked in 2003 on what was to become a five-year research project. This chapter begins by describing the processes we went through in gaining access to the giant firms that feature in the book. It then goes on to cover the methodology and theory that underpin our study.

Access to the firms across the countries did at times prove difficult, but in general it was far from insurmountable. Many companies in the UK and the USA declined to give assistance. In Japan, our access was dependent almost entirely on what our intermediaries could arrange for us. What we found extremely rewarding, however, was that once companies had agreed to put forward their senior and middle managers to meet us, the vast majority of them were extremely candid, open and

---

[1] *Tatemae* means surface level behaviour and language, or the way in which a person is supposed to behave in public or in official roles. On the other hand, *honne* refers to the more genuine feelings that a person tends to keep private. For a detailed discussion of the *honne-tatemae* distinction in Japan see Graham (2003: 233–7). The frustrations experienced by a Westerner working in this kind of environment are described well by Mehri (2006).

39

opinionated. This was also true in Japan, although the staff we spoke to there were sometimes less forthcoming than British and American respondents. Having said that, they still provided a wealth of fascinating information about the restructuring measures taken in Japan and their own opinions on their effects.

Across the three countries we deliberately chose large firms for our case studies, because typically they have histories of bureaucratic, hierarchical management systems. We chose to omit newer firms (such as IT start-ups or venture capital-funded ones – although some of our firms produced decidedly high-tech products) because we were particularly interested in assessing the extent of change to more traditional bureaucratic forms. Although some of the literature on high-tech firms paints a picture of dramatic, but not necessarily negative, change for employees (Barley and Kunda 2004; Best 2001), the focus on eye-catching, 'leading edge' firms might not be representative of what was being experienced more generally. The aim across the three countries was to access firms in the following sectors: automotive manufacturing, banking, business services, electronics, engineering, steelmaking, utilities and, finally, from the public sector, healthcare and local government.

Once we had arranged access, on our first visit we would hold a group interview between the three authors and each organisation's senior HR representatives. Occasionally, the HR person was accompanied by another member of the HR staff (such as at UKSteel), while at one of our case companies (UKDrinks) we were granted access to the entire senior management team on the site, including the heads of HR and Finance. In the Japanese cases, we always met with at least two people at a time, typically both at *kachō* level, although occasionally a *buchō* would attend (for more on Japanese hierarchies, see Chapter 5). Over the course of sixty to ninety minutes, these managers provided overviews of the organisational changes that have taken place in the recent past. In particular, our managers provided details on organisational structures before and after restructuring, the motivations for change and its results, and on middle managers' work tasks, pay, conditions and future prospects. The managers were all provided with a project overview and a semi-structured interview schedule in advance of the meetings. Extensive company documentation was also gathered.

Secondly, the case organisations were revisited at later dates in order to conduct hour-long, one-to-one interviews with up to ten middle managers, using a second semi-structured interview schedule. We interviewed middle managers themselves in order to understand the views of those directly affected by change. We did not wish to rely solely on senior managers' accounts, as we felt that their views may be overly optimistic about the effects of change, given their distanced position from middle managers' work tasks and experiences. The middle managers were drawn from a variety of functions of the business and volunteered to take part having previously been contacted by their organisation's HR or Personnel department. The vast majority of the interviews were conducted in company time and on company premises; we promised not to reveal any names of people or companies in publications arising from the study.

While we were unable to make exact demands on the case study organisations as to whom we wished to interview, the senior HR representatives were familiar with our topics of interest and, having been provided with our research project outline, easily grasped our intentions. We are confident therefore that the differences in the process of gaining access did not compromise the quality of the data. Most of the middle managers who were made available to us had considerable levels of experience (some as long as twenty years' service). As longer-term stakeholders in the organisations they were able to provide in-depth accounts of the personal impacts of restructuring, the motivations for top management's pursuit of change and the results of change over the years. We made it clear that all interviews would be private and confidential and our managers were almost universally extremely candid and forthcoming, with few signs of the respondents providing watered-down accounts for fear of subsequent consumption by senior management.

Access to Japanese companies was harder to arrange than it was to British or American ones. Ultimately, in Japan, we managed to secure access to two automotive companies (JAutoGroup and JAutoComps), a heavy manufacturing firm (JEngineering), an electronics manufacturing company (JElectronics), a city council (JCity) and a very important integrated steel manufacturer (JSteel). We were not provided with a bank case study through this formal channel, but we were able to get around this through personal contacts, and ultimately conducted unauthorised interviews with two younger Japanese consultants at the Tokyo offices of a major American investment bank (JUSBank). Unfortunately we could not get access to a utilities firm or a hospital.

Progress in gaining these meetings was slow, meaning that each trip usually meant no more than four to five companies being visited during our four stays of two to three weeks in Japan. However, once these intermediary contacts were cemented (roughly two years into the research programme) access became substantially easier as our hosts had come to realise, in more depth, what exactly we wanted to gain from these meetings. Despite our fears that the Japanese respondents would not open up to us, they often provided candid responses, and were very conversant with the general themes of company restructuring and workplace pressures. Although they were generally more conservative than the Western participants of the study, our Japanese respondents still provided a great deal of interesting answers to what were, at times, fairly sensitive questions. Virtually all of the interviews, including those in Japan, were tape-recorded, and only on a few occasions were concerns raised about the recording process.

Access to companies in the USA was a simpler task. We decided to pursue our inquiries in very large firms in the traditional sectors of automotive, banking, electronics, utilities, steelmaking, brewing and engineering. We also gained access to one large retail firm (USRetail) and one firm in business services (which turned out to be USRecruit, a world-famous employment agency). Our efforts to gain access began by searching for names of senior HR managers in a range of companies operating in these sectors which had headquarters located in cities that were convenient for us. This search was carried out through the Hoovers database[2] which contained up-to-date details of senior HR people, mainly with executive vice-president or senior vice-president job titles.

Having introduced our methods of study and access, we will now explain the theoretical questions that underpin our analysis. Throughout each case study, the aim was, firstly, to explore what kinds of restructuring had taken place, and what senior management's motivations were. Subsequently, we delved deeper into the organisations, uncovering middle managers' own, often highly personal, accounts of what restructuring has meant for the quality of their working lives. In exploring these themes, we attempt to construct a neo-Marxist, critical analysis of the structures of large capitalist firms, and the human costs of restructuring in the three countries. Our central avenue of inquiry is the changing demands that contemporary international capital places on organisations and its ranks of managers. In doing so, we hope to contribute to the development of a realist account of the contemporary

---

[2] www.hoovers.com/free/

labour process of managerial employees. The rest of this chapter discusses our theoretical background and influences in more detail.

Theorising the organisation and control of managerial labour

We noted in Chapter 1 the contribution made by C. Wright Mills to our understanding of middle managers in the period of classical administration. Although many of his observations are now dated, his overall rationale and methodology has remained extremely relevant. He claimed that it is 'one of the great tasks of social studies today to describe the larger economic and political situation in terms of its meaning for the inner life and the external career of the individual' (Mills 1953: xx). This neatly describes our approach to studying white-collar workers in this study.

Mills' classic text on white-collar workers is one of a small number in which middle managers are the centre of the analysis. However, his work is very polemical, and is typical of the long-term inclination of much of the literature to offer caricatured or highly politicised pieces of work on middle managers, a trend that continues to this day. Critical literature often has little to say about middle managers, tending to focus on the travails of the blue-collar worker, or the hubris of those at the top.[3] One of the foundation stones of critical Marxist analysis of capitalist organisation, management and work is Harry Braverman's *Labor and Monopoly Capital* (1974/1998). It has had a huge influence on debates about Taylorism, work degradation and employee exploitation, especially at blue-collar levels, and signalled the onset of an academic boom in Labour Process Theory (LPT). 'Bravermanian' analysis has been further developed by theorists such as Friedman (1977), Edwards (1979), Littler (1982), Meiksins (1994), Thompson and Ackroyd (1995, 2005) and Thompson (2003), in so doing building a substantial canon of LPT theory. This has been heavily influenced by writing elsewhere in Marxist social science concerning the onset of 'monopoly capitalism', the rise of the giant firms that Marx had envisaged but had

---

[3] This point is well made by Werther (2003) in his short article on Enron – we all know about Ken Lay and Jeff Skilling, but to what extent were other, less senior, executives and professionals involved? What did they know? Did they knowingly or unwittingly contribute to the fraud and collapse?

not lived to see, and a capitalism based not on competition between small firms, but by the wholesale economic dominance of major corporate bureaucracies (Baran and Sweezy 1966: 19–20; Mandel 1971/1999). Indeed, the key stated goal of Braverman's writing was to provide the analysis of labour process that was missing in the corpus of Marxist literature on monopoly capital (Baran and Sweezy 1966: 22).

Essentially LPT builds on Marx's concept of valorisation, demonstrating how the extraction of surplus value takes place directly within workplace settings, providing local detail to complement the macroeconomic abstraction of Marx's Volume One of *Capital*. The central point is that the Taylorian revolution in scientific-technical control over industrial labour in the twentieth century wrested the means of work control from employees and into the hands of managers, with the result that labour is cheapened and work becomes a site of drudgery, alienation and insecurity for the working class. A narrow elite of managers reaps the benefits, both in terms of higher productivity and increased personal rewards (salaries, fringe benefits, more rewarding work). Numerous workplace studies have contributed to this viewpoint across several time periods and across industrial and service settings (see for example Beynon, 1986, on the car industry in the 1970s, and Korczynski, 2001, on contemporary retail service work in the 1990s).

There have been many counter-arguments against LPT. A predictable backlash comes from managerialist authors, who assert that Braverman's critique of capital is groundless and politicised. According to this viewpoint, work has not been systematically degraded. Instead, increasing skill levels and worker participation schemes are widespread, serving to reduce both worker alienation and low productivity. This argument resurfaces, in more critical form, in the 'high-performance work systems' paradigm (Appelbaum *et al.* 2000), which essentially argues that, although these win–win situations do not yet exist in the majority of firms, enlightened, forward-thinking senior managers can and should make it work. In more theoretical discussions, a post-modernist/post-structuralist critique of LPT has also been influential, to the extent that Braverman became a tragicomic figure in some circles, sounding, like many Marxian political economy traditions, 'hopelessly passé' (Ray and Sayer 1999). Post-structuralist-inclined critics would suggest that LPT rests on an entirely inappropriate and elitist assertion of *a priori* structural categories onto a fluid, chaotic, unclear working world, in which individual workers are not subjugated as objects into alienation and resignation, but are active players in a much more complex and subjective world, enacting performances of acceptance and resistance (O'Doherty and Wilmott 2001). Others have suggested that LPT, while 'not entirely exhausted', struggles to describe the post-industrial, service-driven 'New Economy' of the 1990s which often involves highly skilled 'knowledge work' whose value is intangible and, unlike pin manufacturing, cannot be Taylorised (Sewell 2005).

We want to rehabilitate Braverman for two main reasons. Firstly, we believe there is much to be gained by locating managerial work within an LPT perspective, particularly because managers were not the subject of his study, and the coverage of managers is unduly thin and caricatured in other classic Marxian accounts (Baran and Sweezy 1966: 40–55). In Braverman, although retail and office work is analysed in detail (1974/1998: 203–59), there is scant coverage of 'the middle layers of employment' (279–83), and the notion of managers as employees barely features. Secondly, many parts of Braverman's core theory remain remarkably accurate, even given the huge structural changes that have been wrought on the economic landscape since the 1970s when he was writing. Of course, time has not been kind to some of his concepts (such as de-skilling). But other ideas drawn from the traditional LPT stable remain extremely useful for explaining the ongoing rationalisation and restructuring of workplaces, and can be applied to managerial labour.

Middle managers are by their very nature a complex and confusing combination of managers and the managed. This topic was taken up by Armstrong (1989). He argues that Braverman's brief coverage of middle managers actually contradicts the main thrust of his own argument. Braverman notes that lower level managers and administrators, key parts of the capitalist functions of control, are themselves drawn into the labour process (1974/1998: 267). According to Armstrong (1989), this means that the distinction (broadly a class distinction) between capital and labour – a key building block of labour process theory as originally envisaged by Marx – collapses, throwing LPT analysis into confusion and circularity. 'While the assumption that management is a labour process can "explain" instances in which managerial work has been "de-skilled" it cannot explain the many cases in which it has *not*, even though de-skilling may have been technically feasible' (Armstrong 1989: 320). Armstrong argues that managerial work is not simply drawn into Taylorian divisions of labour in the same way as workers on the line. Instead he concludes that 'the relationship between manager and employer, between junior and senior manager is an *agency* relationship' (*ibid.*).

We would agree that it is simplistic and inaccurate to describe middle managerial work as a labour process subjected to the same processes of rationalisation and degradation as blue-collar work.[4] Nevertheless, our analysis of middle management work in the three countries studied does strongly point in the direction of work intensification and the cutting of entitlements, entailing a more pressured and less collegial atmosphere for middle managers than in the days before large-scale restructuring and cost-reduction policies. Contrary to certain arguments of the strategic management literature, which assert that middle managers can and should influence top management strategy (Balogun 2003; Dutton and Ashford 1993; Dutton *et al.* 1997), we found scant evidence of this. Middle management work was becoming more sophisticated and complex, and middle managers were trusted with wider spans of control, but they almost universally possessed little or no influence on decisions that came down from the top. There was a clear division of labour and authority between middle management and executives. According to our interviewees it was clear where the real power lies – at the top. While it would be simplistic and misleading to assert that such a division might be class-based (as a traditional Braverman interpretation could imply), in a narrow sense this division does resemble the divisions of labour Braverman based his analysis around, and it is not solely an 'agency relationship' as Armstrong suggests. In other words, while we agree with Armstrong that middle management is not a labour process in a strict sense, we also suggest that the subordinate position of middle management labour in the chain of command does expose middle managers to many of the rationalising pressures that labour process theorists usually describe in relation to front-line staff and supervisors.

Of course the complex and contradictory status of middle managers – simultaneously contributing to the control of the enterprise while also being subjected to it – surfaced regularly in middle managers' descriptions of their own working lives. How closely do they identify themselves with the aims and cultures of senior managers or with subordinates? Do middle managers join a union, for instance? And if they do, can they go out on strike with the hourly paid workers? Our approach was to

---

[4] Of course, many have disputed Braverman's claim that de-skilling occurs even at blue-collar level (Penn and Scattergood 1985: 613–4).

conduct semi-structured interviews with those involved in an attempt to learn from the field, to collect stories about organisational change and its impact on middle managers' careers and work tasks. We did not go into the field with a theoretical framework in mind that places middle managers into certain *a priori* analytical positions. Rather, we wanted to embrace the complexity of being at once a manager and one of the managed, and attempt to understand it from the standpoints of those involved. Our observations from the field support some, but crucially not all, parts of Braverman's worldview. Middle management work was not being 'degraded' as such; in fact, the work was almost universally increasing in responsibility and skill level. This is not to say, however, that middle managers necessarily received what they saw as appropriate rewards or recognition for this effort. Therefore, 'work degradation' partly captures the widespread sense of unease that middle managers felt about workplace change, but not in the Taylorian sense of de-skilling and separation of planning from execution that Braverman analysed. Where Braverman's interpretation is much more relevant is in the progressive intensification and rationalisation of middle management labour. This was supported very strongly in our interviews.

Ongoing theoretical work in this area is relevant to our discussion. Recently Adler (2007) criticised traditional Bravermanian LPT for ignoring the long-term upgrading of employee skills which, he claims, is an inherent feature of the growing complexities of modern capitalism. Our analysis of middle managers would closely support this element of Adler's argument: the managers in this study have experienced considerable role and skill expansion. However, skills upgrading was not always looked on favourably by middle managers, who typically regarded the increase in work skill as going hand-in-hand with wider responsibilities, heavier workloads and increased pressure. This viewpoint is consistent with a comprehensive array of survey data analysed by Green (2006). We would argue that many of the underlying concepts of LPT remain useful even in the era of huge technical complexity and even as applied to highly sophisticated, professional work. The concept of de-skilling has always been contentious, and is particularly unsuited to an analysis of highly skilled managerial labour. Nevertheless, de-skilling need not form the centrepiece of a labour-process inspired analysis of organisation, management and work (McKinlay 2005: 247; Thompson and Ackroyd 2005: 707). If the focus is trained more on the changing demands that international competition makes of organisations, and on how this affects the lives and careers of workers (as Mills, 1953 envisaged), then LPT analysis can be very insightful. Its strength lies in connecting the analysis of organisational change to broader economic changes. Authors such as Beynon *et al.* (2002), Thompson (2003) and Jenkins (2007) take similar approaches. The main background to Braverman's analysis, and the fundamental drivers of capitalism that he identifies, were, we would argue, broadly correct. However, these drivers have experienced considerable intensification in several discrete but connected ways.[5]

Firstly, the internationalisation of capital has developed considerably since Braverman's day. Crucially, this entails the entry of millions of Chinese, Indian and eastern European workers into world labour markets, creating new possibilities and imperatives for cost reduction. The international expansion of large firms, in terms of access to new markets or through supply chain rationalisation, has grown substantially throughout the twentieth century (Bartlett and Ghoshal 1998). A crucial component of this has been the exponential growth and fundamental adaptation of international financial markets, which have been central components of the construction of a new international architecture in which large firms operate, an architecture which is vastly more powerful (and disconcerting) than the relatively rudimentary and parochial money systems that feature (minimally) in Braverman's coverage of the large, monopolistic bureaucracy. *Labor and Monopoly Capital* predates many important changes in the financial sphere, which amount to an opening of a Pandora's box of reforms in all major economies. New financial forces have been unleashed which firms and governments increasingly struggle to control (Glyn 2006). Such changes include the growth in importance of investment banking, leveraged buyouts and venture capital, widespread privatisation and 'big bang' style liberalisation, and markets in 'new financial instruments'. In all countries there are now fewer 'national champions' and monopolies, a far greater degree of competition on an international scale between large firms, and, until the 2008 global recession, a general retreat of the state from direct economic involvement. Braverman's worldview is very similar to that of Baran and Sweezy (1966) which, while convincing on the steady rise of the scale and dominance of large firms over the economic landscape, underplays

---

[5] Andrew Glyn, before his untimely death, provided an excellent Marxist overview of these and other trends in the OECD nations (Glyn 2006).

the severity of competition between them at an international level, and overplays their financial independence from investment banks (Baran and Sweezy 1966: 29–30).

The second change, which is perhaps the most important, has been the steady ramping up of competitive pressures, especially since the onset of Chinese growth. Competition on the basis of price and quality has contributed to rising expectations of consumers (who can increasingly look elsewhere). Product demand becomes more fragmented and harder to predict – a major change from the monopolistic, Fordist era that Braverman and many of the earlier classics (Marxist or otherwise), such as Mills (1953), March and Simon (1958), Whyte (1960) and Mintzberg (1973) describe. In addition, the steady advance of 'financialisation', that is, the dependence of large firms on equity finance or 'stock-market capitalism' (Dore 2000), has increasingly affected firm strategy in the USA and the UK (Froud *et al.* 2006; Glyn 2006; Golding 2003; Lazonick and O'Sullivan 2000).[6]

The third major change to large-firm structure in recent years has been the substantial job cuts and reorganisations targeted specifically at managers (in addition to the long-standing threats to operatives). This has included the reduction of managerial layers as part of a broader process of streamlining and rationalising the firm. Related changes include the outsourcing of non-core back-office activities (such as payroll), and the increasingly complex interactions of firms with international supply chains and overseas production. This also runs counter to Braverman's (and many of the classic authors such as Mills and Whyte) assertions that large firms were continuing to grow in scale and scope. Although the impact of restructuring and globalisation on employee numbers is debated back and forth, it is certainly the case that many large firms have scaled back their operations as cost pressures have forced them to focus on core competencies, and the increased technological sophistication of industries and services has led to progressive waves of outsourcing into complex webs of interconnected supply chains.[7] Firms

---

[6] Although there are signs of financialization in Japan, the process has been far slower (Dore 2000; Jacoby 2005).

[7] The car industry is perhaps the best example. As the technological sophistication and complexity of automobiles continues to increase, it is simply not within the capacity of a company such as Ford to vertically integrate the production of such complex systems as electronics, software and drivetrain (see Maxton and Wormald 2004: 140).

are also more likely to engage in joint ventures and strategic alliances, forming partnerships with other firms that further increase the complexity of organisation forms and inter-relations (Sako 2006).

Fourth, as the organisation and its environment become more competitive and complex, work itself becomes more demanding. A key finding of our study is the increasing skill and time demands being made of middle managers. Partly these demands could be explained by the impetus for firms to engage their middle managers in high-tech, knowledge-intensive work, along the lines of the organisational holy grail that is 'high performance work systems' (Appelbaum *et al.* 2000).[8] It is certainly true that middle management employees are now compelled to know a great deal more about the business in its entirety than they once did. Much of the heavy work demands, however, appeared in our study to be the result of far more mundane organisational features, such as the 'firefighting' that ensues with the often chaotic pace of work and the frequency of errors that need correcting, or simply work overload due to wider spans of control and fewer managers among whom the task burden is divided.

Fifth, all of the above are partly driven and partly enabled by the massive increase in sophistication and prevalence of ICT systems, which generate new abilities for information sharing, outsourcing and coordination of work across broader geographical and organisational boundaries. Although the 'network society' idea can be very easily overstated, the influence of new ICT developments has permeated many areas of organisational life. This has potentially profound implications for removing traditional white-collar jobs and for changing how surviving white-collar work is controlled and executed, including for example homeworking (Castells 2000; White *et al.* 2004: 89–99).

Sixth, and finally, traditional gender relations have been disrupted in recent decades. Female labour participation rates have climbed significantly, bringing into question fundamental debates about careers, work and family time, especially in the rapidly growing number of dual-career households. While women have certainly not reached parity with men in terms of their access to senior management jobs, in the USA and the UK there are now many in middle management positions, which were formerly the preserve of men (although Japan lags some way behind

---

[8] Interestingly for us, the HPWS concept is modelled closely on Japanese work and management systems (see Chapter 5 below).

other OECD nations). Millions of female university graduates fully expect to have long and meaningful professional careers. Large firms have increasingly recognised that they cannot afford to restrict themselves to selecting their management levels only from the ranks of men, as they miss out on a wide array of female managerial talent.

Work-life balance has become a complex and thorny issue for organisations and families as difficult negotiations are made between employees and workplaces, and between cohabiting couples: balancing paid work, domestic work and family time. Related to this issue is what we call 'the Hochschild syndrome'. This is when employees invest so much of their time and effort into their career that the boundary between work and home becomes blurred (Hochschild 1997, 2003). White-collar workers may actually 'escape into work' to avoid the burdens, frustrations and illogics of family life and care commitments. The ubiquity of 'home offices' containing PCs and broadband connections symbolises the invasion of work into home; a process that firms and employees have both tended to encourage. The phenomenon of employees willingly devoting so such time and personal investment into work is probably related to the growth of the intrinsic value and interest in the job as the skill level of middle management work increases. Others point to a darker element, in that 'presenteeism' on the job and taking work home is a manifestation of employee insecurity and management by fear (Fraser 2001; Rapoport *et al.* 2002; Watts 2009). However, long hours are not simply the result of senior managers impelling subordinates to stay at work for lengthy periods (although this certainly occurs, especially in Japan). It is more the case that the growing scale of the workload necessitates long working days and weeks if managers are ever to feel in control or 'on top' of it all. UK journalist Madeleine Bunting captured this idea well in the title of her book *Willing Slaves* (2004).

There is also something more subtle going on here. Middle management work can be very challenging, engaging and enjoyable. Many of our respondents claimed that their work was extremely demanding, even overwhelming, but many claimed also to love their work. A lively, collegiate, positive organisational culture can, in some cases, contribute to long hours and 'escaping into work'. Moreover, there can be a desire on the part of employees to deliver good quality work and to be proud of a job well done. This element of job reward is absent from a lot of critical literature in the LPT tradition. For whatever reason, or combination of reasons, middle managers are, on average, spending a great deal more time and effort on their jobs than in the era of classical, bureaucratic administration.

Broadly speaking these six macro trends affected all of the companies featured in our study, from New York to London to Tokyo. All three societies are mature, OECD countries enmeshed in the new impetus for cost reduction. All of the private sector firms are large companies exposed to international competition. Despite the existence of different national employment systems, financial systems and forms of corporate governance (as per the varieties of capitalism literature), the fundamental forces at work in these case study companies are very similar. Braverman or the monopoly capital theorists cannot be faulted for their inability to clearly predict these trends any more than any other classical theorists. Our intention in describing these six trends is not to discredit this paradigm, but to update it. The underlying concepts of Marxian analysis, such as surplus generation, rationalisation, exploitation and alienation are critically important issues which are all clearly demonstrated in our research on middle managers.

Before we started our fieldwork, our position was one of scepticism surrounding the 'convergence' of business systems, but we found more evidence of it than we had anticipated. It depends on where you want to look. If analysts are interested in corporate governance or relatively abstract national institutions, then they might tend to find limited change and continued diversity between Anglo-Saxon and Japanese forms (Amable 2003; Whitley 1999). Looking deeper at firm behaviour, and, in particular, at the results of organisational reforms on managerial employers, then a different picture emerges: of managerial staff across three nations facing common challenges, frustrations and difficulties.

Our study does, therefore, indicate a degree of convergence of business systems around an Anglo-Saxon model. We would never argue that the distinctive features of the UK, the USA and (mostly obviously) Japan will disappear. As we shall see, these features remain very relevant to the underlying logics of the versions of capitalism at work. In a sense, just as Jacoby concludes his study (2005: 174) there is evidence in support for both convergence and continued divergence. Corporate governance, for example, remains considerably different in Japan from the USA and the UK. Japanese firms were also far less concerned with shareholder value logic than their Western counterparts, and, also as expected, they refused to abandon policies of long-term employment and complex internal career development systems presaged on staff spending their working lifetime inside the company.

Although we are rather sceptical about excited claims of a radically changed environment characterised by globalisation, post-bureaucracy and the convergence on Anglo-Saxon norms, we were surprised by the amount of change to organisational design, work systems and middle managers' tasks and responsibilities that had taken place. Large workplaces had indeed gone through substantial transformations. And large workplaces in America, Britain and Japan have undergone a degree of 'convergence'. What we see is not so much the destruction or change of institutions, but their increasing marginalisation as large multinationals augment their abilities to operate, transform and expand in response to major economic pressures.

Indeed, we find it somewhat odd that varieties of capitalism authors, who tend to focus on giant firms, find so little change. One might expect the largest firms to be at the forefront of adaptation and transformation, and that their executives would describe change, not stability, especially as some giant firms possess huge capacity for internationalisation. Giant firms claim to be genuinely global ones, with global strategies and visions (Sklair 2001), and they find such a focus on national contingencies somewhat tangential to the real business of multinational operations. This attitude occasionally surfaced during our efforts to negotiate access to these companies, notably for example at USElectronics. In our attempts to visit its head office in the United States, we had originally contacted the Senior Vice-President for HR based in the Midwest, who, before he could commit himself to meeting us, had to seek approval from elsewhere in the chain of command. This led to a telephone call from USElectronic's Global Head of HR to Manchester Business School, in which he sought explanation from us about what we were doing and why. He was somewhat nonplussed about our insistence on the international comparative element – why were we replicating the study with similar firms based in Japan and the UK? What did we expect to learn from doing this? He said something along the lines of, 'we are a global firm, which operates globally, searching for the best staff from wherever we can find them'. This experience seemed to support this mainstream picture of a globalised, borderless world (Giddens 2000; Ohmae 1994) and a global HR strategy. The Global Head of HR for USElectronics was based in London, and the access we were seeking was in the USA. While he did concede that national legal environments differ, he was sceptical that we would find any substantial differences across the three countries as regards change and the imperatives for change.

Although this director's viewpoint might sound overly simplistic, it is hard to disagree with the main thrust. However, the argument needs tempering somewhat – national institutional structures can be a lot more durable and powerful than this executive believes, and our data does demonstrate this. On the other hand, our interviews with managers also described considerable forces of change that have pushed multinationals further down the road to internationalisation, as they both react to, and contribute to, globalisation. We suggest that it is important to move beyond the narrow academic debates over 'convergence or divergence of business systems'. These debates are unlikely to be resolved, and they distract attention away from the impact of macroeconomic and organisational change on employees, something we consider to be a much more important issue.

Finally, in the Appendix, we present brief details on the turnover and headcount of our main case study organisations at the time we commenced research in 2003. The real, in-depth story of these organisations, however, is provided in the next three chapters, as we turn our attention to explaining the 'real world' of corporate restructuring and managerial work in America, Britain and Japan. In these chapters we do not attempt to cover all of the cases we researched in the course of research study; instead, we focus on just a few organisations from each country in order to provide a detailed qualitative analysis of corporate restructuring and managers' interpretations of change.

3 | *Living in the house that Jack built: Management restructuring in America*

[S]pecific companies, especially in the late 1990s at the height of the cult, implemented copies of what they imagined Jack [Welch] did.

(Froud *et al.*, 2006: 365)

Nowhere has the discussion about the changing fortunes of large corporations had a higher profile than in the USA. America is the historical home of the Chandlerian giant firm, the birthplace of business schools, MBAs, management consulting and 'change gurus'. It is where downsizing and business process re-engineering (BPR) first emerged, and also where the backlash against these phenomena has been most vivid, both in academic literature (such as Cascio 1993; Heckscher 1996; Smith, 1990) and popular culture (Bakan 2005; Moore 1997).

The USA and its large firms continue to be at the forefront of debates around economic shifts since the 1970s, and the more specific impact of the restructuring of capital on firms and employees. Traditional Marxist literature focuses strongly on the US model (Baran and Sweezy 1966; Braverman 1974/1998). There is a reasonably well-established concept of the core features of a giant corporation in most parts of the world, and this concept is largely modelled on the publicly listed, divisionalised, US bureaucratic firm. This idealised firm has, of course, been through significant changes. Business and labour historians such as Alfred Chandler and Sanford Jacoby have written widely on the makeup and purpose of the large firm, especially since the New Deal era, in which US firms were bureaucratic, often vertically integrated and paternalistic, with large internal hierarchies of lifetime employees and many layers of white-collar management. The large firm is thus a managerial firm, manipulated more by Chandler's 'visible hand' of scientific-rational white-collar control systems than Smith's 'invisible hand' of market forces. Many classical organisational analyses argued that managerial control insulates the firm from external chaos, but at the same time makes it more responsive to its internal stakeholders, especially to its white-collar staff, which becomes a bounded community working in concert to further collective interests. The focus on profit maximisation supposedly takes a back seat to wider, technical-organisational concerns (March and Simon 1958). Classical literature such as Berle and Means (1933) expected the large firm to develop into 'a purely neutral technocracy'. Kaysen (1957: 314) even described a 'soulful corporation', something that sounds very similar to the traditional, conservative Japanese 'firm as family', or an old-fashioned, elitist British bureaucracy before the 'Big Bang', along the lines of an ICI or a preprivatisation British Telecom.

Such managerialist concepts as 'satisficing' or the 'soulful corporation' have however been heavily criticised by Marxist authors such as Baran and Sweezy (1966: 33–40), who instead describe the real interests of a firm in terms of capital accumulation, rationalisation, incessant drives for higher profits and robust cost control. They describe a wide range of new technical systems that have emerged to push harder and faster for greater profitability.[1] Rather than the mainstream interpretation of a classical US firm operating in the best interests of a broad set of stakeholders, Marxist authors describe large firms as insider-controlled, with top management's interests overshadowing all others.

Of course, this classical 1960s model, however interpreted, is now widely considered a thing of the past. A long-term process of dismantling New Deal bureaucracy has moved the typical large US firm down a quite different road, in the direction of much more openness, flexibility and risk-taking (Jacoby 2005). An enormous literature has grown in recent decades around the relative merits of the US 'business system'. Throughout the 1980s, as the Japanese system flourished before its

---

[1] Baran and Sweezy (1966: 36–9) draw heavily on the work of James Earley (1956), parts of which still sound extraordinarily apt. Rejecting Herbert Simon's view that corporations are forced, by their size and complexity, to focus on complying with the wishes of a broad coalition of interests ('satisficing' behaviour), Earley points to 'so-called "excellently managed" corporations' insatiable appetite for more, and quicker, profits. He describes 'a systematic focus on cost reduction, the expansion of revenue, and the increase in profits. There is, of course, much reference to standards, and to the need of remedying unsatisfactory situations. The drive is always toward the better and frequently the best, not just the good. [...] The exemplary man of management seems to have 'More!' for at least one of his mottoes.' He also points to 'the rapidly growing use of economists, market analysts, other types of specialists, and management consultants'. Benchmarking, consulting and restructuring, it seems, are not such recent developments after all.

1990s slump, the received wisdom was that the structures of US capitalism were in desperate need of change. In taking apart the 'soulful corporation' of the earlier part of the century, the USA was left with firms that were far too focused on short-term financial gain, rather than the steady, disciplined, patient behaviour of, say, Japan or Germany. The highly influential studies on competitiveness by Porter (1990), for example, had little positive to say about US firms which:

[H]ire and fire with impunity and underinvest in human resources. [...] The biggest problem is a lost focus on investment and innovation. Instead of innovating, companies merge. Instead of innovating, they source products and components abroad that could be made more efficiently using improved technology at home. (Porter 1990: 731)

Best's work (1990) pointed in similarly depressing directions. US firms appear far too preoccupied with short-term financial re-engineering than with genuine attempts to generate value in product markets. This dire prognosis would be exemplified by 'value-destroying' industrials such as Ford or General Motors. Struggling industrial firms such as these became notorious not only for poor financial performance, but also for uncompetitive product development, low worker morale and regular battles between management and labour (Milkman 1997; Hamper 1992). The US union movement has also been in serious decline since the 1970s, as lay-offs, outsourcing, offshoring and concessionary bargaining took a major toll on membership (Sallaz 2004).

Yet, much like Japan after its own recession in the 1990s, the US model was written off far too early. A wholly unexpected recovery took place from around 1993 to 2000, especially in electronics and IT (see Best 2001; Barley and Kunda 2004), as the radical paradigm of the 'New Economy' came into circulation, based on new technologies, venture capital and new financial instruments. Many long-suffering large firms were swept along on this wave of change, engaging in harsh, but arguably successful, organisational surgery. While downsizing and restructuring were prolonged and painful processes for firms and employees – for example, Burke and Nelson (1997: 325) state that more than 43 million US jobs were eliminated between 1979 and 1996 – they were also essential for economic revival. The 'high-performance work systems' literature (such as Appelbaum *et al.* 2000) also tended to be upbeat about the prospects for successful reform of US companies' employment policies. The New Economy tech-stock bubble burst in 2000–1, but the resurgence of corporate America remained generally impressive to most observers, to the extent that Germany and Japan lost their 'model' status, with the mantle passing back to liberalised, footloose Anglo-Saxon economies (Amable 2003: 2–3). Such is the extent of recent change that the real story of Jacoby's comparative work on the USA and Japan (2005) is not the piecemeal change of Japanese firms in the 1990s, but the radical transformation of the US companies during that time to a position even further from traditional New Deal bureaucracy, effectively widening the distance between the Japanese and US models. The scandals and collapses of a number of firms which were former stars of the New Economy scene, such as Enron and WorldCom, brought on much soul-searching in the US system of corporate governance (Werther 2003; Leavitt 2007; Froud *et al.* 2006: 35, 52–4). And at the time of writing (late 2008), stock markets continue to take batterings as the fallout from the sub-prime mortgages crisis envelopes the US financial system.[2]

Amid the hyperbole of the 1990s boom, critical voices continued to point to the dominance of short-term, capital-market pressures on giant firms (Lazonick and O'Sullivan 2000); the weak performance of much of US industry (Appelbaum and Batt 1994); the development of an 'hourglass economy' in which middle-earning jobs are squeezed out (Appelbaum *et al.* 2000); poor returns on investment, even in supposedly high-value, cutting-edge firms which have been through continual restructuring (Froud *et al.* 2006: 11–20, 299–368); and to the generally slow uptake of high-performance work systems in US firms (Milkman 1998). Many of the new financial innovations, such as large-scale private equity buyouts, amount to 'value extraction' for top management, rather than value creation (Froud and Williams 2007). Many of the contributors to Cornfield *et al.*'s volume (2001) on workplace

---

[2] US investment banks, which played a major role in the resurgence of corporate America in the 1990s, were complicit in this crisis and sustained heavy damage. During 2008, many announced deep job cuts and the ousting of top executives, including Merrill Lynch cutting one in ten of its employees, and over 60,000 jobs scheduled for termination at Citigroup. Most dramatic of all were the collapse of Lehman Brothers and the last-ditch takeover of Merrill Lynch by Bank of America over one weekend in September 2008, events which sent financial markets into shock and depression. The long-term effects of the sub-prime mortgage crisis are as yet unknown, but are likely to be grave, especially for financial services employees. Short-term impacts have already been seen in job cuts in other industries, especially automotive and electronics (see Chapter 1).

change were also unimpressed, indicating that the long boom in the USA depended in part on a serious harshening of the terms and conditions of workers and managers, including increased work effort, reduced security and longer working hours (see also Schor 1992). Dudley (1994) captured in great detail the personal changes that have confronted workers displaced from manufacturing in large numbers. Downs' controversial book *Corporate Executions* (1995) provides probably the most damning appraisal so far of the human and organisational costs of American downsizing. Osterman (1996) and colleagues (2001) are also generally downbeat, demonstrating how traditional, New-Deal type employment systems have been eradicated, leading to a re-establishment of senior management prerogative in large firms, and the erosion of step-wise promotion up corporate hierarchies. In short, workplaces have become more demanding, less forgiving, more unequal and more pressured. These problems have the potential to be more severe for American workers than for European (including British) ones, given the US tradition of so-called 'employment at will'.

Others suggest that not much substantial change has really taken place. Gordon (1996) argues that corporate management has not been slimmed down, and that front-line operatives are the ones who have really experienced cuts and squeezes. Baumol *et al.* (2003), in the first major study devoted to the topic of downsizing in the USA, also suggest limited real change outside of the manufacturing industry (which has been in slow decline since the 1960s), and nothing more than moderate returns to capital across most of the US economy.

How to make sense of these competing claims? What are the salient features of the US corporate scene? We argue that US firms have indeed been through substantial changes. Our interviews with US middle managers and senior HR executives provided a picture of repeated transformations, with managerial workers confronted by a wide range of new experiences. While some of this change was welcome, middle managers almost universally expressed concern about work overload and reduced support. Many elements of change threatened and challenged middle managers, creating feelings of anxiety and uncertainty. This wasn't simply fear of change or resistance to change, but concrete examples of where organisational change had clearly worsened middle managers' quality of working life. Employees' opinions about the effectiveness of change ranged from guarded support, through ambivalence, to outright hostility. Amid the tightening of financial discipline, the cutting of entitlements and the intensification of work, there were some more welcome changes. Female middle managers in the USA tended to be somewhat more positive about their prospects than those in the UK and much more so than in Japan, reflecting the generally better state of gender equality in US firms than in many other OECD nations.[3]

The US business scene is traditionally distrustful of any limitations placed on managerial authority, whether emanating from state or federal government, trade unions, or elsewhere. Anything sounding like the core European social market model can expect heavy criticism from mainstream sources. North America is the home of the celebrity CEO, of unquestioning corporate loyalty, huge financial bonuses and powerful brand identities. Large US firms tend to expect their employees not just to demonstrate pride in working for the company, but somehow to embody the firm and its values (see Bunting 2004: 89–118, on what she calls 'missionary management'). The enthusiasm and hard work expected of, and shown by, many American staff is not far from the traditional caricature of Japanese 'willing slaves'. Of course, when this devotion is genuine on the part of employees it makes restructuring harder to bear.

The institutional structure of the US economy is widely described as the most liberal of all the OECD nations. Unlike Japan (or, for example, Germany) there are few institutional constraints on top management's actions and strategies. Progressive liberalisation and deregulation in the USA has created a highly open, highly competitive economy, with few of the long-standing reciprocal arrangements visible in, for example, Japanese corporate governance. Jacoby (2005) argues that these changes have removed the ground from under the feet of human resource departments, as financial divisions increasingly become the real centres of power in US corporations. On the other hand, he also demonstrates considerable diversity. There are firms that buck this trend, that do genuinely focus on staff development and product and service quality rather than stock-market performance. Indeed, the USA is also the place where the HRM and HPWS literature first emanated, a literature that has a lot in common with writing on 'responsible restructuring' (see Cascio 2002a, 2002b, 2006). Such writing argues that employees should be the central focus of the firm and, if treated well, can become the basis of a firm's competitive strength. We do not find

---

[3] However, some serious problems persist in this area (Roth 2007).

fault with this idea. However, this literature tends to be very utopian and managerialist. In general it fails to pass comment on the broader issue of the restructuring of capital and the pressures this places on firms. Broader forces are at work that render the humanistic intentions of HR literature unrealistic. According to our interviews, white-collar employees are continually buffeted by these forces of change in a savagely competitive environment where history, tradition and reputation count for little.

Moreover, there is a darker, colder side to this supposedly 'employee-favouring' literature. Cascio, the main figure in the 'responsible restructuring' school, who is usually more circumspect when it comes to assessing the positive effects of new organisational developments, in fact speaks glowingly of Motorola (which has carried out deep cuts to its employment profile in the last twenty years) and the budget retailer CostCo (with its reputed anti-union stance). He claims that firms should 'park' the best employees and 'respect the rest' (2002: 87) thereby endorsing robust restructuring measures. Fundamentally, the HR literature supports the promotion of managerialist interventions to 'improve organisational performance' and has a serious tendency to downplay the damage that restructuring so frequently causes to employees' quality of life. Pfeffer even praises Wal-Mart, a firm renowned for low pay and union-bashing, for its 'long-term' perspective resulting from its large share of family ownership (Pfeffer 1995/2005: 95, 103).[4]

Our position is that there have been important changes to traditional career structures in large organisations, but that they do not amount to a fundamental shift from bureaucracies to networks. Large firms remain bureaucratic and authoritarian. They may have fewer layers of management than before, but they are also not 'flat' – the key strategy decisions are taken at the top, just as before. The main change has been the widespread and continual increase in work pressure (combined with a reduction of support for managerial employees). In many cases, middle managers were left 'all at sea', to sink or swim in a difficult new environment. This story supports an LPT interpretation; not in a sense of direct senior management control over and de-skilling of middle management labour – middle managers in general do not need direct supervision – but through ongoing processes of rationalisation, cost

---

[4] For much more critical reviews of Wal-Mart's employment practices, see Fishman (2006) and Bunting (2004: 102–7).

control and role expansion. What was particularly interesting about the US cases was the similarity of so much of what we were told; notably about the challenges the company faces and the systems put in place to combat them. In particular these included some very familiar, 'off-the-shelf solutions', such as Six Sigma or Balanced Scorecard. The senior executives in these US firms have seemingly followed a similar set of prescriptions. In order to demonstrate this, we now turn to our in-depth discussion of five major US corporations,[5] starting with a *Fortune* 500 listed, multinational recruitment firm.

USRecruit: 'You had a job for life, even if you stunk'

USRecruit is a major HR/recruitment agency headquartered in the USA with a worldwide presence. Our main contact at USRecruit was the Director of Employment Law, Employee Relations and Litigation Management (D of E). Interestingly, given the highly litigious nature of the USA, and its tradition of 'employment at will', the person put in charge of many of the HR issues was actually a lawyer. The thinking behind this was that she would be able to prepare the firm for any employment law-related problems that restructuring could create. In a highly candid and open interview, she gave a detailed account of the pressures facing this famous firm. Her story was full of references to the difficulties both she and the firm confront as they face up to dealing with intense competition in the sector, and to the difficult task of removing many of the company's employee entitlements, notably job security. She mentioned that their main competitor, a major European recruitment multinational, was 'pretty much spanking us right now', largely because of the lack of clarity and rationalisation of her firm's existing systems.

USRecruit was, until fairly recently, a family-owned firm that had grown quickly without much strategic thought given to its organisational form or scope. As a result it was described as 'just too cumbersome' and 'too expensive'. Up until the D of E's appointment, the firm did not even have an HR department. A new CEO, appointed in 1997, immediately set about the task of tackling some of these inefficiencies. Attempts at organisational change (not always achieved) have taken place on just about an annual basis since then. The D of E began by

---

[5] Four of these case corporations are US-owned, and one, USBank2, is historically American, but was acquired by a Canadian multinational.

explaining the recent changes and the drivers behind them. What was particularly interesting about this interview was that it neatly captured both the threatening and possibly liberating elements of fundamental workplace change:

So [name] came in as the new CEO, the first time really somebody new at the helm, and within a few years he brought in a new executive vice-president of North America. [...] She – in essence she's the President of North America – she runs all of North America. Within five months she reorganised what she calls her lead team out of the US headquarters. There were about ten VPs that reported directly to her. And she restructured it so that she only had seven VPs. [...] [USRecruit]'s kind of messy structurally speaking; we've always been focused from the inception on selling and we've never focused on the internal structure. It's always been, 'Let's get as big as we possibly can, let's get in as many countries, let's have as many temps out there as we possibly can and all this stuff will take care of itself', which it actually did. The stuff you do in the booms of the 1990s they were just ... the company just did extraordinarily well. But what's interesting about our industry is that we are the tell-tale signs of when the economy's going to sink and when the economy's going to be great. And so I got here [...] and we could see that, we knew it was coming, I mean it's the harbinger. So the first two quarters of 2000 were awful for us – it hadn't caught up to the rest of the economy but we knew it was coming because, you know, [other companies] stopped using us. We still haven't seen a turnaround, you know, we get these weekly updates, everybody in the company gets weekly updates and some weeks are better than others. But, you know, in 2002 there was a period where it started going up again, but we're in the double dip again, you know, we went into a double dip. So let's get back on track, so [EVP North America] restructured her team and ten VPs were reduced to seven, and what she tried to do is to align it so it makes sense. Nobody had ever really thought about the structure, they were just busy getting bigger, so she tried to line all of marketing under marketing, all of IT under IT, I mean this sounds pretty common sense but it's pretty revolutionary. And out of it the next phase was that we've always had, we've always sort of run home office, the headquarters, we're here to support the field. But the field's so far away that home office thinks that it's most important, you know, and the field thinks it's most important, and I think you'll see that in most organisations, you'll see that kind of tension. [...] We've got something like 150 departments, I can't even begin to tell you what they all do and why we have so many and why we spent the money that way. And for once it's actually being looked at. I mean we're starting to align departments and we're really asking managers and directors in all these different functions to look at who they are, and do we need to, and does it make sense? It's kind of the first time in our history that we've actually gotten there, so the lead team got restructured.

Although this may sound very context-specific, the problem of a firm growing so large without much thought being given to the organisational shape was a fairly common finding in our study. It is not unlike the situation in Japan during the bubble era, when expansion continued without much thought about its longer-term logic. The only surprise in this example is that the change had come about so late on, and that USRecruit had carried on so far without engaging in change until the onset of the dotcom crash era of 2000–2. The phrases the manager used were highly reminiscent of the current discussions in Japan about the 'end of the era of high growth' when nearly all core staff were guaranteed a job and recruitment continued with minimal thought given to the cost or even the purpose of it (see Chapter 5). The new CEO was described as being in favour of Balanced Scorecard, which had been used in his previous post in Canada, and there was talk of bringing this in. The D of E noted that it was 'almost embarrasing to say out loud' that they 'don't have basic metrics'. When such changes finally did come about at USRecruit, many of them had major implications. She was candid enough to admit that the real reasons for restructuring – cost cutting and rationalisation – are not spoken about openly, 'except at the highest levels'. The D of E described what happened after restructuring the lead team:

The next thing that [EVP, North America] started to take a look at was the field. The field was run by two senior vice-presidents, a senior vice-president for the west and a senior vice-president for the east and they were really sort of the operational folks. And then there were VPs that reported to them, so we had fifteen field VPs reports to the two SVPs. Just this May, out of those two VPs, one retired and one went into a new role and we brought in a new chief operating officer. He was actually somebody who had run our Canadian operation. He was asked to come down, and just about two weeks in he eliminated six of the field VPs, so that we are down to nine VPs in the field. [...] It was just too cumbersome, it was too expensive. What's really driving it, and it's not said out loud a lot except for at the most senior levels, is that we had a lot of people, I mean fourteen or fifteen VPs that operate in the field, and they've never been really asked to operate on that level. They're very highly compensated and yet they really worked at this almost like a middle manager level, you know, and nobody really knows what they do. They opened up offices wherever they wanted to, you know, for example they would open offices in these little small towns where there's probably no work for [USRecruit] but because it was their home town. I mean so there's nobody even watching them to make sure that they're really making good business decisions. And so [new chief operating officer] wanted to thin them out [and] he did an evaluation about who he thought would actually be successful in this new role. Because it is a bigger role, they're going to have to operate in a completely new way and, you know, between the three of us, some of them are going to make it and some of them are not. I think some of them we're going to be asking them to operate in a way that we've never asked them to operate in.

Asking people to operate in a new way was complicated, controversial and potentially disturbing. Such was the potential for a collapse in morale that these issues had to be dealt with carefully and, to a degree, secretly. Broader trends in the governance and structure of the firm reinforced the sense of turmoil. After restructuring, things would never be the same again. USRecruit senior managers and employees would both have to accept that certain individuals will not survive in the new era. Today's harsher climate had no room for traditional paternalism. In fact, the very concept of a 'family firm' and all that it entails came in for specific attack. Families can be 'too traditional', 'too cosy' and 'too tolerant of misconduct or laziness':

[USRecruit]'s always operated like a family, I mean you go back to [previous CEO] and this being a family-owned business. Once you came to [USRecruit] you pretty much had a job for life even if you stunk; I mean, you had to engage in pretty serious misconduct to not be here any more. [...] And so what was announced by [new CEO] and the EVP at the annual meeting was huge, I can't tell you how huge it was. You could have heard a pin drop. She announced that [USRecruit] is no longer to be a family business [and] that we're going to be a team-driven business now. [...] She went on to explain that when you're a family, you know, people have a bad time, so that people aren't doing what they need to do, you kind of just let it go because they're family, you know? And you accept a lot more and you're too patient and all those sorts of things, whereas in a team, you know, think back, and she talked about this, think back to your best coach and think about what that coach said. That coach motivated you to be the best, and if you were slacking that coach kicked your butt and said, 'Stop it, and if you don't stop it you're not going to have a place in my team'. And so she really announced this huge cultural shift. [...] And it's going to be interesting to see how that pans out. [...] She freaked out tons of people at this meeting, but at this meeting it's only area managers and directors and above are invited. So sort of the front-line folks aren't invited to this meeting, so what I always wondered, you know, what did those area managers go back and communicate, you know, if they were so freaked out did they just shut up? So that will be interesting to see, but what we're going to start seeing is that people are going to be held accountable for numbers. I mean for the first time ever we are putting [in] metrics. In order to be a successful branch manager you have to have this much business and you personally have to bring in this much business. And if you don't we're not going to consider you successful. We've never done it that way; for the first time we're actually putting together a sales force. 'Cos in some respects it doesn't make sense to have branch managers both being sales people and operations people 'cos there's not enough time. And we have such a strong brand that our business has traditionally come to us so people will just go to Yellow Pages and find [USRecruit] and just call us. That doesn't work any more and so we really are putting together a sales function and so we have this new job called business development manager.

Three of the central planks of the reform agenda (in keeping with many of the service organisations we visited) were the shift of the firm from a servicing to a retailing operation, the reduction of managerial layers and the introduction of new metrics for employee control and performance monitoring. These new metrics would include a modified version of Balanced Scorecard, known in USRecruit senior management circles as 'Visioning':

And so I think this 'Visioning' stuff is tweaking that, I think it's a little less complicated. I think it seems like people don't understand Balanced Scorecard is not just a measurement, it's also the strategy piece. [...] We're involved in something called the Balanced Scorecard community, with [name]; he now has a consulting business. And so what our HR department is doing is we're working with seven other companies across America [names several large service firms] and really big companies who are part of this community where we are going to come out with an HR scorecard. [...] I'm going to have to be a judge tomorrow and Thursday to see what the difference is between Visioning and the Balanced Scorecard. Now all of this is new to me 'cos I'm a lawyer, I mean seriously I'm a lawyer who's playing at HR, so this is always very interesting to me, you know, it's my indoctrination into some of the HR stuff.

Much of this 'HR stuff' was reminiscent of the language of the 'best practice' systems. Moreover, in USRecruit, flattening the management structure was easier said than done. Part of the difficulty lay with the problems the centre had in trying to keep control of the scale and scope of the company's operations:

I should tell you that [...] in between area manager and branch manager there's something called the DM, district manager. Now the reason I forgot it is because it was supposed to go away about a year ago, a year and a half ago, and we've just uncovered the fact that it hasn't gone away at all. And so one of my next big projects is going to be to eliminate those across the country, because it's an extra layer. The reason that it exists is that the field wanted more layers. You know, because there hasn't been an HR department there's been no career pathing or succession planning or any of that good stuff. So whenever anybody wanted to reward somebody they would say, so if you wanted to reward a branch manager who does a great job but there's no area manager opening, they created this new thing called district manager. And it really was a way to pay these folks more money and give them a little bit more prestige and, you know, it's just a way to reward. There's also a senior staffing specialist which I forget and again it's that same thing where those are supposed to have gone away and they haven't. And so what salary banding is going to do is that it's going to be my worst nightmare I think, because what's going to be unleashed on this organisation who may not be ready for it, I mean we need to do it whether or not we're ready. But what we're going to be unleashing on this organisation is the fact that we want to have fewer levels, we want to get thinner.

'Getting thinner' implied increased demands on those who managed to survive. Workloads and work intensity were on the rise at USRecruit, and the newly established HR community in the firm was eager to assure that existing staff were able to increase their skill levels to meet the expansion of their roles. This can have differential impacts on people, with some being 'energised' and others 'demoralised':

So it's interesting to see how some of this works out, so it's not just the people part that's in flux, pretty much everything about [USRecruit] is in flux. It's all scary, and it's exciting, I mean I think that you find a lot of people are really energised by that, but you also find a lot of people that are really, especially in the field right now, they are pretty demoralised, their whole leadership has changed. The area managers, you know, within the last three weeks realised that if their VPs have changed, guess what? – they're next, you know? And as soon as something happens with area managers the branch managers are going to know they're next and then you've got the staffing specialists who are just trying to survive every day.

With a new organisational form came new career paths. The firm had made some effort at improving the quality of working life, but this had not been easy. Senior managers had started to give due attention to the serious issues around burn-out, career development and staff retention, particularly in the context whereby ranks were being cut away and the traditional ethos of long-term employment and stepwise promotion were being eroded by organisational restructuring and pay regrading:

I've got a team of four employment lawyers, they're called managers in [USRecruit], and I had to call them managers so I could pay them what I needed so they would have the right benefits. So part of the salary banding process is to get rid of that whole model. [...] There's going to be two career paths, there's going to be sort of the manager career path, [...] then there's going to be sort of the technical specialist career path. And for like my lawyers they'll lose that manager title 'cos it's dumb; they'll be a sort of a senior consultant in the senior consultant level and they'll be in the same band as the managers but they won't have to be managers; it'll sort of eradicate some of the falseness of that. How do we incentivise great managers to stay? I think that there will actually be some more room to give them better compensation and I think we'll have more room to give them increased training, and there'll be more room to say: 'Look, when this area manager, when this position opens up or there's a position throughout anywhere in the country, an open area manager position, we're going to be willing to consider you for it.' One thing that we haven't been good at is if there's an opening up in Seattle and we have this awesome branch manager down in Florida we haven't been connecting those, we haven't been saying, you know, 'Let's use our talent and move them up here'.

As we have argued elsewhere (Hassard *et al.* 2007), it is striking that, despite the clear differences between societies and organisations, there is so much similarity in the demands for large organisations to change in the face of such severe financial and competition-related pressures. Many of the Japanese firms we visited (see Chapter 5), for example, even though they possessed powerful traditions of lifetime employment and seniority-based pay, strongly emphasised the need to restructure old-style career paths in the hope that this would allow for more flexibility and more varied and rewarding careers for staff given that the expectation of a steady climb up internal career ladders had diminished significantly following organisational change and job cuts. The discussion of the need for a 'manager' employment track and a 'technical specialist' employment track at USRecruit was very similar to what we saw in Japanese manufacturing companies which, once again, highlights the features of restructuring that these multinational firms have in common under pressures to be profitable.

On a more positive note, the D of E mentioned that, even though restructuring had caused morale problems, it had not, so far, eradicated the feelings of goodwill in the company, which are mostly derived from the nature of the work itself:

One of the questions is why do people stay in [USRecruit]? There is this amazing weird culture that I adore. You are sucked in and you just adore this place, and it has this weird unique charm that you just are sucked in. And a lot of it is 'cos our front-line folks really sort of believe that they are the job people, they believe that they are out there everyday fighting the battle of giving the unemployed employment, of giving the underemployed better employment, of training folks who have no idea how to get a job and be an employee. It's almost, our front line are almost like a social service and they all have this great fire in their belly, sort of, do the right thing and get people the best job and make sure our customers treat our people the way that they should be treated. I mean it's just amazing, amazing ...

It would be critical for USRecruit to ensure that, somehow, this feeling of goodwill can survive despite the changes. The D of E demonstrated the conflict and trauma associated with organisational change, particularly when forced through in such a hurried manner. Authors such as Cascio (2002a, 2002b) would argue that this is an example of a poorly thought-out and risky strategy, one that risks alienating surviving staff. His ideas about 'responsible restructuring', while in many ways laudable, are somewhat optimistic. Even when organisational change has been carried out in a less radical fashion, and even when an 'amazing' atmosphere has somehow survived more or less intact, increasing workplace pressures, heavier workloads and the removal of traditional seniority-based employment and jobs for life are almost inevitable results of cost-control measures. It is then incumbent on the employees themselves to cope with the new environment. In the above case, the D of E seemed to be enthused by the challenge and although at times highly critical of her firm, also spoke in glowing terms of the culture of the workplace, claiming to enjoy the challenge of work and change. The tension between the goal of modernising the firm while limiting the 'collateral damage' was clearly highlighted in this case. But so too was the secrecy at the highest levels as to the real reason for restructuring – cost rationalisation and tighter organisational control over managerial labour.

USElectronics: 'Cutting and caring'

Our second case company, USElectronics, was another major American corporation. It has long been a global competitor in the highly competitive mobile communications sector, being one of the world's largest major manufacturers of cellular telephones and paging devices. It also has a large presence in global markets for automotive components and semi-conductors. At the time of our fieldwork it had almost 85,000 employees, down from around 150,000 at its peak. In recent decades the corporation has competed with major Japanese, Korean and European electronics manufacturers, both winning and losing high-profile commercial and technological battles.

Senior informants at USElectronics suggested that, in the 1980s, the corporation dominated the emerging domestic market for cellular phones and pagers. However, during the late 1980s and early 1990s, with the trend for Japanese manufacturers to swamp the American market with low-priced, high-quality products, USElectronics became uncompetitive. The corporation's initial response was to consider abandoning a range of businesses, even to the extent of mooting the merger of its semiconductor operations with those of a major Japanese competitor. Instead, however, it decided to compete with the Japanese in an attempt to recapture lost market share. This strategy saw USElectronics attempting to learn from Japanese operational capabilities in order to compete more effectively.

In enacting this strategy, senior executives devised a series of generic goals that essentially committed the firm to lowering its cost base while attempting to improve quality levels. USElectronics executives and managers were sent on missions to Japan; the results seeing the corporation significantly enhance its R&D budget while at the same time making plans to close several plants with the intention of later opening new ones. At the level of personnel, a subsequent organisational development programme saw an emphasis on training in a range of corporation-wide quality-management techniques. Notably this included a major commitment to the Six Sigma methodology, for which it won major national quality awards.

At the time our association with the corporation began, in late 2003, senior executives suggested the corporation was now experiencing a period of relative competitive success, following a very difficult period of 'unprecedented shrinking sales' from around 2000. In the second half of 2003, overseas operations appeared buoyant, with the firm even having, for example, twenty offices and more than 3,000 employees in Japan where, at the time, it held third place in terms of market share both in pagers and cellular telephones, and was approaching second. In terms of global sales, at this time USElectronics controlled around 45 per cent of the total market for these products, having regained its number two position in semiconductor sales. More than 55 per cent of its revenues were being generated abroad, with the corporation suggesting that its short-term goal was for 75 per cent of revenues to come from overseas markets.

Recent years (2006 onwards), however, have seen another period of competitive decline for the corporation. The success of one of its handset products around the time of our field research projected USElectronics into a position where it became a major force in the market. Corporation informants have suggested to us recently though that a significant profit decline in late 2006 brought about a major restructuring exercise in 2007, when once again core manufacturing plants were earmarked for closure and non-core divisions divested. Indeed, in 2007 one of the corporation's long-standing South Korean competitors overtook USElectronics as the world's second-largest handset maker, with another Korean manufacturer now being poised to take over USElectronics' third position.

During our time at USElectronics we were fortunate in being granted access to executives at the very top of the corporation. In particular we gained much insight into corporate strategy from senior executives in human resources, and especially from the Senior Vice-President for Human Resources (SVP HR), who had spent the last ten years of his twenty-seven with USElectronics in this role. Our discussions with him brought into clear perspective the harsh realities surrounding strategic and operational decisions. Decisions taken had drastic implications for managerial labour, including recurrent rounds of corporate reform, restructuring and change. The HR executive described the recent history of the corporation in terms of an economic and technological 'rollercoaster', although one moving, in his words, at the speed of a 'rocketship ride':

If you haven't looked at the charts, the growth charts of the semiconductor industry it's an amazing thing to look at; I would encourage you to get them because it is a rollercoaster. And you can almost predict that in about three more quarters the semiconductor industry will go back into a dip, and, you know, it'll hit bottom and then it'll come bouncing right back. And so it's not this gentle kind of a curve, it's Mount Everest and, you know, Mount McKinley, and what you don't know is how deep is the pit, the trough, right, and how high is the peak? So from the trough to the peak is probably a 100 per cent sales growth, right? So from a 40 per cent negative to a 60 per cent positive and it'll all happen in about a two-year period of time. And so, you know, that hits you at the same time, and then some mistakes, I mean just, you know, the execution mistakes that we made. Not responding to some of the consumer trends as fast, having great competitors like [names of three competitors], so on and so forth. You know, all those things kind of combined to say, 'Well, we've just got to start taking out cost or we won't survive'.

A rollercoaster ride will feature many frightening twists, dips and swerves. For USElectronics, almost all of these challenges derived from the need to take out costs. The firm followed the costly pattern described by Downs (1995) of a 'binge and purge cycle'. Recurrently, new technologies were developed only to be all too soon abandoned. New divisions were bought only to be quickly 'spun off'. New workforces were hired only for a large percentage to be 'transitioned' or 'outplaced'. The peaks and troughs of overall firm staffing levels in recent decades were especially marked:

Taking [USElectronics] from a peak of about a 155 [thousand employees] approximately to a current state of somewhere around eighty-five and to a future state once we spin off. We've announced we're spinning off our semiconductor business to become an independent company called [name of company]. When that is done [USElectronics] ends up somewhere around 65,000 employees, sixty to sixty-five, somewhere in that range. So I mean when you think about that kind of a change, so 155 approximately, a peak of 150 let's call it, down to sixty-five, you know, not all through forced reductions, right, but through strategic transactions, selling the government business, spinning off the semiconductor business, having sold off previously a part of the semiconductor business. You know, we sold off manufacturing facilities to third-party outsourcers, you know, including one in [a major city in the British Isles] and the like. You know, there's a lot that has happened where jobs didn't – people didn't all lose their jobs is my point, right – we did the best we could to try to, you know, have continued employment for our people, give them a future that would be there for them to help them create with the new company. But then there's been a lot that have just, the people who have retired or left or, you know, we've closed facilities or whatever it may be.

The metaphor regularly employed by the SVP HR, of divisions or sub-companies being 'spun off' by the parent, is an interesting one. It brings to mind the image of a spinning top which, initially (and perhaps casually) set free and given motion by its host to operate in independent space, works quite steadily for a period before, as the level of independent motion decreases, it begins to veer in a number of seemingly random and unpredictable directions prior, finally, to coming to a complete and sudden stop. This is reminiscent of the histories of many divisions and sub-companies set free by parent companies in the post-industrial break-up of large manufacturing groups in the USA and the UK during the 1980s and 1990s, where units initially released to operate in the same product market, but under a different, independent name, were seen, over a relatively short period of time, to take on a range of new names, identities and ownership forms, and manufacture a range of new products for different markets in order to survive, before ultimately going into liquidation.

The SVP HR's early training appeared to immerse him into USElectronics' form of corporate style and appraise him as to the realities and norms of an industry where sentiment and loyalty appear to count for little where matters of operational cost-effectiveness are concerned. Our senior executive outlined, for example, how an early role for USElectronics saw him charged with getting a small British operation in a 'sleepy' country town 'up to speed' in order to handle a new product line. However, the (then) junior HR executive became actively involved in the English plant's closure and subsequent transfer of operations to a site 400 miles away, in Scotland, with this new site, in turn, being 'spun off' independently less than three years later.

My first assignment outside the USA was to help bring up to speed a plant in England which was an automobile plant in [name of small town], sleepy old [name of town] [...] it was a plant that had been making some automotive equipment, parts for the motor industry and had extra capacity. So [USElectronics] decided to start building cell phones there and then. So it was a very interesting kind of transition to take; the automotive industry as you know, while it has a lot of technology, is very, very cost sensitive. So all of a sudden these cellular folks come in and, you know, we're seeing volume going through the roof, it was a real interesting transition for that town taking that plant from about 200 people to about 2,000 people and never, never ever being large enough to be able to handle that, and then ultimately moving that plant to Scotland.

The 'hyper-competitive' nature of the global electronics market and its impact on organisational development and structuring was a theme that framed many of our discussions at USElectronics. Much of the logic for the rapid purchase and divestment of divisions on a global basis seemed to rest squarely on the issue of whether or not the 'cost base worked'. During the 1990s, the transitional economies of China, Russia and Eastern Europe seemed to offer plenty of opportunities for USElectronics to establish production sites in potentially low cost base locations, and thus to expand its global empire through experimenting in new markets and products:

You know, seeing China emerge, seeing the rest of the Asian economies emerge and helping [USElectronics] really, you know, get into those kind of countries. Eastern Europe when that opened up, right, and a lot of work in Russia and, you know, the other Eastern European countries and the Middle East and then Latin America. You see the same thing happen in Latin America with expansion in Brazil and in Mexico and so on and so forth. So it was an unbelievable experience to kind of build that business and opportunities that were presented way before anyone would have imagined just because the place was exploding.

But as this rapid 1990s expansion into new markets, products and economies was developed, it too ultimately began to reflect the extremely corrugated pattern of USElectronics' recent corporate history and experience. This was nowhere better demonstrated than when, late in the decade, the firm got into serious economic difficulties in its attempts to create a series of industries that failed to take off:

Some of the opportunities to create new industries didn't work, like [name of satellite phone technology]. You know, not a technology failure by any means, in fact a technological wonder by many accounts, still being used today which is sort of the part that people don't know about, but a lot of that traffic that's coming from Iraq and radio stations and televisions are still using the [name of technology] network which is up and flying above the earth. But a business failure, no doubt a business failure because the time it took to develop the technology was so long that in essence cellular developed at a speed that made that unnecessary. That and probably a mismatch of markets, trying to sell that as the world travelling phone, or the phone for the world traveller was misplaced, it really was communications in those places where there were no other options is really the market it should have been after. But then the cost base didn't work and so on and so forth. So that, living through that, and the telecom bust, you know, the 2000s, the paging industry going away, merger with cellular, the cellular industry becoming hyper-competitive, and the emergence of [names of three major competitors] and the like, you know, and still holding on to the number two position but at one point in time obviously having a number one position, you know, and then seeing [name of major competitor] kind of jump over and, you know, become the dominant player there.

Given such techno-economic turbulence and uncertainty, the timescale for making major decisions on, for example, divisional or technological divestments was often extremely short. Massively important decisions were taken on the basis of figures from a few years' trading or from trends extrapolated from quarterly results. Moreover, the basis for decisions upon which some of the major downsizing exercises that took place at USElectronics around the turn of the century appeared simply to include elements of strategic 'feel' or 'guesstimate' for an industry or product as much as cold economic and technological evaluation. As the 'hyper-competitive' and uncertain environment of 'world economics' seemed (perhaps ironically) to represent something of a metaphorical *longue durée* for USElectronics executives, so there appeared almost an acceptance of a degree of serendipity in terms of what the future status of the business would look like in wake of the types of decisions taken. Such corporate happenstance, however, rested somewhat uneasily with the reality of tens of thousands of employees being potentially or actually laid off. Whatever the basis of the corporate decision logic deployed – be it objective economic forecasting or subjective executive feel, or a mixture of both – the post-hoc justification appeared pretty much the same; that is, corporate statements suggesting USElectronics must be consistently engaged in 're-engineering' in order to be more 'agile', 'leaner' and ultimately 'fitter'. Metaphors of battle and war are regularly used. These are apt given some of the lines of business that USElectronics has worked in, calling to mind the neo-Marxist logic of the 'Permanent Arms Economy' (Baran and Sweezy 1966; Mandel 1971: 274–309) into which many large multinationals are connected:

It's been a tough road for the last five years approximately, you know, the journey's not over, right, nor is the competitive battle, if you will, and, you know, the last quarter of last year, the first quarter of this year shows some great signs. And so you begin to see now a much leaner, much less costly, much more agile company beginning to emerge, and, you know, one of the things that I watch as the senior HR leader is so through all of that downsizing, right, all that kind of trauma and pain were we able to preserve a culture that can respond now that we have some hot products and we have some pretty big opportunities. So that's probably what I feel best about, you know, so if I kind of hung it tomorrow and said, you know, I'm kind of done with this, time to go do something else, I would feel that would be my biggest

accomplishment was to try to get the organisation through the pain that we
had to go through. Which was awful quite frankly and absolutely no fun to
be in HR when you have to take out that number of people. But to have
preserved the company, preserved its independence when it could have been
swallowed up by someone else and sold off in pieces, and then to see it be able
to emerge stronger hopefully. And that jury is still out, right, we don't know
that that's going to happen, the signs are extremely positive and Q1 was great,
Q2 I think we have a very good chance and then we'll see what happens with
the world economies in the second half of the year. But certainly growing
market share, biggest gains in your home market in Europe with the emergence of some new phones and, you know, it's great to see that you can come
battling back. Now, you know, the question is – does the workforce, the team,
the leadership have the stamina to continue the battle? Because it's been so
hard and only time will answer that question.

Often the feeling we came away with from such discussions was that
when corporate times were bad it was (deterministic) factors such as
'world markets', factors apparently beyond executive control, that
tended to be highlighted, whereas when times were good it was the
(voluntaristic) strategic choices of senior executives that were placed
more centrally on the stage of corporate affairs and fortunes. However,
this was not exclusively so. Mistakes were admitted to; decisions taken
at one point were based on the best information available at the time,
but in hindsight they appear as serious mistakes. When a major government electronics business was divested by USElectronics, the explicit
rationale for disinvestment was that the division was not 'strategically
well aligned' with 'core competencies'. Nevertheless, there are clear
signs that this management-speak glosses over the real reason: the
urgent need for cash to shore up the balance sheet. Indeed, the executive admits that this short-term move was in hindsight a mistake. It is
likely that top management had taken this decision under pressure
to follow the trend for 'unbundling' large firms into simpler structures
which capital market investors can, supposedly, better understand (see
Froud *et al.* 2006: 305). This episode reflects the tendency for Anglo-
Saxon firms to take drastic action, something the Japanese firms in our
study were much less willing to do. The possibilities for parts of the firm
being spun off or sold always hung in the air, and it must be difficult for
staff to know where they stand given the likelihood of such radical
change. Decisions for changes of this nature take place a long way
above middle managers in the hierarchy, indicating the rather limited

sense in which they are really included in strategic decision-making, in contrast to some of the more optimistic strategy literature (Balogun, 2003; Dutton and Ashford 1993):

And so all of a sudden you've got, you know, a looming kind of a crisis, and although we never quite frankly did get in trouble but were close enough where you began to say, 'wow, you know, we've got to look at our balance sheet' at the same time. And so everything was turned open to say, 'we've got to go take a look at this', so the kind of things that we did, you know, was to first make hard decisions about what businesses you want to be in. A good example of that is we had a very profitable, very successful government electronics business that made equipment for the Department of Defense. Every mission, every NASA mission has had [USElectronics] communications equipment on it. So, you know, lunar rovers, the Mars probes, you know, all of the things on the moon, all that communications equipment was made by [USElectronics]. And so a very attractive business, fairly stable, reasonably profitable but not strategically well aligned, and so a decision was made to sell that, it was bought by [name of corporation] and so, you know, all of the leadership team, all of the people, so on and so forth went with that and that was a few thousand, you know, three, four thousand people and over a billion dollars in sales, so an example of a very healthy business that you would say, you know, should go. Interestingly enough, if we would have known about September 11th, we probably wouldn't have sold that business.

In attempting to stabilise the balance sheet and turn the business around amidst the profitability crisis, USElectronics executives operationalised a range of corporate strategies, goals and programmes, including Six Sigma and cost rationalisations. The philosophy for turnaround would not, supposedly, take recourse exclusively to the traditional American organisational change techniques of 'the butcher' as, for example, in deploying the 'rank and yank' method used so commonly by US corporations to remove annually the lowest performing 10 per cent of staff.[6]

---

[6] 'Rank and yank' is a commonly used slang term for a very robust labour management technique made famous at General Electric under Jack Welch. It is also known as the '20/70/10' system of annual employee appraisal, or a system of 'forced ranking'. The top 20 per cent performers are the company's most precious human assets that it must hang onto and reward highly. The middle 70 are meeting acceptable standards of performance. The bottom ten are not and, in all likelihood, will be swiftly 'transitioned out' of the company. Welch was a 'celebrity CEO' well known for his cost slashing, but also highly respected for overseeing a very long run of earnings growth. Perhaps because of this success, the narrative that was constructed around GE at the time was very favourable, and many of Welch's tactics have gone on to be

Instead, the 'techniques of the surgeon' would represent USElectronics' motif for radical HR change; the corporation thereby predominantly seeking to take 'vertical' rather than 'horizontal' slices out of the business:

So it was not any one single thing, is what I'm going to say to you, it wasn't any 'we're going to take 10 per cent across the board' or 'we're going to take 40 per cent across the board'. It was a series of strategic decisions by the business in trying to say, 'so how do we get leaner, how do we get more cost effective, how do we lower our breakeven?' And we were setting goals like lower our breakeven by five billion dollars, you know, so big humungous goals, and then saying, 'all right, here's what we have to go and do about that'. Another way that we did it was simply to look at real estate – how many facilities do we have and where are they and let's consolidate, let's shrink. And, you know, some people were able to physically move locations to a new facility. Others we said goodbye to with respect as they were leaving. Other tools that we would have used would be to say, 'how do we cut an organisation?' Not, you know, kind of by horizontal slices but by vertical slice, right? So how do we say you can't just take out, you know, the 10 per cent lowest paid or the 10 per cent worst performing, you have to also say well, do you have too many managers, you know, do you have too many finance people, do you have too many HR people, do you have too many engineers? And really sort of, it's the analogy would be, you don't do this by the techniques of a butcher, you do this by the techniques of a surgeon, right? You say to yourself, if you do it right you do it that way, right, you say to yourself, so I need a healthy patient at the end so I can't cut out the heart, you know, but how do I cut out some of the fat, you know, how do I really sort of make this a leaner, healthier organisation. And you can't just sort of say, 'well, OK we're going to lose fifty pounds, chop off a leg', you know, you've got to think of it in that sort of a mind frame.

Historically USElectronics has been a non-union corporation which believed in its own paternal benevolence. Senior HR executives were thus at pains to stress that during the downsizing process the 'transition[ing] of people to their future' had to be carried out in a positive and compassionate manner. The awkward phrase used to describe this process was 'cutting and caring'. The extent of USElectronics' expression of direct corporate welfare during this period, however, remains moot given that

hugely influential. 'Rank and yank' has been used in many *Fortune* 500 firms. In McLean and Elkind's book on the collapse of Enron (2004), some of the former executives critically describe this exact system. See Froud *et al.* (2006) for an analysis of the 'narrative management' tools employed by and around GE.

an external HR consultancy was hired to take the major role in the 'invest(ment) in outplacement' process in USElectronics plants worldwide. The key instruction to this HR consultancy was to 'get them [redundant staff] to wherever they're going to go next as fast as we can'; this being directly related to USElectronics' desire to avoid any subsequent class action suits or union-organising drives. The risk of litigation appears to be the key factor influencing the need to take 'care' when cutting:

The other couple of things that we always kept in mind is this is a non-union company, right, and for seventy-five years that's been a tenet of this company – to be able to treat people as individuals with dignity and with respect. And so keeping that value in your mind and saying that's something we want to preserve long term, now, how do we go about this in a way that we treat the people as well as we possibly can on the way out and yet make sure that those who survive also look at that and go, you know, 'I could be next, and if I am at least I know I'll be treated fairly and so I'm going to give it my best to turn this thing around'. So that was always a consideration for us as well; tools that we used along the way would be, we felt, important to transition the leaving employees to their future as fast as we could. And so we invested in outplacement for every employee, and so we hired, we negotiated a national contract in several countries around the world and used [name of an HR consultancy firm] as a supplier in most of the countries to say we want to help every employee move on to the next event in their lives. If that's retirement, great, but for a lot of them it was the next job, or it was, you know, education to a new profession or whatever it may be. So we didn't just think of this as 'so how much money are we going to give them to leave'; we always had in our mind the idea that says, 'we've got to get them to wherever they're going to go next as fast as we can'. And the faster we do that the better it is for the employee, the better it is for those who survive these cuts and the better it is for us in terms of surviving any legal challenges that may come our way. And, knocking on wood, we've had no union-organising drives and we've had no serious class action suits along the way. And so I think this speaks to cutting and caring, right, so it's the surgeon's approach, right? Like, I don't want to cut you open and I don't want to hurt you, right, but I have to save your life. [...] The analogy of the butcher and the surgeon is not one I'm using just today, I mean that's the mental picture that we tried to paint in terms of the leadership of the organisation and the kind of things that we did.

In terms of the practical technology (or 'tools') driving this approach to downsizing and de-layering the corporation, the SVP HR offered a detailed explanation of USElectronics' preferred method of 'spans and layers analysis'. In so doing he outlined some of the 'worst case' scenarios, where layers in divisions could number as many as 'fourteen or fifteen', but where spans of control could be large at the top and the bottom, but relatively small in the middle. This, he explained, was poor structuring in an environment where the corporation was getting progressively 'smaller and smaller':

And we've developed some very good tools to just sort of say, 'OK, well, how many layers are there between, you know, the CEO of [USElectronics] or the CEO of a particular business line that we call sectors and the lowest level employee', right, and just count them. And then, you know, go into your system and say so how many managers report to each layer and what's the average span or how many people report to each manager and what's the average span? So, you know, what we found when we first did this at the top you would have a span of, say, one to eighteen – pretty big – at the bottom you could have a span of one to forty, and in the middle you had tons of one to two, one to three, one to four, you know. And I think the worse case we found was like fourteen or fifteen levels, right, and so we just said we're going to set a target; we're going to get to seven levels, right? And we just started driving, you know, through reporting and saying, 'look, if we're doing something stupid stop us and tell us, right? But unless you tell us we're doing something stupid it doesn't make sense to us that we would have fifteen levels', especially as we keep getting smaller and smaller and smaller.

The goal of the corporation was to get to layers in 'single figures', although specific circumstances (particularly based on geographical factors) would possibly result in exceptions being made to the benchmark figure of divisions having a maximum of six layers from the chief executive to the lowest ranked employee. As the SVP HR explained, this was simply business common sense when you consider the massive overall reduction in staff that took place at USElectronics:

You know, our goal now is basically to get to five. [...] So the CEO is zero, right, the lowest level employee is five, so six total levels. [...] And, you know, we're there in some places but not everywhere, and where we're not we understand why, right, because I know HR the best, in some places it's just pure geography, right? If you're going to have, you know, this little plant somewhere in China, someone's got to be looking out after the HR needs and it's going to be a small span and an extra layer. But there were lots of things that just didn't make sense any more, you know, there were lots of processes and programmes that were put in when you were 150,000 employees and 40 billion dollars of sales that don't make sense when you're 85,000 employees and 27–8 billion dollars of sales. So there was a lot of, kind of, cleaning up to do on that one, too, and we still look at that, right? We still look at that as a tool.

As we have found in other case companies in our research, such dramatic de-layering tends to bring with it significant role expansion throughout a corporation. At USElectronics the need to radically downsize and de-layer one of its historically important product divisions led to a particularly challenging environment for those middle managers that remained in post:

But we in essence went, we took out somewhere between in the max case probably seven or eight layers, in most cases three or four layers. And then just said make the jobs bigger, make them more challenging, put the best people in them, and in some of our business, you know, we literally would take out, in the semiconductor business we took out 1,200 managers. And we either classified them as individual contributors or some of them just decided to move on, so that was a tool that we used.

The marked reduction in management layers also had a significant impact on career development at USElectronics. We observed techniques being employed that were essentially similar to those we had observed in other major US and UK corporations, notably concerning the 'rotation' of promising managers to different jobs at the same organisational level but at various geographical locations. This approach was felt crucial to avoiding promising management staff perceiving themselves as having become 'stuck' in the middle reaches of a de-layered organisation, where possibilities for career progression were now significantly reduced:

What we've done in essence is to really work on rotational assignments as development for people. So that's the way we've tried to address it is to say for those most effective people, 'we're going to move you'. I set a goal in my organisation to move almost 20 per cent of the talent every year, and not just the great talent right, the great talent are obviously the easy ones to move, well, usually easy. But all the talent we're going to move, you know, it's about 250 people approximately this year. And we're going to track that every quarter and let people know how we're doing, so that people get a signal that says, 'OK, well, you know, I'm trying to develop and I'm trying to do something'.

However, perceptions of 'treading water' career-wise among some of USElectronics' promising managerial talent prompted the corporation to consider a more purposive strategy for career development. In so doing it developed the popular notion in HR circles of a 'pipeline of management talent' to complement its rotational strategy. Here key personnel are given clear indications of what their 'destination' role will be after undertaking several rotational postings:

We've added also pipeline programmes. So we've said so we have the destination job, the destination job is to be a director or HR for a large business, which we would call a group. Who are the people that we see that have those skills and what are we doing to move them towards that level, and, you know, plotting their careers, planning their experiences and then tracking them as they go through? And that's been done for other big destination jobs in the corporation too. So a lot of emphasis on rotation as development, coaching and then lastly training. Those are the three pillars of our development strategy.

USElectronics did not only deploy the tools of downsizing and de-layering for use on middle and lower levels of the organisation. In addition the corporation has made significant headcount reductions among its senior officers. The SVP HR suggested this was a particularly 'painful' and 'tough' exercise for USElectronics, given that such executives had generally risen to senior positions because they had 'done pretty significant things for the organisation'. Nevertheless, the corporation takes recourse to a basic percentage benchmark ratio of senior officers to total workforce and this – together with comparative industry data – suggested that further reductions in senior executive headcount needed to be made:

And then the last thing I guess I would highlight is in the course of doing all that you also have to look at the most senior levels in the organisation, right? And so we looked at officers for the company, and at the peak of the company we had 550 officers; we now have about 345 and we're moving down to about 300. And so, you know, we just sort of said if we're taking our workforce down by approximately 25 per cent the officer corps ought to reflect that. And so again it's this idea of looking at our organisation, you know, this way and not just this way, right? And so that was very painful too, because you don't become an officer unless you've done pretty significant things for the organisation. [...] Moving out a couple of hundred officers was tough, to be honest with you. We're back at it now because as we look at the spin-off of the semiconductor business now you say, 'holy smoke, 62,000 employees'. We have a ratio we use to say, you know, officers should be less than a half a per cent of full employment or something like that, just a guideline. [...] We got some data from outside, surveys that we do and those kinds of things, and so

we had to say if you look at the officer corps, you know, with the semiconductor business it's about 345, if you look at the officers it should be about
345, if you look at the officer quota without the semiconductor business it
should be about 300. And it says we're going to go after another fifty-six or
fifty officers, so anyway those are some of the things that we tried to do and
the mentality that we had going into it. And it wasn't perfect but I think all in
all we did OK.

This senior HR executive felt all of the measures taken during the period
of radical de-layering and downsizing were consistent with the corporation's traditional culture and philosophy:

Principles have really stayed constant, right, so this company talks about two
values – I've mentioned one – 'respect for the individual', or sometimes we call
it 'constant respect for people'; we use both of those terms. The other is
'uncompromising integrity'. So it's always trying to do the right things in
terms of representing the company. [...] And I think, you know, in general
[USElectronics] has an image as a global player who's trying hard to do the
right thing, and, you know, if we have problems we fix them quickly and
move on.

However, one element of the paternalist ethos that had to be altered
during this difficult period was to facilitate a change in belief systems on
the part of lower level employees from an 'egalitarian and entitlement'
culture to one based firmly on 'performance rigour'. This was not always
an easy exercise to effect, given uncertainty on the part of employees as
to whether this signalled a major change in cultural 'principle' or merely
a change in operational 'practice'.

The perception for many, many years at [USElectronics] was that if you had
been here ten years you could not be laid off, right? Well, that got shattered
because we had to go do that and we had to, you know, make tough decisions
on people who just weren't performing no matter how long they had been
with us. We always treated them well on the way and in fact we based most of
our severance plans on how long you had been with us, so, you know, that
was another way to try to demonstrate [respect for the individual]. But we
didn't avoid the issues, we addressed them, and so that was probably perceived by employees as a change in principle, but I would say to you never a
change in principle, a change in practice and a change in the way that the
principle's reflected. But in honesty, if I was to be honest with you, if you were
to go and ask that question to an employee they would say, 'oh man, yeah that
was awful, all these people just had to go'. The other thing that we did, we
needed to do to change this culture is we added much more performance

rigour, so much more performance management than what we had seen before in the company. And both the absolute scales, so 'what did you say you were going to do, now how did you do?' And then a relative scale, so, you know, 'did OK on what you said you were going to be but when I compare you, in my case, when I compare you to our competitors out there, how are we doing in our people practices relative to [names of three major competitors], or whatever'. And that was a change, right, because we had a very team-oriented kind of a culture, and when you're exploding as a business, you know, that's the only way that you can survive is to have that. And now all of a sudden you added an edge to the organisation that said, you know, 'we really like you but we like you better and so we're going to pay you more than we pay you'. And that was a bit of a culture shock and a very tough change to make.

Ultimately, a major step in bringing about this greater performance rigour at USElectronics involved the performance-rating system being redesigned in such a way as to add a 'force distribution' component. However, when the SVP HR executive described the way in which USElectronics subsequently operationised the system, he appeared to contradict completely the views he expressed elsewhere concerning the corporation's 'surgical' approach to restructuring and its critique of 'rank and yank' methods as practiced at other major US corporations:

So when we looked at it, we had a five-point performance rating scale not unlike most companies; we were using two points on a five-point scale, right. So 96 per cent of our people, approximately, were one or two ratings, which means you have no differentiation, right? You have no idea who to pay more or who to pay less, and if you do pay someone more or less you can't justify it if you're challenged. And so we said 'that's got to go', and we kept a four-point absolute score against your goals, and then we added a force distribution. And we said about 20 per cent of you are going to be considered our top most effective performers, 70 per cent of you are going to be considered our solidly effective performers and 10 per cent of you are going to be considered those who need improvement or are relatively speaking least effective. That was tough, really, really tough, and, you know, you would get the phraseology like, you know, 'rank and yank', so 'rank us and then yank us out', because at the same time we were downsizing. So I mean if I had it to do again I would implement that system in a peak performance time, right, as opposed to a down performance time. On the other hand, at least I had data to help decide who were the people who should go, and so I can argue that kind of from both sides. I mean, what we're trying to do now is keep the differentiation but soften the edge a little bit, right? And so we've made some modifications to that process so that, you know, we'll still kind of have four different categories, you know, kind of a top 10 per cent, the next 20 per cent, the solidly effective 60 and then the 10 per cent that needs improvement. But we won't do it to the same kind of standard that we did before, still getting to differentiating pay and differentiating rewards. So that was also a big change in terms of people perception that we've changed the culture and maybe, you know, changed some of the principles.

USBank2: 'Love and trust in the matrix'

Our third case study from the USA is a large retail and corporate bank based in a major city in the Midwest. This was the second retail bank we researched in our study of large US corporations. Once again, in seeking to understand this organisation's recent history in terms of restructuring, change and development, we were fortunate in gaining access to senior executives within the corporation, especially to senior human resources officers, and centrally the Senior HR Executive for the United States (SHR US).

In terms of corporate history, USBank2 was established in the 1880s as a 'trust and savings' operation, the corporation's origins lying in the drive to assist American expansion westward. Originally a family-owned business, the bank was established in a period when the state in which it is located permitted only 'one bank to one location'. Such was the desire to take maximum advantage of having but one city building, that the financial district of the city in which the bank is based houses a number of extremely impressive banking institutions, many of which occupy an entire city block.

The progressive relaxing of state and inter-state banking regulations from the 1970s, however, saw USBank2 engage in a major programme of bank acquisitions that continues to this day. This has mainly involved acquiring banks with small- to medium-sized capitalisation. Indeed, the bank has gained an industry reputation for being an extremely aggressive purchaser of small banking operations (in the drive for greater market share, USBank2 even acquired a bank that had only two branches). Today the company is itself owned by a Canadian multinational bank. USBank2 has a large number of affiliated businesses and divisions, operating across ten states. In its wider metropolitan city area it has well over 200 locations, with a further forty in an adjoining northern state.

During the time of our fieldwork, USBank2 was in the midst of a major corporate restructuring exercise. This programme seemed at first rather gradual in comparison to some of our other case corporations, but later we came to understand this as extremely radical when the full details emerged. Our main contact, the SHR US, was playing a major role in this exercise, and he explained how the structural side of the business had evolved from the time he joined USBank2 in the mid-1990s:

I got here about eight years ago and we had what I would call the empire model, and that's where all the, sort of, lines of production report to one person. Non-matrix [...] you have a very traditional kind of organisational structure, and the CEO and Chairman has got all of the lines reporting to him. I'd say about six years ago, and I'll get this wrong in terms of time frames, but over a period of time, bit by bit, we went to a more matrix organisation.

The SHR US was at pains to stress the competitive advantages that a move to a matrix form offered for an organisation such as USBank2. He suggested that this model would allow it to obtain significant 'corporate leverage' while at the same time retaining its 'local advantage' with the wider metropolitan area:

The [Canadian parent bank] is a mega-bank, so we were trying to take advantage of what we called 'corporate leverage and local advantage'. We had very clear advantages in each of the communities because we had community banks. You know, each one had a president and all that kind of stuff, and the good news is that, you know, we've come a long way to going into the matrix world where you're trying to get the economies of scale. [USBank2] is too big to be small and too small to be big. So we've got to latch onto the economies of a North American strategy and not just a US strategy.

The basis for the new matrix form therefore very much reflected this desire on the part of bank executives to get the 'best of both worlds' – to couple the leverage of its Canadian parent on its North American business lines with its significant local presence in the metropolitan area:

So you now have a whole series of lines of business that run North American wide. Pardon the expression, but, you know, we've gone from the emperor model to the matrix weeny model, you know, and [the CEO] still has a very significant presence in that he runs [USBank2], which is all our retail and our commercial banking, you know, industrial, commercial business. But we have a private client group that is North American, we have an investment banking group that's North American, our infrastructural technology area is all North American, human resources is a high part of a North American operation. So the matrix really is, you know, the columns represent your North American strategy, the rows of the matrix is you want to have a local presence. A lot of people, to our great delight, in [city of USBank2's location] wouldn't be able to tell you that we have a foreign parent. And we're very happy to keep it that way, you know, in the sense that, you know, if we can provide the service without people feeling that, 'oh gosh, I'm dealing with a foreign bank', you know, it's just to our advantage.

Nevertheless, such a major structural redesign, from functional to matrix, has presented the corporation in general, and the HR function in particular, with major challenges, not least of which relate to the restructuring of middle management operations:

Historically though what we've had is a full infrastructure in the US which meant that we would have a reasonably senior marketing person. In other words, if you were to go into a bank of [USBank2's] size that was an independent bank, that person would be a senior executive. I sit on this guy's executive committee, so it depends on, you know, sort of you get to that height and then you get to the top and, oops, it's not the top, there's another, you know? And businesses all over the world I'm sure are just going, with all the acquisitions going on, plus the trends in organisation structures so they're going through the same thing. So all of a sudden my biggest challenge is to look at the middle management structure, and again I loosely describe it as that, and say 'OK, how are we going to evolve from the empire model to the matrix lean model?' Because if you were starting from scratch you probably wouldn't hire the same group of people, in fact there might be some positions you wouldn't even have.

Indeed, many of USBank2's business arrangements tended to suggest a major tension between much of its day-to-day retail operations and the structural form it wished to promote at the corporate level. When the legacy of USBank2's traditional state banking experience is coupled with its recent history of acquiring small to medium sized indigenous businesses, the business portfolio of much of its retail side suggests a range of local businesses operating primarily on traditional structural lines. Such arrangements thus contrast sharply with the recent history of major corporate functions, such as HR, which have seen qualitative changes as the matrix logic has taken effect. As the SHR US suggested, there have been 'many casualties' along the restructuring road from empire to matrix:

So the big challenge we have here is we have some indigenous businesses, which is our retail business, in that we have a more traditional structure. We have a branch network, we have regional presidents and we have two people who run the major hunks of our retail function. On all the support functions I report to the Head of HR for the whole enterprise in Canada and my job used to be I ran a fully integrated human resources function. So I've had to change with all of the other functions and, quite frankly, and this may be a little melodramatic, with the exception of the general council and me, we are the only persons in this executive floor that were here when I got here. And, you know, some of it is retirement, some of it. But some of it is, you know, you don't just turn the axis of an organisation and expect everybody to fit, and the more senior the officers are the more likely you're going to have someone who, in a Darwinian sense, evolves into something and is no longer what you're looking for.

A major problem for USBank2's HR executives related to the spans of control under the move from empire to matrix. A particular problem for the SHR US was realising USBank2's philosophy that there should be greater role expansion in the middle layers of the organisation. Specifically, USBank2 wished to promote the concept of middle managers moving from being 'supervisors' to 'player-coaches', or from being people who 'run things' to people who 'move dirt too'.[7] There was a clear impetus for expanding the spans of control for middle managers (downwards in this case), because of the cost rationalisation it promised. The following excerpt provides strong support for an LPT interpretation of organisational restructuring. New metrics and systems were developed and discussed among senior executives as they attempted to tackle perceived inefficiencies in managerial labour. Senior management will continually use and develop new technologies to analyse where labour costs can be minimised, and will squeeze as far as it logically can:

We are not happy at this point with our spans of control. We've done some analysis and what a matrix does is you get a shift from – and this is really what I'm talking about here – from people who run the place to what I call player-coaches, where, yeah, you're going to run the place but you're going to move dirt too. And so as a consequence you'll get small work groups where it looks like your span of control is horrible in the conventional measurement sense.

---

[7] The middle manager as 'player-coach' metaphor was used by several of our respondents in the Japanese case study organisations (see Chapter 5 and also McCann *et al.* 2004: 34).

And so we're under the gun for SG&A [Selling, General and Administrative] expenses, so I'll be putting another conference call at the end of the morning where we are talking about some analytics we've done on expanding control, particularly expanding control. We think we've got our lines of business right but now we've got to squeeze this thing again to see if we can get some costs out of it, and expanding control is one place to look.

However, HR executives at USBank2 appeared somewhat sceptical about how far they could achieve this particular element of restructuring the business from 'traditional' organising, despite the promise such role expansion appeared to hold for 'squeezing' more cost out of the business:

I'm not sure we're going to get too far because with the whole idea that, you know, your player-coaches move dirt as well as supervise, that kind of redefines what span of control means. So you have to look at each individual piece and say 'wait a minute', you know, 'you've got somebody managing there and you can clear the management position down to two people if you want'. But wait a minute, there's enough work there that, you know, I don't know how we would replace them but we'd sure replace them, it's not as if, hey, you can get rid of that layer and have someone else have a seven-person span of control instead of two, and you're kidding yourself, you've just gone back more to the traditional organisation.

This process at USBank2, as with other organisations we researched undertaking major restructuring exercises, suggests an emerging problem with the motivation of middle managers in terms of their career progression in corporations with fewer levels and where roles have been expanded significantly. At USBank2, as with so many other organisations in this book, the emphasis was placed increasingly on the potential for motivation through undertaking wider role responsibilities or more interesting work, or by rotating staff laterally, given the failure of de-layered organisations to provide sufficient rungs on the ladder for motivation by step-wise corporate career progression. The SHR US, however, was quite candid about this situation and acknowledged that the practice of moving mid-level staff laterally was not solely a motivational or developmental device, but also one that would allow him to hang on to promising staff for perhaps a few years more, given the lack of advancement opportunities in the organisation as a whole. USBank2 executives also felt this problem was particularly acute in their situation, given the organisation was owned by a foreign parent:

So more and more we're seeing middle management where it's the nature of the work that's going to challenge them as opposed to the next rung up the ladder. And that's been really magnified down here because frankly most of the masters are in Canada running it from Toronto. So my challenge, for example, within the HR structure is to take my middle management and [explain that] I have now got two alternatives [for them]. One is advancement in the firm and the other is 'see you around' because you'll find the opportunities elsewhere. The ladder was one that, you know, you'd sort of spin on and say, 'you know, well, we don't work that way'. Now I almost have to manage with that in mind because I'm not going to have the challenges for them on the professional side unless I move them laterally into something that they wouldn't be able to recruit for outside the bank because they don't have the background. I'm willing to take a risk on them, and it buys me a couple more years of a talented person, but I don't have the rungs in the ladder any more to amuse them and to allow them to move up.

However, despite the significant changes that had taken place during the ('non-traditional') restructuring process, with a new organisational philosophy being advanced by the corporation overall, we were assured by HR executives at USBank2 that underlying the changes there remained elements of traditional 'hierarchical' organising. What was significant, though, was that the restructuring programme had allowed senior executives to take a significant amount of cost out of the business, with de-layering, new performance management metrics and outsourcing technologies at the heart of this process:

Because we're in a bank and part of our DNA is hierarchy, you know, I mean we will never drop that and, let's face it, nobody ever really drops it. [But] when I came down I took about 40 per cent of the cost out of HR. I took a layer of management out and so that, what that did for me, and by the way we have just outsourced the transactional end of our HR activities; that has eliminated some layers as well. But we went from one, two, probably in the sense of professional people, four layers of management, and then we went to probably three if not two. Now one thing you've got to remember, though, my role has become matrix, so the person in Compensation is more junior now here but has a relationship with me and also the Czar or the Czarina of Compensation in Toronto. So, you know, we certainly created a more professional organisation and of course we got the geography piece. And that is that person here in Compensation now has to think of a jump and do they want to live in Toronto. And so there are other challenges as well. [...] I would say easily we've taken a layer out and that would be the empire managers because we don't need them anymore. I need dirt movers.

Overall, the process of taking 'cost' out of USBank2 in terms of layers and positions had been operated under a general corporate strategy that advocated greater 'focus' as far as its various lines of business were concerned. This philosophy reflected forms of strategic realignment we have encountered at other case corporations under the guise of championing 'core competences'. At USBank2, the re-examination of business competences suggested a radical 'tearing apart' or re-engineering of traditional business lines prior to their reassembly under matrix. This was an approach that appeared to sit particularly well with USBank2 executives, for in the subsequent reassembly of operations under the matrix model they were able to ensure that the 'columns' of business lines didn't dominate the 'rows' of geographical business territories:

Basically we were finding that to be competitive you've got to focus. And to focus you can't run fifteen lines of business. So we said, 'so let's focus on the lines of business'. And we've had all of the offshoots of that, ranging from some of the angst that we've had in the change management side, you know, where we've had misfits and all that kind of stuff, right through to probably more siloing than we had before in the sense that you do have people who are on a mission from God in their line of business and they don't give a stuff about any other line of business. […] Now that's naturally starting to come back together, so the trick of this whole thing is you tear it apart, you reconstitute it such that they gain their self-confidence in terms of we have a viable line of business. And then you start to put it back together such that your matrix isn't totally dominated by the columns of the matrix, that you actually have 'geography matters' stuff and it pulls back together. And we're starting to feel like we're coming into harvest time.

As the SVP US indicated, this radical restructuring process was accompanied by expressions of significant cultural resistance. A climate of corporate 'destabilisation' was realised in expressions of job insecurity. Some managers reacted by reinforcing their territorial boundaries. As the re-engineering process 'restabilised' under matrix, and surviving senior managers apparently began to realise they, and their operations, had a 'justifiable existence', confidence was said to have returned to the lines of business. Indeed, a degree of destabilisation was described as necessary given the complexity and fluidity of contemporary market conditions:

Who is it said avarice is the root of all evil? I think organisational insecurity is the root of all evil, and you get somebody who's destabilised because of a reorganisation, what do they want to do? They want to grab territory and build a wall, and as that goes away people get more confident in the fact that they actually do have a justifiable existence. And all of a sudden the lines of business start to cooperate because, you know, the market place doesn't give a damn, you know? Customers don't come in with barcodes on their foreheads saying, 'I am a private banking client'. So if you don't have a way that, you know, fuzzies that relationship, such that your distribution system finds them and then your professionals take care of them, they just walk out the door.

Despite the 'instability' at USBank2 brought about through the re-engineering process, the pressure remains to 'slim down' the business further. Indeed, the SHR US suggested that the notion of a business process 'revolution' that has framed the recent change programme was not entirely appropriate for USBank2. Instead, and again in keeping with the expectations of LPT, the demands of the cost environment and the perceived expectations of shareholders determine that senior managers at USBank2 have to monitor productivity ratios constantly and assiduously in order to 'squeeze' and 'trim' its 'chubby' operations:

All of a sudden we're supposed to revolutionise? Well, that's naïve, you know? Our cost environment you've got to just keep squeezing and squeezing and squeezing. 'Cos one of our biggest challenges is our productivity ratio. Yeah, we watch our productivity like a hawk, and so […] we have a very good reputation on the revenue side. People like what we're doing in the various lines of business, but there's always the footnote that, you know, they're a little chubby. […] We'll find some bits and pieces where I think we can trim.

The productivity revolution promised by the re-engineering process, also in line with LPT, involved the application of new performance management and employee incentivisation measures. Similar to the USEngineering case (see below), senior figures in USBank2 were unhappy with the stock-based payment plan for managers, as this was considered too generous, and did not differentiate between the best employees and others. In place of an incentive plan that was related to the overall performance of USBank2, incentive rewards are now driven predominantly by the performance of business lines. As such, generic profit sharing has given way to incentive plans that relate more to the performance monitoring of an independent business unit within a business line:

So the first thing that happens is they [management performance measures] become very much driven by the line of business. And so where you used to have, for the sake of argument, everybody had a multiplier in the incentive compensation that related to USBank2, that doesn't exist any more. In fact at one point we had profit sharing up until about four years ago. Well, you know, that was, I describe it as, you know, sort of nobody had any sense of 'I'm going to try harder today'. Because of that, you know, it was sort of 'see when you opened up [the box and] the turkey dropped on your desk' and you had no idea why, you know? And so, you know, we shifted from that and put it where it made more sense. So then, within the context of the line of business, you then have incentive plans that relate to [for example] an independent firm in that line of business. So again [for example] your investment banking people are driven in the same way as an ordinary investment banker on the street would be, as opposed to having a bank incentive plan. [...] I would suggest that the biggest change was that it was far more driven by the line of business now.

At the heart of re-engineering changes in USBank2's performance management and objective setting systems has been the adoption of the 'Balanced Scorecard' framework developed by Kaplan and Norton in the 1990s (Kaplan and Norton 1996), a performance management technology we have seen employed in many of our case corporations. Balanced Scorecard, which is basically a strategic management system based upon measuring key performance indicators across all aspects and areas of an enterprise, has been applied throughout the USBank2 corporation. As with other firms in our research sample, however, USBank2 has attempted to customise the Balanced Scorecard method to suit its own needs:

We're moving to a Balanced Scorecard, and it's one of those things that, you know, probably 200 key performance indicators is a few too many than I want to be measured on. So that you boil and boil and boil, and this is going to be a real, almost a silly statement but we have four quadrants that, you know, relate to financial, customer, human resources and the community. And then I add a fifth quadrant, which I realise doesn't make sense, but that is people's personal objectives on what they want to do themselves. And we dropped key performance indicators into each of the quadrants and those are agreed to at the beginning of the year. And those go right up to the Board, you know, I spend far too much time in my opinion, you know, looking at our CEO's objectives as to how they're going to be fed to the CEO in Canada and subject only to the Board. But, you know, the HR committee of the Board of [parent company] is very interested in the top [...] people's objectives and they look at them.

The re-engineering changes outlined above have impacted significantly on the self-identity of senior and middle managers at USBank2. In particular the traditional role of the manager in the middle reaches of the organisation has been subject to major changes in the move from empire to matrix. In a passage strongly reminiscent of views expressed by an ex-manager of UKBank (see Chapter 4), the SHR US discussed the general loss of 'points of authority' that has accompanied the restructuring and which has resulted in a significant number of middle managers leaving the corporation. This cultural turn has also seen traditional authority norms of the empire model give way to the 'love and trust' needed to operate in the 'cells' of a lean matrix. As the SHR US suggested, in many respects such turnover has been the logical response of re-engineered managers saying 'that's not what I grew up to be':

This is all part of the nature of the leaner syndrome. [...] You need a lot of love and trust in a matrix, and so as a consequence you'll have people who are perhaps even more influential. Because again you're eliminating layers and there's an inherent influence of what people do, and so to the extent that they influence they probably have more impact than they have in the past, and that's the whole idea. As far as authority is concerned, because you have reduced the points of authority there are times when you say, 'hey, wait a minute,' you know, 'just how high do we have to go to get this thing done' when you start getting things of a broader nature? [...] We had a fair amount of turnover within our middle management ranks. You've got these bank presidents out there, they think they run a bank and historically they've been right, [but] now we're trying to move them into more of a distribution, sales management job. And they're saying 'that's not what I grew up to be', and you'll see them migrating to some of the small independents. Some of the ironies are that, you know, within a couple of years of when they move over into an independent bank, we buy them!

The significant culture change at the bank, however, was due as much to USBank2's strategic realignment through, for example, acquisitions, alliances and outsourcing, as to the effects of generic corporate re-engineering. In recent years USBank2 has outsourced, for example, HR transactions, payroll, a call centre, custodial activities, credit card services and systems support. Like other firms in our sample, the narrative favoured by senior executives at USBank2 suggests that a formally 'paternalistic' culture has been forced to give way to one more attuned to the harsh ('leaner and fitter') realities of the times. Nevertheless, the narrative of senior management at USBank2, as with that previously at USElectronics, claims that whereas the 'culture' may have changed, the basic 'values' of the corporation have not, with the treatment of those forced out being 'humane'. Once again, though, the desire to avoid litigation is probably the subtext to this narrative:

We've had a lot, a lot of people who have either, you know, been terminated or they've gone over to our outsourcers. And historically our culture has been, probably to a fault, depending on how you want to describe it, maternalistic or paternalistic, you know, 'stick with us and you'll be OK', to [the situation now] where people have truly seen the evidence of you'd better fast forward your resume, fix it up such that you've got marketable skills. I would say very strongly though we've stuck to our values, you know, even in the sort of heat of having to get rid of people. I would say that we have a very, very established and protective way of dealing with that. Now people don't want the outcome but they wouldn't say, 'all of a sudden, you know, I had all my stuff thrown in a cardboard box and I was frog-marched out of the building'.

The above case of major organisational upheavals with a large percentage of the managerial workforce having been downsized amid a significant realignment of its business operations shares a great deal with what we have already seen at USRecruit and USElectronics. The drama played out by senior HR executives at USBank2 follows a similar script of 'crisis – countermeasures – partial resolution'. In this regard, restructuring is both a form of 'narrative management' (Froud *et al.* 2006) and a 'mechanism of hope' (Brunsson 2006) in that it provides a sense of rationality and structure to a rapidly changing world. Senior management tells a good story, containing struggle, battle and unfortunate but inevitable casualties. The old system was creaking and needed replacing. New systems and technologies were introduced that were basically (often mildly adapted) versions of 'best practice' elsewhere. Some of these introductions, however, were resisted. The future is looking rosier, but the threats have not been nullified. There is never time to be complacent. At least at USBank2 and USElectronics there was some optimism, and some of this may be warranted. Unfortunately the small pockets of optimism that existed at our next case seemed less credible, given the massive challenges the corporation faced.

USAuto: 'Not empowered, just more responsible'

USAuto is one of the largest auto manufacturers in the world. At the time of our research, the corporation comprised a global workforce of around 300,000 and had an annual turnover of $164 billion. It is an iconic corporation, with a history spanning more than a hundred years, and is truly symbolic of American capitalism, especially in the heyday of the 'old economy' of mass industrial output. Its eminence today is far less clear given long-run financial deficits, poor shareholder returns, low levels of customer satisfaction and competition from the currently very successful Japanese firms. We visited one of its major engine plants in the Midwest, where we were given some excellent access. This plant (which was in fact split into Engine Plant 1 and Engine Plant 2) in keeping with so many in the industry worldwide, had gone through major workforce reductions recently. When we first visited in 2003 it had 240 salaried employees (managers of one kind of another). Two years later, this had come down to 109. On the blue-collar, hourly side, it had 1,800 in 2003, but just 1,200 in 2005. We interviewed the Plant Manager, a senior manager in charge of lean manufacturing systems, and four other middle managers drawn from across the plant. Finally, USAuto management granted access to blue-collar, hourly supervisors who had taken on several managerial responsibilities in return for a slightly increased hourly rate. Interestingly, management would not allow us to tape-record these interviews with unionised, hourly supervisors, so we had to rely on note-taking in our discussions with them. With the exception of one of the blue-collar supervisors, all our respondents were male.

Our discussions with the Plant Manager provided a good background to the case. He had nineteen years of experience in USAuto, but was still relatively young for such a senior position, just two rungs below corporate senior vice-president.[8] He was an extremely impressive and persuasive communicator. Perhaps his climb up the ranks could be explained by his combination of 'people skills', engineering expertise and a passion for the company and its goals. In different ways, all of the people we interviewed at USAuto shared a lot of passion and pride for the firm – they desperately wanted it to succeed, but adopted slightly different perspectives. The Plant Manager placed particular emphasis on the familiar theme of the intensity of international competition. He consistently emphasised the importance of 'impressing the customer', with all the major auto players having to relentlessly develop 'exciting new designs', while retaining sight of 'quality and reliability'.

---

[8] For more detail on USAuto's hierarchy, see Chapter 4, where UKAuto (a subsidiary of USAuto) is discussed.

He mentioned many other competitors in the interview, underlining the toughness of the industry:[9]

I guess my view of the business – and I've been with [USAuto] now for nineteen years – is the industry has never been as competitive as it is today. If you look at our competitors in general – and I tend to take in the auto shows and things of that nature to look at just the vehicles that are being provided – the powertrains, the engines, the transmissions, they are all very good. I mean, our worst competitor is extremely good to be able to compete in the way the global industry is now. So what we are struggling with for lack of a better description, and I think every auto maker struggles with the same thing, is how do you maintain your position in that field, 'cos you have to be constantly improving, right? And depending on what's going on in the economy in general, meaning what are your strongest markets, what currently do you deal with, right? So things like fluctuations in the yen, things like a market that might soften where you are kind of your strongest, you could become the best and drop quickly to the worst of the major players pretty quickly without a lot of, things out of your own control, right? So how do you position yourself to be able to balance all that? How do you enter emerging markets, right? How do you maintain your strength in North America if that's your strongest market, right? How do you improve your quality to the point where you're becoming significantly better than your competitors, right? And you're always looking for that competitive advantage, right? (Engine Plant Manager)

He went on to discuss the importance of the 'people side' of the business with regard both to 'transitioning' the firm to a more profitable future:

So to me the focus for us as an organisation always has to be in our workforce and our work groups and just kind of solicit the important strength of our people. That has to be our strength because that has not traditionally been our strength, so we've been trying to transition that way for the last few years, but invariably we've been an organisation for the most part run by middle and upper management. So that is our transition, and when I look at the business that's one part of it, in North America I think the biggest opportunities is you have to draw people into your showroom. So you have to constantly be introducing new product and, as you introduce new product, if you can work

---

[9] Once again, military or hunting metaphors appeared in this interview with the Plant Manager, for example he said: 'We really have to identify who the enemy is, or what the enemy is. And sometimes, you know, we spend a lot of time thinking it's us, among ourselves or it's one of our sister plants. [...] Really we need to identify what we're going after, right?'

on, kind of, the other things. You have to continue to improve your quality, but just doing those things without introducing new product, something that kind of excites, surprises and delights the customer, you won't be successful, right? So it's a combination of how do I launch product and get people excited about that? And then how do I work on the basics underneath that, the foundation which is to significantly improve my quality [to] make sure I've got a workforce that understand and is aligned to the business, right? And if you do one without the other you don't achieve as great a level of success. (Engine Plant Manager)

Throughout our time at USAuto (the longest we spent at any of our case companies) we formed the impression that there could be no faulting the staff for effort and commitment. The shared dedication in trying to make the firm a success was very evident. However, dedication and hard work are necessary, but not sufficient, conditions for success. We were somewhat concerned that the Plant Manager appeared to have a view of 'continual' launch of 'new product' as the saviour of the company. His examples of a famous sports car and a well-known pickup truck manufactured by USAuto as 'great models' that the company needed to build on seemed to us unfortunate, given the current trend for moving away from high-consumption vehicles with poor environmental standards. Moreover, the suggestion that USAuto should somehow gamble and beat the market with exciting new products seemed a risky approach given the massive cost structure throughout the business. This 'strategy', while containing some obvious seeds of truth, seemed to be based more on hope than expectation, even with a hint of desperation, particularly as the Plant Manager had no firm explanation for how other competitors had managed to 'surprise the industry' with rapid improvements in their performance. Indeed, the suggestion was that automakers across the world are actually converging on increased levels of sophistication and quality improvements. As such, Japan, in this view, is not necessarily destined to remain considerably ahead of the USA on quality:

If I look at [JAuto], [JAuto], right, is the darling or one of the darlings of the industry right? Now in 2000 [JAuto] was bankrupt, they were literally bankrupt, right, so what was their formula for success, right? They said, 'the products that we're not making money on we're going to discontinue', right? 'We're going to realign our capacity with what we're actually selling', and what they've been able to do is launch some exciting product. Now if you look at [JAuto's] products they're significantly different, right? Now they've got to continue to work on their quality but they are making billion of dollars, and I think per unit produced are by far the most profitable automobile company right now, right? So four years ago they were nearly bankrupt, right? So things can change very, very quickly. The other thing is where we used to look at specific competitors and maybe know what we'd expect, that's no longer the case. So you look a few years ago, Hyundai came into the market and [was] almost a laughing stock, right? It was poor. If you look at their improvement in the last three years, it's phenomenal, it's phenomenal, right? Where we used to think, 'Jeez, we've got to chase Toyota to be the best in the world', now I've got to believe that Toyota and Ford and General Motors are saying, 'boy, how has Hyundai done this in the last three years, you know, how have they turned things around?' So I look at the industry as just this kind of constant up and down, and I see five years from now that we all continue to close the gap on quality, so you start looking at the numbers and everybody is kind of coming, you know, they all are improving at different rates to get to the point where they'll all be pretty much at the same level. And now you have to really work on continuous improvement in your cost structure, right, always need to work through that. And then how do you develop this exciting product that kind of gets people, you know, in a case that says, 'I look at that and I love it', right? And if I look at [USAuto] we have some vehicles that do that, the [sports car] is one, the [pickup truck] is another. People identify with those vehicles and it's kind of this love relationship that you say, 'boy, how do you get that?' But when you have it you know there's that bond with people. And every industry kind of has them, well, not every industry but every auto-maker has them with certain vehicles, right? There's certain cars that kind of inspire that. You have to really try and develop that, if you can, with every car that you make. (Engine Plant Manager)

In effecting organisational change USAuto had widely adopted lean manufacturing systems, and especially Six Sigma processing. As a large body of academic literature explains, adoption of these new techniques is extremely hard – an ongoing change process as opposed to a quick-fix solution. In fact, some of the more zealous advocates of 'lean' describe it as a philosophy that requires revolutionary change at all levels of the firm (Liker and Morgan 2006; Womack *et al.* 1990, 2007). Many of the managers at USAuto were under no illusions that the change process had to be radical. In the words of the Plant Manager, 'our term is "rolling the triangle"'. Senior managers, in general, while recognising the huge challenge of this change, tended to be much more optimistic about its viability, and at times appeared frustrated at the slowness of the transformation. The Plant Manager believed that all the facilities in USAuto 'are on that journey towards lean', but were at different places in that journey. Various USAuto workplaces needed a 'significant emotional event that will allow you to maybe motivate your workforce at a little more of an accelerated pace'. This kind of utopian, visionary approach to management was clearly important to some senior managers in the firm. It was less evident with some of the middle managers, however, even though they definitely shared the passion for the firm and the desire for it to be successful. Overall the middle managers were much more downbeat than the Plant Manager, and also seemingly a great deal more pragmatic in their views.

The Plant Manager was keen to point out that success in the firm would not come about through old-style authoritarian command and control. Instead, lean systems could only work effectively if they contained a real commitment to listening to employee input:

Any kind of employee can sit in this room and talk to us, they can work with any level of the hourly workforce, they can work all the way through middle management and go up the organisation, down the organisation, just by, you know, listening, interacting. And so that's one of the skills that is huge, and then I'm not sure if [Senior Manager for Lean Manufacturing] took you through what we refer to as our 'lean behaviours' and 'respect for people' and, you know, 'continuous improvement', but that whole behaviour around respect for people, listening is obviously one element of that. But it's very large in an organisation in transition, right, as we're trying to draw more people in. You know, feeling valued in the organisation is, and I think you see it in every study, right? You know, what do people come to come work for? Well, yeah, they want to get paid, but that's not necessarily the biggest motivator, right? Do I feel valued? Do I have the opportunity to use my skill set and to create that type of environment for people I think is very big, very big. (Engine Plant Manager)

The Plant Manager spoke impressively on this issue of fair treatment and dignity, and there is nothing wrong with the sentiment. There are questions to raise, however, as to whether this picture is genuinely experienced by staff further down the hierarchy. We were also given a highly detailed presentation by a senior manager, in charge of Lean Manufacturing and Competitive Business, who had been recently brought to the engine plant from another USAuto facility. He explained to us a highly complex series of diagrams displayed on the walls of the boardroom, detailing all of the sophisticated processes he had championed in his short time at this plant:

So what we've done as a company is we've delivered a couple of very important tools, one is this whole Six Sigma philosophy or process, you know. And I like to think of Six Sigma kind of as manufacturing calculus, right? For the most of us who made it through engineering, right, 90 per cent of us aren't going to use a whole lot of calculus but it teaches you how to think, right? It teaches you, it sets up your thought process in a way that you can think through any problem. You know, if you can get through calculus three or four, right, you can usually figure out just about anything else, right? So Six Sigma's the same way, 90 per cent of the people we deliver green belt training or black belt training to aren't going to use the formalised process, right? But they're going to learn that, 'heck, here's a problem, I've got to define my problem, I've got to measure what my problem is, then I've got to analyse it', and here's some tools. And so you go out on the floor now and you begin to see middle managers asking for wishbones [wishbone diagrams], which I think is a huge leap forward because those guys never talked about it, right, they just were, 'hey, just go do it', right? So that's one key deliverable that I think as we foster that middle management role, and then it goes back to the cookbook as far as a very simple list of what to go and do. And what we've done here is we as a company have broken it down into eleven sections of the cookbook [...] in a very simple way, using inputs and outputs right back to the Six Sigma training. And if you do the inputs you get the outputs, so what we've done is we've broken the cookbook up into eleven sections with leadership, our SHARP, which is our safety, health programme, our quality operating system and station process control, our synchronised material flow, right, there's our [USAuto] Total Production Maintenance, manufacturing engineering, indirect material, industrial materials, workgroups, training and environmental. So each one of those arrows has a list of ingredients, and if you do the ingredients you get to the level that we're striving for, and several of these sections have ten levels. (Manager of Lean Manufacturing/Competitive Business)

While this manager had clearly invested a huge amount of his time and energy into establishing and defending this system, it seems debatable whether such a technical, numbers-based system can offer genuine 'toolkits' and 'solutions' for middle managers, supervisors and operatives. What it certainly can do, however, is to discipline managers quite effectively. All of the Six Sigma process results were displayed openly in the boardroom, the context in which the regular management meetings and our interviews were held. Managers' performance scores, therefore, were displayed for all to see:

So right now we're shooting for level six and I'm a firm believer, we're going back to accountability, right? You put the person's name up and then it drives it to them. So this week you'll see those blank squares be populated by the name on the bottom and what level they're at, and this is where we have all of our meetings, so this is where the bosses all show up, this is where the managers all show up. So the last thing that anyone wants to do in this row of middle managers is to have them showing that their name is at a level two, because that just begs the question. So it's that accountability portion of it that I said earlier that, you know, we don't do a very good job of. So if you do all those inputs that brings out to the outputs, and the outputs are here, this is the scorecard and this is what [Plant HR manager] was saying, this links into our major pushes, right? Safety, quality, delivery, cost, morale and environment. So if we as a plant go and deliver all these then we've got what we need to do here. And the link is that as a middle manager you look at all this and say, 'well, how in the world am I supposed to do any of this, you know this is bloody awful, there's so many different ones here, yeah, what am I supposed to do?' There's your cookbook, right, so if you follow the steps, the simple steps, it should deliver the results. And what we do is we set up targets that the workgroups in a future state and certainly in several facilities within [USAuto] internally, the actual targets are set by that middle management level. So now not only do you have accountability but you've got ownership, which is critical, because if you don't own it then you're not going to push and strive for it. (Manager of Lean Manufacturing/Competitive Business)

It is interesting to see how senior management can readily connect what are basically systems designed for accelerated throughput (lean manufacturing, process engineering, Six Sigma) with the goal of also increasing employee dignity and morale through 'ownership' and 'accountability' – a classic 'win–win' situation, perhaps. This upbeat picture, however, did not synchronise with the reality experienced by some middle managers. The message from them was that empowerment and devolution simply meant heavier workloads through greater responsibility. Rather than an open environment with more, and better, communication, they tended to describe disconnection and isolation. As roles were stripped out, the distance between managers increased. One of the middle managers at USAuto's engine plant described how the 'journey towards lean' meant the removal of the role of general foreman or manufacturing planning specialist – basically a level that operated as a 'buffer' between supervisor and superintendent. This change has seen the workload of the supervisor of hourly employees expanded significantly to include, for example, an increased range of planning, scheduling and 'interactive' roles. In addition, the supervisor of hourly paid employees now has a more isolated position in the hierarchy, given that team managers are difficult to consult with because their own roles have been intensified ('tenfold more') and they personally are 'notoriously busy':

Well, the change in the supervisor of hourly employees is that there's one level of management that has been disbanded, right, and that's the level of either the general foreman or manufacturing planning specialist or whoever that might be, that would be the buffer between the supervisor of hourly people and the superintendent over team manager. That job has gone, so now you have to fold into your duties whatever that guy was doing, right? So you have to do your planning, you have to do your scheduling of maintenance, you have to do your interaction with the quality departments, you have to do your interaction with all the other departments. You have nobody else to go to except your team manager and the team manager is notoriously busy because his job has changed immensely. So for as much as a supervisor of hourly people's job has changed, that team manager's job or the superintendent's job has changed tenfold more. So the duties, even though the same amount of hours are in a day, the duties have grown and you just have to be more efficient with your time, I guess, is the best way to put it. (Middle Manager)

The message from the blue-collar supervisors was even more pessimistic. Although wishing to find solutions to USAuto's problems, they saw little potential for the solution to appear in a system of flow diagrams, however sophisticated or scientific. They were UAW (United Auto Workers union) members and reluctant to embrace management's new techniques, even as they adopted some managerial roles themselves. They were somewhat dismissive, for example, of the Lean Manufacturing Manager's utopian description of lean and Six Sigma technologies. They commented along the lines of: 'We've seen all this before. It's good that you're talking to us, too, if you want to get a real picture of this place. Because he's only been here a year, and he'll be gone in six months.' The 'real' work, according to them, clearly went on 'down on the line', and they saw little value or meaning in these complex, abstract Six Sigma diagrams.[10]

---

[10] Unfortunately, we were not allowed to tape-record our brief meeting with the two blue-collar supervisors, so we cannot comment further on their views. The comment we attribute to them is based on our handwritten notes, and is not a verbatim quotation.

The middle managers in USAuto pointed to considerable work intensification in recent years amid a story of regular 'crises'. Some of these
managers had risen from line work; others were career managers hired
with (usually) engineering degrees. Many of the middle managers had
chequered careers, containing periods of unemployment as the plant
was closed and retooled. One interviewee, a mid-level manager in his
early fifties, has been a USAuto employee 'on and off' since the 1970s:

I was hired in '76 as an hourly employee, worked hourly for a year, year and a
half. Took a supervisory job, worked on that job for a few years, three years,
four years. Was bounced around the plant for a while, went through a
downturn in the '80s, the early '80s, got laid off, laid off for eleven months.
Came back to work for a couple of months, got laid off again, so I was laid off
for a total of thirteen, fourteen months over a two-year period of time. At that
point in time I realised I'd better get my education, because things were just
not going to be the same when I went back to work. So came back to work,
was told that when I come back to work, by a person that I particularly
trusted, that seemed to have taken me under his wing, said if I find another job
I should take it. Was here for a short period of time, three months, four
months max and I haven't left. So that was, '83, '82, so it's been a long four
months! (Middle Manager)

During his three periods of employment with USAuto, this middle
manager had been employed in a wider variety of roles. Again, typical
of manufacturing, many of these roles have been in functions no longer
operational at USAuto; roles and functions that have 'melted away':

I've got a background in, worked in such areas as statistical quality analysis
when they had a department as such here. Worked as a process engineer for
a number of years – seven, eight years. And then I went on the floor and
started working in production again. Took a promotion to the floor, the
promotion was a supervisor of salary personnel in a production line, I think
I'd had five direct report supervisors and an afternoon shift to direct. From
that time I took a job in this plant, transferred to this plant and started
supervising hourly employees again, because the job that I had before
had been melted away. Hence the changes in manufacturing, right? Now as
a supervisor of hourly people I was directly reporting to a superintendent, of
which it wasn't uncommon anyhow because I'd been reporting to a superintendent for a few years, so that change wasn't very difficult, in fact it was
no change at all. The change was that I had to go back and start supervising
hourly people versus salaried people; a difference, a distinct difference if
I could say in a unionised shop. So from there bounced through a couple of

departments, went through a couple of launches [promotions], and here I am. (Middle Manager)

Similar to discussions at other corporations where middle managers were asked to take on technical tasks in addition to managing, so the middle managers described how superintendents' role at USAuto had been expanded to include a far greater interaction with hourly paid employees. Given the philosophy of superintendents operating an 'open door policy' to aid communication and accessibility, plus the need to interact with hourly paid employees as well as engineers, the superintendent had been forced to adopt a 'different mindset':

The superintendent now interfaces more with the hourly people than he ever, ever has. His direct line to the hourly people has become sharper, right? Because you've actually lost a layer of management in between, which makes you more accessible. On top of that the thoughts of an open door policy, the thoughts that an hourly person should know as much about the business as the next person, makes him inherently more accessible. He's got to be, he can't, he doesn't have a choice, he has to. On top of that, the structure of the company has laid many, many more different job types into his lap. A case in point is there used to be a separate process engineering, manufacturing engineering area. Electrical engineering [also] used to be handled by a different manager. Now the team manager has an electrical engineer, has a mechanical engineer along with the supervisor of hourly people. So he has to be able to manage engineers, which again is different than managing hourly people and it's different than managing people that manage hourly people. It's just a different mindset, so that has changed massively. (Middle Manager)

If this trend continued, our middle manager suggested that, in addition to the removal of the general foreman, the supervisor of hourly paid employees may be another level to be de-layered. This, he suggested, was the logical conclusion to the current policy for creating hourly team leaders or coordinators; employees whose roles, if progressively enlarged, would gradually encroach on tasks that were previously within the domain of the production supervisor:

If I were to guess, if evolution keeps going the way it's going now, the team manager will directly, the hourly people will directly, report to the team manager and the supervisor will go away. [...] Now the way that's going to happen or can happen would be that the hourly workforce also has developed a job that's called a team leader or coordinator, now that coordinator has taken up some of the duties of the production supervisor. So as that job grows, as that job begins to mature, then it's possible in the future that a team manager won't have a supervisor any more, he'll hand most of those duties off to the hourly coordinator. (Middle Manager)

This middle manager suggested that rounds of de-layering at USAuto had seen work intensify at all levels, with one of the characteristic features of this intensification being the large amounts of information now available to managers and workers to process. Such information processing brought with it 'immense responsibility'. He was unequivocal about how global competitive pressures impact directly onto workers and managers in their day-to-day lives. There is no slack in the system, especially in a 'lean' one:

If you're running production, on any given minute virtually all hell could break loose, right? There are no straightforward jobs, and that would include the team manager's job, it would include the production manager's job, it would include the assistant plant manager's job and the plant manager's job. And they handle tons of information, more information than we've ever seen before. And they're responsible for much, much more capital outlay than we've ever been responsible for. I mean, a plant like this could virtually bring [USAuto] to a standstill in a lot of their automotive lines just by a wrong answer to a question. Immense responsibility, more now than ever, and the reason being is that inventory levels are down. Nobody wants to spend that kind of money to keep an extra 2,000 engines or an extra 20,000 engines or an extra 30,000 engines somewhere in case we just don't run good. So they could run a month on the float – it just doesn't work that way any more. You have a bad afternoon and you feel the ripple the next day. It's a lot of pressure and the pressure goes down to the floor level too. (Middle Manager)

However, although de-layering has meant that this manager's role had been expanded to include 'more responsibility', this did not mean he was personally more 'empowered' and motivated. De-layering, when combined with new ('immediate') technologies, such as email and pagers, had simply given him more tasks to accomplish in a generally 'hurried' situation:

I've been entrusted with more responsibility but it doesn't mean I'm empowered more, it just means I have more responsibility. Could I say 'no' to any one of the items that are handed to me? Sure I've tried, [name of colleague] knows I tried. In this day and age of emails and pagers and phones and, you know, immediate questions and immediate responses it's awfully easy, terribly easy for anybody to get an assignment from anybody. I'm sure that [name of colleague] goes through it all day long, he gets pages off people that are asking him to do stuff and sometimes the pages sound like they're telling him to do stuff. Because there's nothing really nice about what comes across that pager, they're just words making their way across the screen and they have no emotion other than if you're in a hurried situation right now and you read it that's the last thing you want to read, you know? So everything is immediate and everybody is your boss and you have to make the right decisions, right? You've only got so much time to react to certain things, and sometimes you just know the decision you make is going to get your butt kicked tomorrow. So you get responsibility. Can I change the business? It's hard to turn that big ship. I'm not a windmill slayer, I'm no Don Quixote, I can't go out there and slay any of the windmills. I just try to do my job and make the decisions that I think are best for [USAuto] production first. And some people are unhappy with that. I come in every morning knowing I'm going to make somebody unhappy today. (Middle Manager)

Other middle managers concurred that their workload in the era of 'high surveillance', 'lean manufacturing' and 'world competitiveness' was large and intense:

Q *So ten-hour, twelve-hour days are pretty common, right?*
A For a lot of salaried folk, yes, yes it is. Especially when you're running a multishift operation. Tonight I'm going to have to stay and talk to hourly employees. [...] The business starts at five in the morning no matter, you know, 'we're going'. We've got the trucks all lined up, we're ready to go and everything's happening real early. When you get to look at the numbers on the factory, look at the value added of what that person's really doing, you know. So this lean manufacturing, this world competitiveness, it can put a big strain on everyone. (Middle Manager)

The strain is particularly intense when employee numbers have been cut so drastically. The Plant HR Manager explained that it was an increasingly tough job assigning work to people who were already over-stretched. Although many work processes were eliminated, some return following subsequent changes. If something has 'come back into play again' then the manager in charge of that task has to ask himself:

'Now who do I give it to', 'cos that person who did it [now] has two jobs, he's got two plants right now with the Engine Plant 1 as well as Engine Plant 2, for instance. So it's resource constraint, and the plant used to have two years ago, 200, almost 240 salaried people. Now we have a 109 people. And the plant used to have 1,800 hourly folks and now we're down to 1,200. (HR Manager)

What is the recognition for all this effort? Like others elsewhere in the study, middle managers at USAuto noted that de-layering had made it more difficult for them to progress through the organisation. As one explained, the lack of posts available for him to progress into essentially meant that his career had 'stalled'. This situation was exacerbated, he felt, by USAuto's decision increasingly to recruit graduate level employees into junior and middle management positions, rather than to develop hourly paid employees:

My career has stalled; it's stalled because of the changes in the way we're managing business now. Like there's a lot fewer jobs to go into, hence the competition is a lot tougher. And there's probably fifty guys smarter out there who can do the job better than what I can do. [...] Don't know that there's fifty guys more dedicated, but there's fifty guys smarter probably. I think that the progression of promotions has virtually, I can't say stalled because it never stalls, right, but it certainly has slowed down to the point where I have no reason to believe that I will be promoted before I retire. No reason to believe. (Middle Manager)

This middle manager felt that the working environment at USAuto was now a very different one from that experienced by his father, who was also a life-long USAuto employee. Many of the sentiments expressed here resonate with those expressed by informants in Japan – brand loyalty, lifetime employment and a younger generation that is less fixed to these ideas:

And if I had one of my sons sitting here and he was in this business for four years or five years and he was asking me, 'What do I do, Dad?' I would tell him 'Start looking somewhere else. If you want to get promoted you start jumping companies.' My dad lived and breathed [USAuto], right, so I was a [USAuto] brat when I was a kid and I got a brand somewhere on my body but I can't see it, it's got [USAuto] on it, so I was a [USAuto] brat. My dad would never ever, ever think of leaving the company, never, right? He was dedicated to [USAuto], he was convinced that [USAuto] was going to take care of him and he was going to take care of [USAuto]. And there was that link together that this was his family away from home, in many, many ways more important, sad to say, right? [...] In my age group there have been a few people that started to jump [i.e. leave USAuto] in order to be promoted, right, looking somewhere else, ready to take the chance and move to be promoted. The younger generation, they're not so dedi-cated to [USAuto] as what, certainly what my dad was and me, too. Is that good? (Middle Manager)

The USAuto case also reflects on senior management's interpretations and justifications of restructuring processes and events. While senior management did acknowledge the contradictory, challenging and even destructive sides of restructuring, they essentially reinforced the idea that change is essential for the firm's survival and is the right option to pursue. At times, the impression was given that robust organisational change, although often unpleasant, was not so much the *right* option but the *only* option given the wider economic forces at play. Given this situation, the response of senior managers and executives was to attempt to shape the path of change as much as they could.

Perhaps they believed that restructuring would have been carried out with or without their input? Such a view would support a traditional LPT interpretation which tends to regard unpleasant effects on employees as inevitable results of capitalism's continual, ratcheting demands for larger and faster returns. While we agree with the main substance of this view, there are more complicated forces at play in that organisational changes need not always be inevitably 'read off' from the demands of international capitalism (see Chapter 2). While partially true, a simple version of this position inadvertently supports the 'there is no alternative' view of senior executives, and is overly generous in its account of the rationality of their behaviour. This chapter suggests that top management does not possess all the power that it wishes to believe it has.

Senior executives in our case companies often seem to read from a shared cultural script of established systems for organisational improvement. In contrast, many of the middle managers at USAuto looked at change with a more critical eye, suggesting at least three main areas of critique. Firstly, there was the widespread claim that the lionised new organisational systems were not 'toolkits' or 'solutions', but in effect oppressive systems for driving more effort out of already overstretched managers and supervisors. Secondly, the USAuto middle managers suggested that senior executives do not always have the right answers, and that we should not assume they are in full control of what they are doing, or even of what they think they are doing. And thirdly, rather than restructuring being 'inevitable' and rational, many of the middle managers pointed out that new systems do not actually serve to increase product quality or enhance workplace communication. Instead, chronic short-staffing and the incessant pace of work actually diminishes what they, and by extension the firm itself, can achieve. The introduction of these systems, therefore, might not be inevitable. Their adoption could actually be an error. These change measures might be mistakes that not only alienate middle management and front-line operatives, but also fail to satisfy top management's intentions for profitability and success.

A further element that problematises a simple LPT version of events is the effort that middle managers put into work despite reservations over senior management's strategy. While there was much resigned compliance among the middle managers as to reduced security, intensified work, tightened surveillance and reduction of promotion opportunities (as an LPT perspective would rightly expect), they also spoke proudly about working for USAuto, and suggested they threw their heart and soul into work; they genuinely wanted USAuto to be a success. This latter point, however, complicates a more traditional LPT viewpoint, which has little to say about the intrinsic reward of work.

Adler's (2007) recent account of workplace changes is considerably more optimistic than that of traditional LPT. In contrast to Braverman's emphasis on progressive de-skilling and work degradation, our analysis would agree with Adler's view that the quality and sophistication of work systems has increased. However, where our analysis differs from Adler's is in our more downbeat account of the working reality of these changes. The lived environment into which these sophisticated systems are introduced and sustained is certainly intensified according to the managers consulted in this study. Moreover, 'degraded' is perhaps quite an apt word to describe the frantic scramble that white-collar work has become in recent years. Interestingly, while obviously a major issue for middle managers who experience it, this kind of environment is probably also self-defeating for top management, because high-quality, innovative work probably cannot be sustained under this climate. (For further discussion of this point, see the discussion of UKAuto in Chapter 4.)

The final case of this chapter, USEngineering, reflects on restructuring from a more senior perspective in the firm, as a senior HR executive tells a cathartic, almost confessional, story of organisational change and its personal costs. Throughout this account, there is a tacit suggestion that things could and perhaps should have been different.

US Engineering: 'Every day is a final exam'

USEngineering is a *Fortune* Global 500 company with around 28,000 employees and turnover of over $9 billion. The company is present in almost every continent and is among the world's largest industrial gas manufacturers. Founded in the early twentieth century, USEngineering has developed processes and technologies that have been at the fore-front of innovation in the industry. In its early years, for example, the company was a prime mover in introducing a distribution system in the USA for liquid gas. Today USEngineering supplies a range of gases, coatings and supply system technologies to a diverse range of customers, such as aerospace, healthcare, beverages, semiconductors, chemicals, refining and metal fabrication. The company practices Six Sigma methodology throughout the organisation.

The corporate history of USEngineering has, however, been far from smooth or untroubled. The heavy emphasis placed in publicity docu-ments on the 'environmental benefits' of the corporation's products stands in sharp contrast with its reputation as one of the world's most infamous industrial polluters. A reading of the corporation's long history finds it replete with instances of serious industrial and environ-mental accidents and violations. In the early 1990s the company was spun off from its parent. As one senior USEngineering manager informed us, in light of the corporation's history of bad press, when making major decisions its senior executives and managers are reminded to take the 'newspaper test' – 'to never do anything you wouldn't want to see in the newspaper the following day'.

At USEngineering we conducted research interviews at the corpora-tion's headquarters, situated in a rural community seventy miles north of a major American city. USEngineering's headquarters is reminiscent more of a university campus or golf and country club than an industrial estate. The corporate headquarters house a number of impressive glass/concrete/steel buildings, dotted over a large acreage of manicured park-land, and linked by a network of winding roads and pathways. On entering the estate, the impression is of an appropriate location for an environmentally sensitive company – azaleas and laurels; peace and tranquillity. A safe and controlled world – one far removed from hazardous gas production in developing nations.

Once again we were fortunate in being granted access to very senior figures in Human Resources and in particular the corporation's Senior Human Resources Executive (SHRE), whose views on corporate restructuring are reproduced in the interview presented below. This executive, perhaps nearing retirement, was a particularly interesting subject. He made it clear from the outset the main reason he had been hired by USEngineering was because 'the CEO wanted to have more teeth in the [HR] system, so he said, "put a system in place that does that", so we did'. Having been headhunted from General Electric, he would certainly know a thing or two about robust performance management systems. He suggested that his close knowledge of 'forced ranking' at GE, and his experience of large-scale corporate de-layering and downsizing, made him an attractive hire. However, he admitted that the performance management approach he imported from his previous employer – to the more 'sleepy and relaxed' culture of USEngineering – had not been met with ready acceptance during his decade with the company. Moreover, he had come to see how forced ranking systems 'can be very debilitating'.

During our initial discussions with this executive, he was keen to put recent trends in American corporate performance into perspective. A major philosophy of recent corporate theory and practice, he suggested, was that management staffing levels were 'too generous'. Before the trend for de-layering and downsizing in America, there existed 'more people than jobs' in the middle management levels of large corporations. In particular, too many individuals were involved in 'peer management' – essentially organising people rather than achieving tasks – an art which was now 'virtually redundant'. To optimise performance in the hyper-competitive environment of global capitalism, USEngineering, like other major American corporations, had realised it had to remove around 50 per cent of its middle management capability:

There was probably an imbalance in terms of jobs versus people, there were more people than there were jobs, okay? Basically the mid-level management jobs certainly were 'management jobs' quote unquote, were peer management jobs and so they managed other people. Nowadays you have no peer management jobs, you have no working management, so you basically have about three-quarters of a person for every job and a half that's out there.

Attempting to rebalance the equation, he suggested there were also negative outcomes of restructuring to reduce middle management layers and numbers. A major downside of the current 'scarcity of management' and 'scramble to get stuff done' was that the 'coaching' or 'counselling' role of middle management, which existed for many decades in American industry (in the form of 'contact' or 'face time'), was now virtually a thing of the past, a luxury that modern corporations could no longer afford. Managers and their subordinates were now more distant and 'remote', due to increased managerial workloads, fewer organisational layers and wider spans of control. This can clearly be detrimental to both individual and organisational development:

So everyone's scrambling as hard as they possibly can to get this stuff done, there's no time to do the kind of coaching, counselling, the sort of middle management kind of role that existed many years ago. And so that's what's unfortunate about the turn of events today for the generation that's entering the workforce, they don't have the face time, they don't have the contact time, the sort of counselling and coaching time that we might have had, that I might have had twenty, thirty years ago. Because I could sit down with a manager and he or she could talk about different issues, about how you handled this, right, or 'why don't you try this or that?' Nowadays you just don't have that kind of face time. [...] They're remote from each other in terms of manager-subordinate, but also just because of the scarcity of management. I mean you've got one manager for, in some places, ten, fifteen direct reports, twenty direct reports, there's just not the ratio there where you can spend any time with them.

The SHRE suggested this 'scarcity' of management was basically a result of the desire among corporations to 'connect' their organisational layers more directly, a communications narrative we had been presented with at many of the US corporations in our study. The metaphor he favoured was unsurprisingly linked to engineering – that of removing layers of 'insulation' in the structure, given that insulation can serve to 'muffle the message'. However, when the corporation engages in de-layering, the SHRE suggested that one of the side-effects can be to 'expose the wires onto the elements' thus 'short circuiting' the organisation:

Yeah, I think we're all trying to direct connect. I think there's a real need to reduce what I call layers. Organisational layers are basically insulation in an organisation, and that insulation muffles the messages very often. And so if we want corporations to be nimble, to be quick, to be connected to the customers in their markets, then we must try to remove as much of that insulation as possible. But that exposes the wires, right? Onto the elements, right? And so basically you've got some short-circuiting that occurs because you don't have the insulation in the case of many more middle management. So it has a downside – an upside and a downside as well.

As with so many other organisations across the three nations studied, the SHRE noted how the reduction in organisational layers had affected the traditional step-wise progression and development of middle management personnel. With fewer management levels, largely the result of the restructuring of narrow occupational 'grades' into broad career 'bands', middle managers at USEngineering remain at a particular level of the organisation far longer that they had done in the past. Like other US case corporations, USEngineering's solution to the problem of retaining and developing middle managers, while at the same time keeping them at the same career level, was to rotate them in an attempt to widen their personal skill bases, a practice which would, in the fullness of time, give middle managers the resources necessary to make significant vertical moves:

Because there's less layers we're asking people to move across levels, so they're going to remain in a level for longer, they have to do multiple jobs to garner the kind of skills that they need to, sort of, move up to the next level. Whereas in the old days when you had grades, many grades, twenty, thirty, forty grades you can measure your progress, okay? But today it's much more, it's much more difficult to see direct progress because there would be what we call band made systems now where you took grades and you banded them to broader levels and whatever you call it, zones [...] companies call it different things.

The Senior HR Executive also suggested that the move from grades to bands was also influenced by the nature of the competitive environment, in that USEngineering's downsized Human Resources function simply did not have the resources to operate anything like the old grade system, especially in terms of managing pay and rewards. The finer detail of human resource accounting that had operated under the grade system had been replaced by a more 'amorphous' but less costly system of role 'profiling'. Like several of the US firms in Jacoby's study (2005), HR systems had been allowed to wither as financial pressures dominate:

But we no longer, even on the compensation side, have all the resources needed to do the old grade system which was, well, you added something to your job or changed your profile, and nowadays people only have profiles. I mean, basically it's just general statements about, directionally about, what they're supposed to do and it's very, you know, it's sort of amorphous in terms of, 'well, you're in marketing, you're going to be connected with customers in this product set'. And then you basically go off and do it, because day to day it changes and there's no way that we can document that to any successful degree.

With the erosion of coaching and 'face time' this did not appear to be a firm that genuinely cared about people management and good treatment of employees. These unwelcome developments had largely been implemented during the decade in which the SHRE had been with USEngineering. Before his arrival in the early 1990s – around the time the corporation was being spun off and renamed in the wake of an environmental disaster – USEngineering had operated with a 'more formal structure' in the sense of 'peer management' being still included in the job ratio. The de-layering and restructuring that has taken place over the last decade has served to 'radically change' this structure into a 'leaner' form and in so doing to reduce the level of bureaucracy and speed up communications, again by reducing the level of 'insulation' and allowing managers to 'direct connect'. According to the SHRE, this has facilitated 'flexible', multilevel communications in an environment previously characterised by managers working through several layers to achieve their objectives. This flexible approach, allowing communication directly with the person who has the necessary information, now enables managers to place their fingers more firmly 'on the pulse' of the business:

I mean basically today it's a much leaner organisation, and again I think the interest here is in connecting with the customer, connecting with the market place, connecting with the work in hand. One of the values we have is having your fingers, sort of, on the pulse of the business, those are the words that we use, so that you [don't need to] speak through three layers of managers, you basically pick up a phone and call people when you need to talk with them. And so you can get a phone call from a CEO, you can get a phone call from the EVP. Very, very thin, sort of, levels of management. So that they can direct connect with the action and can have, sort of, fingers on the pulse, know what's going on all the time. Whereas in the old days you had two or three levels sprinkled in, it was muffling basically, wrapping in insulation and muffling on the sound and you couldn't put your fingers on what was going on directly, you had to work through several layers of people. Here you don't do that, just direct connect. So if I want to find out what's happening in, say, our eastern region or our western region of the US I can call. I talked to Europe this morning, I call direct, you don't have to go through layers.

Moving from a formal to a leaner and more flexible structure, however, had involved significant downsizing. This had been directed primarily at the removal of so-called 'non-productive' work, with the management of formal cost structures within the corporation being directed at the ratio of such work being either reduced or at least remaining the same:

Sure there's been downsizing but, and we do watch SG&A [Selling, General and Administrative expenses], you know, what we're always looking for is non-productive kind of work, we're always trying to look at that ratio of the total cost structure and say, 'we don't want that to grow, we want it to at least remain the same'. [...] I think there's a genuine interest in just being very effective in what you do, and we find that the more people you have, sometimes, yeah, you can get more work done but you're not necessarily more effective in what you do. And so you're trying to reach that optimal balance between the number of people you have doing work and making sure you're direct connecting with the critical tasks that need to be done for that function or business or whatever.

The SHRE expanded further and more concretely on how this philosophy for reducing 'non-productive' work had affected reporting structures, managerial responsibilities and hours of work at USEngineering. In terms of reporting structures:

Well, clearly more people [are] reporting in to the positions, in fact very few positions are without seven, ten, twelve people reporting in to them. [...] Years ago you would have a manager that could potentially have two or three direct reports. It's very rare nowadays, I mean now they're going to have seven, ten, twelve direct reports.

In terms of managerial responsibilities, US Engineering was similar to other US case corporations in seeking to increase the ratio of direct to indirect work in a middle manager's role:

They would have a set of responsibilities, we call them working managers, but they would have a set of responsibilities uniquely for themselves. I mean in terms of projects or if they're in the sales marketing area it would be accounts that they would have to handle. And they would also handle people in the field, should have them report in to them who are doing similar kinds of work.

And in terms of working hours, again they were extremely long in comparison to traditional levels. The environment appeared very uncompromising:

Well, I never get home before ten o'clock at night, so it's like you're here from early in the morning till very late at night with dinner time, and then we have a meal service here that's available. So we'll have our meals here and we don't go home, I would say that's an anomaly, that's not the standard piece, but I would say people work at least fifty if not, you know, fifty-five, sixty hours a week, it's quite a lot, quite a lot. [...] Here in this building it's almost religious because our senior management likes people here at eight o'clock, it's very early, and you'll see people here very late.

Interestingly, the company was now apparently not completely happy with many of the features he described following restructuring. Despite the positive appraisal of how USEngineering was achieving its currently high levels of 'shareholder return' through eliminating non-productive work, reducing layers and broadening bands, he went on to disclose that the corporation was actually starting to rethink its grading structures and to consider a move to relayering in the face of perceived problems with management career progression and the absence of face time, coaching and collegiality:

There's a move afoot right now to sort of relook at the five bands and maybe build, say, a ten-level kind of a system, not [to] go back to grades where there were thirty or forty but maybe put some demarcations in the bands. Maybe, you know, a couple demarcations per band or maybe a few, maybe one or two more in a few of the bands, but basically to address that issue. So that people understand there's distinct levels that they can cross and can get over to, for nowadays people can stay in a band for four, five, six, seven years. And sometimes it feels they're not, they're treading water but they're not making improvements in their career, although they're gaining skills [...] So there is a human component here that says while from an organisational perspective we're indifferent, we're agnostic about whether one system is better than the other there's a human component here that says they'd like to see some improvement, some change. So we [need to] build into the system some additional sort of demarcations that allow people to feel they're making progress.

Nevertheless USEngineering was not overly worried about losing staff through natural wastage. Turnover levels had consistently remained very low in recent years. The SHRE felt there was an unsatisfactory reason for this. The extensive nature of stock-based compensation among USEngineering's executive and senior management staff meant that during a period when the company had made significant returns to shareholders, the problem at the higher levels of the corporation was more one of 'pushing people out' than losing them through 'natural attrition'. Even in the face of more 'demanding' performance management and workload systems, executives and senior managers were often unwilling to leave given the implications of losing financial returns on their stock. This scenario emerged similarly in discussions with executives and senior managers at a number of other large US corporations, where experienced managers and executives would suggest in confidence that although they were alienated from the hard grind of their corporate working environment, they were ultimately tied to their corporation through the rewards from stock-based compensation:

Our turnover is pretty consistent, it's only about, including retirements, it's only about 6 or 7 per cent which is very, very low, it really is very low. In fact we do more, especially in the upper level, of pushing people out than we do losing people through natural attrition. It's a very demanding organisation. It's one that takes performance management very, very seriously. We have a forced kind of system, a structure in place. And so we don't require the bottom 10 per cent to leave every year. [But] we do certainly put them on a very stringent development plan so that people understand performance needs to come up to scratch if they want to remain. But I think we've been so successful financially, and we have been, and in terms of total shareholder return we've been making between 15 and 18 per cent a year per year for the last ten, twelve years. That's a very good record, I mean, regardless of the economy, how many companies can you talk to where the population, if they invest in the stock, they're going to make 15, 18 per cent a year, year over year? That's a company that you'd probably want to invest in, right? And so that's a very tough argument – to back up or leave? I mean we found this, no matter how difficult the environment might be in terms of just workload, and just demand, if you're getting that kind of financial return people say, 'well what am I here for?' […] And that's a pretty hard argument to fight against. So we don't consequently lose many people.

Whereas a pattern of low executive turnover influenced by stock-based compensation was understandable, the SHRE admitted there were sides to the 'psychology' of middle managers at USEngineering that he hadn't anticipated on joining the corporation. One issue in particular – of middle managers seeking to 'satisfice' rather than 'optimise' in their performance levels and career aspirations – was one he described as alien to his previous corporate experience at GE. The problem, he felt, stemmed in large part from a decision he himself had taken five years previously to revise the performance-related compensation system. The goal was to deploy a system that would more adequately differentiate between managers on the same band level. In particular it would break a pattern whereby 'about 90 per cent of the population was getting the same thing'. However, when the 'very flexible' revised policy began to provide for 'huge' compensation differences within bands, to the extent that bands were almost overlapping,

then unforeseen problems started to arise as some managers started to
give up on the prospect of pushing themselves harder for more seniority
and status:

Now we're providing an incentive for people not to stretch and grow to a
certain degree, because if you're consistently above standard in a particular
role we'd encourage you to take on a larger role. But you're going to say to
yourself, 'well, wait a minute, I know this space pretty well, I've got it nailed',
right? And so some of the people who are less risk averse probably don't have
the profile for big leadership, they're going to say, 'no, I'm going to camp out
here and I'm going to be pretty safe because I know this territory pretty well'.
And I never really thought about that side of people, but there are some folks
that are like that. [...] I was always thinking, 'well, the people who are going
to exceed expectations will want to step up and take on a bigger role and make
progress'. The problem, if you make that big step, now your competitive
group is just, you know, a bigger job, it's tougher. And sometimes when
you're new to it you're not as superior and you're not going to show as well
as, say, people who have been in it for a while. [...] There is a considerable
number of people in there who camp out and find some space that they're
pretty good at, do it very well and there's not much to say about their
contribution, it's there, clear. But they're not going to push themselves into
something bigger. [...] So these systems, while they're meant to sort of bring
out the best in us, some people will figure out self-interest, 'what's best for
me', and sometimes take some of the power away from the system, and I think
it's human nature.

He also noted other forms of middle management reluctance or resistance, notably in response to the corporation's desire to rotate managers
around a variety of roles in a number of geographical locations as their
operations grew globally. The issue of maintaining work-life balance
was becoming more important to a percentage of middle managers than
it had been in the recent history of corporate America:

I was talking this morning with a colleague of mine who is of my age, she
is from Columbia University. I'd known her for years, and she was out here
and we were talking about some development programmes for some of our
people, and she said, 'what's your big challenge right now?' And I said, 'well,
it's always growth'. I said growth is always an issue because the more you
grow the bigger you are and the more they expect, and so it's an engine that
keeps speeding itself. So I said now we've got eleven geographies around the
world and [...] we're looking for the twelfth, you know, we're looking for
growth in the other eleven. And I said, the interesting thing is the younger
people, whereas when I was coming up they said, they told me, 'we have a new

plant in Turkey, we want you to go there for six months or a year', you'd go, and 'okay fine'. You were living in some provincial [Turkish] town and it was dirty and dusty but it was fascinating, and you'd do it and say, 'hey – cool'. Or you'd go to Europe for this or go wherever they told you. Nowadays we're having a harder time because they say 'oh, you know, my family is here in Buffalo and I really don't want to leave', and 'it's too expensive up there', and you're looking at them like 'what?!' But increasingly we're getting that kind of feedback where people are saying 'no, I want this whole life, not just work'. [...] Increasingly you're seeing people are saying, 'I don't know if I want to do that', and it's like we've had situations where the CEO has got fairly substantial managers saying, 'I really don't want to go to X, Y, Z to do this and I have to think about it'.

Showing such resistance and reluctance to be posted to positions in other USEngineering plants has generally been frowned upon by the corporation's senior executives. Much like the traditional Japanese firm, the overall cultural norm is still for managers to be posted to locations near or far almost at the drop of a senior executive's hat:

We never want anyone to feel they have a rock-solid seat at the table. I mean, maybe it's my years at GE but it's always like every day is a final exam. I always like to have a little tension in the system because you never want complacency to set in, and maybe that's strong, I don't know, but it certainly is the way we like to run things here.

This case shares much in common with other industrial firms in the sample: the intense international pressures, robust performance management, long-hours culture and hugely demanding work. It also had an ageing workforce and low management turnover. This might suggest working pride and intrinsic reward for middle managers, but is also indicative of the stock-based compensation system that ties people into the firm's future. It was interesting to hear share-based reward systems being criticised. Perhaps it reflects an individualised culture that had developed at this organisation and others we studied. The company perhaps suffered from a reduced level of collegiality, as the SHRE bemoaned the lack of personal development and the erosion of 'face time'. This senior executive had contributed to the dismantling of the old system, but was never completely happy with the development of the new. Like all the other companies in this chapter, it was an established player, with enormous income and technological capacity. But the HR restructuring did not appear to have caused that many improvements, and has apparently created new difficulties. Perhaps highly skilled, committed experts tend not to look too favourably on forced ranking or other such off-the-shelf systems. Time and again, top executives are attracted to magic bullets that don't always hit their targets.

The Senior HR Executive we interviewed had overseen a ten-year period of serious challenges for people management. His tenure came in the wake of the appalling shock of an environmental disaster, and it is understandable that significant changes would be brought about during this time. The conversation we had with him was almost cathartic in nature. At times he appeared to be apologising for some of the GE-style systems he put in place. This downbeat assessment of events was by no means unique, for it was shared by many other managers in our sample, even if senior figures mostly favoured a more optimistic gloss.[11]

Conclusions

Throughout this chapter we have drawn attention to the similarities of the stories at senior and middle management levels. Top management depended on white-collar employees' goodwill in regularly working

---

[11] Further evidence for the spread of GE-influenced 'best practice' ideas came during our study of USHospital. Six Sigma had been widely adopted in this case, and hospital management had employed a 'master black belt' to help them build this process improvement philosophy into all kinds of operational projects. When discussing the systems for employee review of managers that they introduced five years ago, the SVP for Human Resources stated that, 'we stole this from GE', describing their systems as 'fabulous'. He also noted the same 'transfer-in' effect described at USEngineering, in that the new CEO of USHospital was formerly chief executive of GE Medical. He explains that:

We basically do an annual talent review, we review every manager, director and individual contributor – we actually stole this from GE, this is what they call their 'Session C' – and this is our fifth year. We have a strategic partnership with GE and we basically, before [name] became CEO, when he was CEO of GE Medical he came to one of our senior management meetings, shared with us how they think about leadership development and they taught us how to do this; it was great best practice. They are fabulous, GE, with this stuff, it's really good, so I would try and get to see them. I'm actually going up to Milwaukee tomorrow doing a presentation at GE Medical. If you can get to see GE, see them. (SVP Human Resources, USHospital)

He went on to mention that the performance appraisal system at USHospital 'clusters people into stars, up-and-comers, solid 'B's, watch list, or out the door'.

well beyond their contracted hours. The pace of work was intense, and collegiality and inter-level contact had often degenerated. On the other hand, there were signs that such demanding work did have intrinsic rewards and, in some cases, large financial ones. Middle managers, while frequently suffering from low morale, almost without exception wanted to be part of a prestigious organisation. But this desire was not always fulfilled. Senior management had frequently become distanced from middle management, with this posing problems with regards to collegiality and support. This could impact on morale, in that middle managers could express scepticism about the effectiveness of top-level executive strategy. Moreover, as middle managers had often given up hope of being promoted into senior positions, there was little prospect of middle managers being able to shape and influence the future direction of the firm.

At a broader level, there were some remarkable similarities in the kinds of restructuring measures and philosophies used, such as Balanced Scorecard, lean production and Six Sigma. When adopted they were often altered to fit the firm's situation, typically being repackaged with a new name. In being generic and off-the-shelf systems, they were frequently of questionable use in dealing with the particular and specific problems that these organisations faced. To borrow Brunssen's (2006) phrase they perhaps operated as 'mechanisms of hope' for top management, providing illusions of control. Middle managers often looked on them sceptically, because it is at their level (and below) where their impact appears the most intense. These systems were part of a broader range of rationalisation measures adopted by large firms, designed principally to reduce costs. As such, they belong to a long heritage of such organisational technologies, as described over fifty years ago by James Earley (1956). An LPT account of organisational change therefore explains the rationale for these systems quite well – they are part of the long-run rationalisation of large firms under the driving hand of international capitalism.

But this rationalisation drive is not as systematic as an LPT interpretation would suggest. Restructuring is clearly concerned with cost-cutting, and employees often bear the brunt of these measures in capitalism's incessant struggle for greater profitability. But the changes did not always work. Increased profits often did not materialise. New systems threw up new problems. In short, restructuring can easily be chaotic and irrational, as senior management struggle to make sense of how best to respond to the forces against them. Managers regularly employed battle metaphors, suggesting a 'fog of war' engulfing large firms, confusing and unhinging the company. Who is the enemy? Where and how, should the firm respond? What is an appropriate use of force? In this sense, it is clear that restructuring pressures never cease. Internal and external threats to the firm are never fully suppressed or even known. We should, therefore, be cautious in ascribing too much power to senior managers and their 'rationalising' systems in our explanations of organisational change. Of course, they monopolise organisational power over the direction of the change measures, intensifying the work and increasing the workloads of staff further down the hierarchy. On the other hand, they are never fully in control of the outcomes of the changes, as witnessed by the often disappointing results of restructuring, the hidden costs of squeezing too hard and overloading staff, and by the perceived emptiness of these off-the-shelf organisational technologies.

The next chapter explores organisational restructuring in Britain. The UK is, of course, a far smaller economy than that of the USA; its economy is linked into a wider range of (notably European) socioeconomic institutions than those that exist in the USA. These have the potential to constrain and dilute managerial power (for example, a much larger percentage of UK managers are union members than in the USA). Nevertheless, large firms in Britain have been through many similar experiences to those described above, and so it is to their restructuring that we now turn.

4 | *Maximising shareholder value: Management restructuring in Britain*

> [T]he shareholders and economics will finally decide what happens.
>
> (Burchill *et al.*, 1999: 58)

It is often suggested that the UK's general economic system closely mirrors that of the United States. The UK is a highly internationalised economy with minimal governmental interference. When it comes to organisational restructuring, large firms in the UK have experienced similar forces of change to those across the Atlantic, involving downsizing, de-layering, a concerted shift towards 'shareholder value logic' and business process re-engineering. The UK economy is decidedly liberal, financialised and globalised.

It wasn't always this way. In the 1970s and 1980s Britain's economy was widely perceived to be in the doldrums. Unemployment, inflation, weak competitiveness of goods and services, low labour productivity and serious industrial relations unrest were readily visible. Much of UK industry was under state ownership, control, or heavy regulation, including at various times the steel, automotive, transport, utilities and telecoms industries. Subsequently, the UK has been at the forefront of economic liberalisation, involving a string of major sell-offs and, controversially, partial privatisations of core parts of the welfare system, including education and health. Until the 2008 economic recession, recent UK governments had retreated from a position of active involvement in industry and national industry policy, preferring 'light-touch' regulation.

The long-term and ongoing deregulation and liberalisation of the financial sector (beginning with the 'Big Bang' in 1986) has been critical to the internationalisation of British financial capital. European Union legislation has subsequently encouraged further liberalisation.[1] At firm

---

[1] Such as MiFID, the EU's Markets in Financial Instruments Directive, which was enacted into UK law in November 2007, ironically just as it was becoming clear how hard the US-born sub-prime mortgage crisis would hit Britain.

level, large publicly listed UK companies have been drawn to US-style financialisation. It is likely that these reforms have stimulated financial growth (although perhaps not the dramatic improvements often described in mainstream sources; see, for example, Glyn 2006 for a very downbeat assessment of the economic results of liberalisation). The dramatic increase in the importance, competition between, and influence of pension funds, international hedge funds and other institutional investors into the UK economic scene has transformed the environment of the City of London into a major world financial player (see Golding 2003 for a detailed account of this transformation; or Augar 2000, for what he calls 'the death of gentlemanly capitalism'). The City of London plays a massively important role in UK and world economic life, particularly as the big US brokerages moved in *en masse* to the Square Mile and Canary Wharf in the 1980s and 1990s. Large UK firms are, therefore, heavily involved in, and exposed to, US-style measures of corporate financial performance such as quarterly returns to investors. This exposure to global finance is likely to have been substantially more intense than that experienced by other European nations, and certainly more so than Japan.

During these decades of change, the UK established a highly liberal economic climate in which the short-term financial demands of the City can easily override longer-term 'stakeholder' concerns. This has served to further encourage investor flight from weakly valued capital-intensive manufacturing sectors (especially steel and cars which had, by the mid-2000s, all but disappeared from UK ownership) and into higher-valued services sectors; for example, insurance, banking, marketing, advertising and publishing. It would appear that large UK PLCs have come to adopt the US-style 'downsize and distribute' mentality, to use Lazonick and O'Sullivan's (2000) famous phrase, and that old-style stakeholder values, such as long-term employment, have fallen down the list of corporate priorities, as finance and accounting departments increasingly dominate top-level strategy (as argued by Jacoby, 2005, in the case of the USA).

The pressures to liberalise are so strong for Porter (1990: 722) to have argued that 'American-style earnings pressures threaten to dominate British management thinking. A long-term bias is in the interest of the national economies. Policies should be adjusted to create one.' Others of a more left-wing persuasion (e.g. Hutton, 1995) were attracted to similar arguments against short-termism and financialisation, citing them as evidence that liberalism and rampant capitalism must be curbed by tighter regulation and revamped socio-economic institutions. The relatively weak economic performance of Britain during the early 1990s added substantial weight to these arguments.

Until the 'credit crunch' of 2008, however, concerns about short-termism were usually ignored in far more upbeat assessments of the performance of the UK and its large firms and financial institutions since the mid- to late-1990s. Mainstream business analysts tended to praise the liberal nature of the UK, certainly in comparison to what were widely regarded as its more heavily regulated and taxed European competitors.[2] Market values of FTSE firms, in general, grew steadily in the twenty years following the 'Big Bang'. Key institutions of the City of London, such as the UK's Financial Services Authority, were described as models that even the USA could learn from.[3] In terms of labour markets and workplace reorganisations, White *et al.* (2004) provide a surprisingly positive assessment of the health of UK PLC, in contrast to the gloom of the 1980s. According to them, large firms in the UK have undergone painful but successful surgery and that the intensity of restructuring appears to have slowed in recent years, with longer-term employment and internal career ladders back on the agenda for sufficiently skilled and committed staff alongside widespread use of temporary and flexible labour.[4]

The 2008 economic downturn notwithstanding, since around the turn of the century a substantial amount of critical literature has emerged which sheds light on the price paid by workers during the decade of economic revival from the mid-1990s. For example: Beynon *et al.* (2002) present a pessimistic view when describing ongoing redundancies, diminution of staff security, reduced recognition for hard work, increased stress and truncated career opportunities; Marchington *et al.* (2004) describe how new technologies and organisational philosophies have enabled the 'fragmentation of work', increasing the complexity, flexibility and porosity of contemporary organisations; Green (2001, 2006) argues, from an analysis of major surveys, that while workplace reforms have led to an increase in UK worker productivity, this has been at the cost of a significant intensification of labour. And Burchill *et al.* (1999: 60)

---

[2] 'German boss urges dose of UK medicine', BBC News, 24 April 2002.
[3] 'US looks to London for regulatory model', *Financial Times*, 14 December 2007.
[4] However, White *et al.* (2004: 102) do certainly acknowledge increasing employee complaints around workload and work pressures.

argue that liberalisation and restructuring 'have strengthened the hands of managers but weakened the position of workers'. Indeed, they claim further that:

[J]ob insecurity is now higher than at any point in the past thirty years. The evidence also suggests that the spread of job insecurity has widened to encompass a growing proportion of non-manual workers. And, within this category, the biggest 'losers' have been professional workers: between 1986 and 1997 they went from being the most secure group of workers to the most insecure.

Quotations from workers in the survey of Burchill *et al.* support this picture of a radically insecure environment, in which many employees have had their workloads increased without adequate reward, and do not trust management to safeguard their jobs: 'I don't trust [management] a great deal because external forces are external forces! Even if they wanted to maintain the headcount, the shareholders and economics will finally decide what happens.' (Burchill *et al.* 1999: 58.)

On the other hand, Burchill *et al.*'s survey is based on a sample of just twenty firms and larger surveys show a more balanced, less traumatic, picture for employees, notably demonstrating a surprising degree of job security (Doogan 2001; Fevre 2007). Findings from a recent WERS survey (Workplace Employment Relations Survey – the most detailed national survey of UK companies available) indicated that employees are increasingly able to make use of various flexible working arrangements (Kersley *et al.* 2006: 249–65) and that the increase in work intensity seemed to have reached a plateau (2006: 101). The UK shares a long-hours culture with the USA and Japan, and WERS demonstrates that UK managerial work continues to be highly demanding. Managerial staff regularly work more than forty-eight hours per week, and this creates particular problems for female managers who are more likely than their male counterparts to perform the juggling acts of domestic and family responsibilities (Kersley *et al.* 2006: 268, 274). Fifty-eight per cent of managers and 60 per cent of professionals agreed with the statement that they 'never seem to have enough time to get [their] work done' (Kersley *et al.* 2006: 100–1).

Alongside excessive work pressure, concerns have also been raised about UK companies' high degree of exposure to overseas takeover. As the UK economy has liberalised, large numbers of UK firms have been purchased by overseas competitors, sovereign wealth funds or private equity, raising once again the issue of the so-called 'Wimbledon effect';[5] i.e. there's no realistic chance of the Wimbledon tennis tournament leaving London, but it was always possible that Sony, for example, could close its electronics plants in South Wales, which it finally did in 2005. This idea was often used as an anecdotal defence for investment into the UK, but it is a rather simplistic concept (Augar 2000: 3)[6]. Widespread overseas ownership of any country's firms and infrastructure will always be prone to the repatriation of profits back to the home country and the very real chance that the owners will close the plants, cutting the jobs. Offshoring has also had a major impact on service jobs (just as in the USA), as telesales and back-office processing jobs have been shifted to low-cost processing centres in India.

Debates also continue about the skills profile of the UK workforce. The policy direction has aimed at continual upgrading to maximise the competitiveness of the workforce, away from cheap, low-skilled work (in which no OECD country can possibly compete with emerging economies) towards high skills (see Brown *et al.* 2001). Of course, countries such as China and India are also upgrading their skills bases, and inflation is pushing up their low wage levels, so this is an extremely competitive race. In recent times, the UK has received a relatively positive review in the business media, one that suggests the UK is no longer the 'sick man of Europe'. This might suggest that other large economies such as Japan, France and Germany are in comparatively weaker positions, with less flexible labour markets and heavier regulatory burdens. According to this logic, these latter countries have liberalised to a degree in recent years but, unlike the UK, they have not been willing or able to push the reforms far enough.[7] Although 'Anglo-Saxon' is used as shorthand for the USA and the UK, it is important to bear in mind that the UK remains significantly different from the USA in certain ways. While Britain's labour markets are substantially more liberal and flexible than the core European nations, they are somewhat more closely regulated than those of the USA. Britain's membership of the EU means that a degree of external regulatory pressure will persist in a way that is absent in the USA. In the OECD's index of the strictness

---

[5] 'Reflecting on the "Wimbledon Effect"' *The Observer*, 2 July 2006.
[6] 'Sony Announce Closure Date for Bridgend Plant', 23 August 2005. www.prnewswire.co.uk/cgi/news/release?id=152072
[7] This, for example, was the general line of the 2007 special report on Japan by *The Economist* magazine. 'Going Hybrid', *The Economist*, 29 November 2007.

of national labour protection laws, for example, the UK scores a very low 0.9, in relation to the USA's 0.7, France's 2.8, Germany's 2.6 and Japan's 2.3 (Rubery and Grimshaw 2002: 166).

Below the macro level, however, a great deal of disconcerting evidence exists regarding the costs of liberalisation and restructuring on employee well-being. The data we have gathered from interviews in large UK firms reflect many of these concerning elements, notably in regard to stress, overwork and insecurity. In some cases (such as the former branch manager at UKBank, below), the stories were of considerable concern. Elsewhere, there is evidence of improvement, such as attempts to move away from a culture of bullying and intimidation, and many of the managers interviewed claimed to enjoy their job, despite the heavy workloads. Even as some managerial experience may have improved, following culture change programmes and attempts at professionalising HR (Kersley *et al.* 2006: 36), the daily work pressures have certainly increased for middle managers, as their spans of control and areas of responsibility have grown while their time horizons for the completion of tasks have shrunk.

Following this overview of changes in the UK economy, we now offer an in-depth analysis of management restructuring at three UK-based case studies. They include a US-owned automobile transplant (UKAuto) and two large British-headquartered PLCs – a major privatised utilities company (UKUtilities) and an insurance firm (UKInsurance). We end the chapter with an interview with a former middle manager at UKBank, who, after struggling with the new post-restructuring era, had chosen to quit corporate life altogether. Unlike the vast majority of interviews conducted in this study, this final one was not organised officially through the company. As will become clear, despite differences in company size, sector, market performance and financial position, the picture of the major restructuring of managerial hierarchies was very consistent across the cases, involving serious challenges for middle managers. We begin with the car manufacturing case study.

UKAuto: 'What is the rationale? The rationale is saving fucking money!'

The automobile industry receives a great deal of attention from business media and academic research, not least because of its enormous degree of internationalisation (Maxton and Warmold 2004). Workers and managers in the industry have been under duress over the last twenty years (at least) as rationalisation pressures have impacted on all of the major car groups, especially US-owned ones which, as we have seen above, have struggled for some time to meet the Japanese challenge. The case study we present here is wholly US owned, although we will refer to it as UKAuto for simplicity. At this company, we were able to secure access to both a major engine plant and the HR division at head office. UKAuto is simply the UK operations of the parent company USAuto, the firm which featured in Chapter 3.

At the UK head office, an HR manager explained the broader organisational changes that have enveloped the company. At the time of our research UKAuto employed around 14,000 staff in Britain. It housed five layers of middle management, from Leadership Level Six (LL6 – the first rung of middle management) to Leadership Level Two (LL2 – very senior positions). The HR manager outlined how the growth in international competition was the major factor impacting on the company's need to restructure, with cost reduction plans being uppermost in senior management's mind. Redundancies and early retirements have been widespread over recent years, although the total number of managers in the UK had actually grown, from 1,370 in 1998 to 1,751 in 2003. The HR manager suggested that in selecting staff an education in business and management, such as that related, for example, to an MBA qualification, was not especially valued. Instead they wanted people with interpersonal and communication skills, an ability to work in a team and a high degree of operational knowledge.[8] She went on to mention that job security and morale for middle managers had certainly decreased somewhat over the last five years, citing, in particular, the increasingly competitive market, tougher business situation, increased individual accountability and more demanding roles and responsibilities.

In general, the view from head office regarding UKAuto's economic fortunes was reasonably sanguine, although problems were noted. A much more concerning picture was presented at the local plant level. We were able to secure interviews at a division that manufactures engines for a range of Auto's models. Its Head of Plant HR granted us an interview, and we were also introduced to other middle managers from

---

[8] This would seem to echo a quotation from an auto employee in Starkey and McKinlay's article : 'It was the Rambo rather than the Einstein who was invariably given the job' (1994: 980).

various sections across the plant. It soon became clear from our discussions that UKAuto was thoroughly caught up in the broader transformations taking place across Auto's facilities worldwide. Whereas the macro numbers provided by HR looked encouraging, when we looked closer at this specific workplace within the corporate group, a far tougher environment was revealed. The Head of HR at the engine plant, who, nearing retirement, had clearly witnessed a lot of change during his time with the company, was particularly outspoken, and appeared not at all interested in rehearsing a glossy 'official line' on Auto's policies and practices.

From what the Head of Plant HR had experienced locally, the restructuring of white-collar ranks had been robust. The number of managers at the engine plant had decreased from thirty-three to just eighteen following years of rationalisation. These eighteen managers were expected to manage a total of 1,500 staff at the plant; this is lean management taken to its limits. The plant HR manager described how there were 'a lot of layers' up until around 1998. Whereas the old structure had twelve layers between first-line supervisor and corporate vice-president level, the new structure had just four levels between them. The old structure at UKAuto had clear grades and sub-positions with an implied career development track inherent in the system. Below is an outline of the old and new white-collar career tracks:

Pre-1998 managerial level	Post-1998 managerial levels
9. Superintendent	Leadership Level Six (LL6)
10. Superintendent (Large Area)	
11. Area Manager	LL5
12. Area Manager (Large Area)	
13. Assistant Plant Manager	LL4
14. Plant Manager	
15. Plant Manager (Large Plot)	LL3
16. Operations Manager	
17. Operations Manager	LL2
18. Operations Manager	
19. Top Management: Corporate Vice-President	
20. Top Management: Corporate Senior Vice-President	LL1
21. Top Management: Corporate Senior Vice-President	

Clearly the new system was much leaner than the old, with more mundane job titles and broader pay banding within the ranks. According to the Head of Plant HR, however, this streamlined structure meant that there was no direct way of learning about a small area under the coaching of a senior. This led to overstretch for less experienced managers:

Not all PTMs [Production Team Managers, at LL6] can get promoted in this lean structure, that's the crux of it. This de-layering has taken out what I call the key development grades. It's all about money. There were thirty-three managers here, now there's eighteen. A superintendent could develop into a bigger superintendent role, but they can't do that now. There have been huge organisational jumps in expectation, almost where they want to promote people to the level of their incompetence: the 'Peter principle'. There are huge levels of risk being taken with people. But the acid test is, it doesn't allow development. Not everyone wants to be on the fast-track scale. Sometimes slow is better for some people. They will get there eventually – don't push too hard, you know? [...] It doesn't matter too much to me. I'm an old fart, and old [UKAuto] hand. I know my way around and I'll be gone in a year or so. But I feel sorry for them. (Plant HR Manager)

Another experienced middle manager also expressed concerns about the heavy demands placed on white-collar staff. He described his own feelings of stress when he first became a manager:

When you're a new manager you're living here in the plant, not going home much, and making sure it's in good shape. Are all the other managers doing what they said they would do, and likewise all the foremen and the engineers and everyone else, you know? So there was a tremendous learning curve which I found very stressful at the beginning, but actually got manageable towards the end, you know? [...] I've never been one that actually was an eight-till-four person anyway. I've always worked extra hours and felt better for it. But now, sometimes, not all the time, sometimes you feel almost guilty going home, you know? There's always something else to do. You don't sleep very well then. [...] I guess my working day is typically seven in the morning till six in the evening. And when you have periods like with the audit that would be all weekend as well. (Training Manager)

Another UKAuto manager – who joined as a form maker in 1985, did his apprenticeship with the company, completed a degree in engineering and 'worked through the ranks' to his present role at Leadership Level 5 – described an 'average working day'. From his account, the level of involvement of a middle manager in this organisation appears exceptionally deep and the level of responsibility exceptionally high. Our middle manager describes, *inter alia*, 'touching base', taking 'snap-shots', doing 'walks', undertaking 'reviews', arranging 'containment' if things go wrong, and constantly keeping in touch with the hourly supervisors and first-line management. Of course, the hours are long, but the intensity during those hours is perhaps the most noticeable element of his story. He even mentions his frustrations of sitting in the office when he needs to be out on the line, where the real work is done. The image created is of a manic environment, where speed is everything. Judge for yourself – is this environment conducive to the development of quality and creativity that world-class firms are sup-posed to embody?

When I arrive in the morning, which varies between six to half past, that's my time to actually check emails, which there tends to be a lot of nowadays. From then on I have a review at seven fifteen and that's a snapshot review of the first hour and fifteen minutes of the shift. And in between that if I can do an area walk and touch base with a supervisor I tend to just have a very quick snapshot, three-minute overview, of any problems and issues and also do my line walk. The seven-fifteen review purely consists of safety issues first, whether we've got our containments in place, the delivery status, the first hour and fifteen minutes, or the first hour there's usually a six to seven score, and then if there's any quality concerns. And that's a very, very quick fifteen-minute snapshot on where we are, do we need help and do we need to put any containment on to prevent further losses in the following hours to come? I then move on to Assembly, another process walk, probably just meeting and discussing a similar focus on safety, quality, delivery with the foreman and with team leaders on the line. And by the time I've completed that it's approaching seven forty-five. At seven forty-five I have a review with the plant manager in Assembly – that lasts for about fifteen minutes. At eight o'clock I do another review with the [section] man which is very similar to or virtually identical to the earlier review – what's happened in the first two hours of the [section] machine shifts, 'cos they start at six, and what's happened in the first hour of assembly, and again it's safety, quality, delivery, and that's a snapshot overview again. There onwards there's a meeting structure set up which is a standardised structure we set up between [various sections]. Eight forty-five there's an in-depth review on, not so much safety, it's really delivery and quality. And that takes place reviewing really what happened the previous day – is there anything we need to learn from that, any permanent fixtures we put in place? Some of the ongoing concerns and actions that we've identified we need to do and we review and receive an update on quality – what we're holding, anything needs sorting and anything that needs repairing. That happens on Assembly from eight to eight forty-five, and then on Machining the same format happens from eight forty-five to nine thirty. I tend not to go to those reviews at this stage purely because that's a PTMs' [Production Team Managers'] meeting. I used to, but it's one of those things, when you're comfortable with the approach, that the manager needs time to actually deal with his teams, and with myself being present at these reviews it tended to be always 'Well, what do you want us to do next?' type of thing. And that's a bad situation to be in because I want the PTMs to take ownership of their areas; I'm there to give to guidance, to have a look at things, you know, coaching the PTMs. So I backed off from the Assembly one. I tend to go into the Machining ones a bit more – but not every day, it's every other day – observe end of the meetings, give a coaching tip to the PTMs saying 'you're sloppy, you're not doing right' or 'you could do better'. Nine thirty we used to have an OCM, that's the Operating Committee Meeting, that's [...] a plant manager's meeting and basically status, any problems, what happened yesterday. It's a similar kind of format, same theory, it's just check the kind of process. And you could say it's a waste of time, it's a waste of my hour. I find it frustrating sometimes that, you know, there's that time I could spend on the floor and do something more productive. But [Plant Manager] changed that now, he's changed the format. [...] He still takes my hour but it's a different focus, like we did one this morning. So from nine thirty to ten thirty we'll do a waste walk in a particular area, and that's really a line-based walk looking at if everything's in its place, is the housekeeping correct, are there any safety concerns we can observe? And that's really, you know, what you see, how can we improve and that's with the supervisors on the shift, it's a process we've just recently kicked off so it's waste walks. And then on a Wednesday we've a planning strategy meeting, and we've kicked it off this week. So you could argue that that hour is probably a bit more productive for me, 'cos I'm spending that hour as my waste walk or safety walk, call it what you like. So I find that useful now as opposed to sitting in an office talking about, it's really talking about not so much strategy, what went wrong or what we want to fix, and you know, I think we do too much of that, and we did recognise that so we've changed that. [...] After ten thirty I then have another walk round the areas and touch base with PTMs, and come back and do a bit more emailing and check on emails. My role at this moment in time has been a dual role as a launch manager and an area manager, and that's been rectified recently. [...] From an organisational perspective we should also have had a launch manager on board. So when [name] took over the position as Plant Manager I stepped into his shoes together with running the normal side of the business. You could argue the handover of these is not ideal. I think it was done very, very quickly. But also it had knock-on effects, because I have to bring myself up to speed with the launch programme. And not having other resources available at that time, the resources are stretched. But we've had to manage. (Area Manager)

Time and again, especially in manufacturing firms, this kind of frenetic, highly stressed picture was described by managerial employees. In the above case, this long monologue flowed from the manager very early in the interview, simply as a response to our question 'what does an average day look like?' During our interviews at UKAuto we were deluged with this kind of outpouring several times, which perhaps suggests that overstretched managers were keen to take advantage of this rare opportunity to relate their experiences to a friendly and independent person.

All of the managerial staff at UKAuto were on 'pay for performance' contracts and thus appraised every six months. According to the Plant HR Manager, 'this again is putting too much pressure on people'. The system of Balanced Scorecards cascaded down from the Plant Manager to each Production Team Manager (first-line management). The HR Manager went on to note that 'on an hourly basis PTMs have the stress of being person plus or minus – they have enormous stress'. His explanation for why this is happening was unequivocal:

What is the rationale? The rationale is saving fucking money. People are doing higher jobs for less money. […] With scorecards and pay for performance, youngsters are going to have to learn quickly. Young managers are going to have to learn quickly. We're putting in bright people – but they are not managers, they are engineers. I get worried, I'm not confident. Engineers aren't 'people' people. They see things in black and white. But work is a quagmire of grey. They think things either work or not, but people are a bit more complex than this. You have to find out what's important for people. (Plant HR Manager)

It was startling to hear an HR manager talk in such depressing terms, and one wonders whether senior management in the UK head office (never mind in Midwest USA) were aware that a senior HR person considered his workplace to be so mismanaged. Even if the corporate centre was aware of what its policies were doing in the localities, it is likely that this would be explained in terms of 'this is what the international market dictates', and 'there is no alternative'. Balanced Scorecard, moreover, is supposed to be welcomed by middle managers as part of their 'toolkit' for getting work done. Indeed, despite the situation described in this plant, according to the terms laid out for it by the parent, USAuto Group, the plant has been a success. A significant part of this, according to the Plant HR Manager, appeared to lie with the 'sensible', 'unionised but moderate' character of the blue-collar workers:

This plant has been very successful. We have a team structure. The unions and managers run the place together. We have incredibly sensible people on the shopfloor. I know this sounds a bit overcooked, but we have a partnership approach and it does work. People are sensible, they know that if people aren't buying cars, there won't be any shift premium or any overtime. (Plant HR Manager)

This picture diverged considerably from the history of labour militancy at UK car plants, such as that described by Beynon (1986) at Ford Halewood, or the infamous shop steward 'Red Robbo' (Derek Robinson) at what was once British Leyland, Longbridge. Workers and managers appear to have had little choice but to 'buy in' to this new culture of high performance and international pressures. Having said this, the middle managers we spoke to appear genuinely proud to be involved at the cutting edge of automotive engineering. The highest skilled and best performing engineers were well rewarded. It is not simply a case of highly skilled staff being bullied into submission from above. Many of these staff are committed and hardworking, and do receive job satisfaction from their high levels of responsibility and involvement in a 'world class' company. However, there was a significant motivation problem for these engineers, as they see promotion to LL5 not only as rare, but frequently as unwanted, given the pressure they are already under. (Almost exactly the same situation was reported in many of our Japanese manufacturing plants: see Chapter 5.)

Some of the LL6 engineers don't want to become managers. They don't want to do anything else. There's been less shit for them in their present jobs. They have company cars and PFP, but on a daily basis they won't get fucking beaten up. But they know they are at the leading edge in [UKAuto]; it's made them more marketable. We don't get much turnover. (HR Manager)

Another middle manager, responsible for coaching and training at the plant, was also concerned about this issue of motivation. As upwards movements were 'few and far between', graduates would have to learn to be satisfied with sideways movements and a wider development of their skills and knowledge:

[UKAuto] has quite a robust selection process for graduates, and we've had to stop offering them sort of 'you will be a manager in five years' type [promises], because we can't deliver that. We've introduced a system called the People Development Framework. And what we've tried to do is give people an opportunity to develop sideways but not necessarily upwards, because of the sharpness of the triangle. [...] And it could well be that somebody that might be in mainstream engineering might see that, you know, a career opportunity is better in production than it would have been staying in engineering. So we've given them the opportunity to go and work in production, or it might be in design or it might be in logistics or systems or whatever. We have to give them the opportunity for the best ones who actually say they want to do that in order to then progress. And they could also end up actually not progressing but just developing theirself as a person to have a wider breadth of knowledge of the business. So we're trying to tackle it that way. (Training Manager)

Middle managers at UKAuto had legitimate complaints about pressure and the absence of upwards movement. The threat of plant closure always hung in the air. But at the same time they wanted the plant to be a success and appeared to put a lot of energy and devotion into their work. To quote the Training Manager again:

There's a much greater expectation that you know a broad knowledge of how the company works. Before, years back, there were traditional chimneys where you actually were expert in your chimney. And now it's you have to be that, but you have to be able to understand the business in its totality, you know?
Q   *Do you work harder, are you working longer or harder?*
Yeah, working longer and harder, more is expected of you. Yeah, a lot more is expected of you. And this can be good as well. I'm not saying it in a negative way; it gives you that satisfaction, a feeling of worth. It overcomes the stress. (Training Manager)

The importance of this kind of non-tangible reward closely mirrors Kanter's (1989b: 92) argument that: 'Project responsibility leads to ownership of the results and sometimes substitutes for other forms of reward.' There is clearly a grain of truth in this. However, mainstream analysts such as Kanter can tend to overplay these effects, and thus give a lower profile to the costs required to receive these rare benefits. Senior management clearly depends for its success on the levels of effort and goodwill that middle managers provide, and it relies on staff to continually work well beyond their contracted hours. Middle management did seem willing to do this, out of professional pride and a genuine concern to help the plant be successful, but senior management can readily exploit this commitment. If performance consistently dropped below acceptable levels, then the nightmare scenario of plant closure could become a reality.

On a more positive note, several middle managers at the plant described an attempted move away from the traditions of intimidation and macho management at all levels of the hierarchy. In this respect, it was suggested that although their traditional weapons have been blunted, the unions on site clearly can still play an important regulatory role. According to an Area Manager at LL5:

Dealing with an organisation where we have trade union involvement from an hourly perspective and a salaried perspective, [...] I wouldn't say it's difficult, [...] it's that you have certain rules to engage with. But you know there's an advantage of having the unions, as well, because if there's something we've jumped into, and we may jump into it too hard, too quick without thinking, so there are instances where the union said 'oh, you haven't really thought this through'. So it's not always [that] the unions are a bad thing, but there are difficulties, you know. I think from a competency level, we're trying to move the needle throughout the [UKAuto] organisation with supervisory staff. [...] More is now being done with coaching, you know, I think the style of management needs to change. [...] And some people go with that mode and they accept it, but there's an old style of management which I'm brought up in and it's just shout, bawl, 'get on with it!' type of thing. And that's short-termism, that's short-termism. It can be effective over the long term, but obviously that has an impact on the individual you're dealing with. So whereas in the past maybe we didn't really focus in on the impact with people – because of some of the environments and the jobs that supervising was always seen as the hard person or even the hard man – now we are seeing more and more women in the organisation, which is good, so I think our role as managers needs to change. But then we need to be given the coaching and the guidance and the training and also the mindset to say 'well, hold on, the role is slightly changing' – we have less and less people, less layers. (Area Manager)

The efforts to improve people management, however, were hampered by the demanding and exacting environment into which they were inserted. This meant that stress always remained a factor:

It's almost a learn by doing, which is not the right way. I mean, there's an element of needing to learn by doing, but if you're doing it in an environment where there isn't blame, you know that you learn by your mistakes and it's accepted that 'that actually didn't go too well, did it?', what do you want to do, learn from that, and that was in the culture, that's fine. But if it's sort of a 'kick arse' mentality I guess [...] that is seen these days as very old-fashioned, it's more about, you know, 'what can we do to help you' school of management. That works really well now rather than, you know, victimisation. [...] It's a hard-nosed business that we're in at the end of the day and you know production is king and quality's king and safety's king, but you know you've got to get the engines out. And that brings with it lots of stress and sometimes people react to stress by being a bully. (Training Manager)

One major change in Anglo-Saxon manufacturing since the time of the very pessimistic literature by a diverse range of authors such as Beynon (1986) and Best (1990) is that the uptake of Japanese-style lean systems appears to have created a strong culture of quality and increased the levels of expertise, effort and care spent on the work by managers and operatives (Adler 2007). In some ways quality improvement has made the workplace safer and more involving than the Taylorist, bullying culture described by Beynon (1986) and Starkey and McKinlay (1994). However, the system remains exceptionally demanding and, on an emotional and technical level, maybe even more so than before. Lean implies that workers and managers have to 'buy into' the system, and are unable to withdraw and resist in the way that Beynon (1986) describes. There is probably less of a 'them and us' culture between white- and blue-collar staff and, although we could not interview them in this case, we were given clues from the middle managers that front-line supervisors and operatives were more technically competent and much more committed than in earlier eras (Lowe *et al.* 2002). The work remains just as demanding, but it makes different demands than before. Not everyone can cope, and bullying and intimidation continue to surface in lean systems (Milkman 1997). Indeed, a critic such as Mehri (2005) would say that lean actually depends on intense and robust treatment of staff. Clearly the atmosphere in UKAuto is very uncompromising.

Nevertheless, these jobs were attractive. There appeared to be considerable demand for workers to join the company, and managerial turnover was low. Plant HR told us that when 600 new posts became available with the opening of a new line, they received 7,000 applications. Higher-end positions at UKAuto were very well-paid, highly sought-after jobs in short supply. The prestige attached to the jobs meant that, although senior management had to tread carefully with some of the top engineers, in general they could continue to exert pressure on managerial and line staff and expect them to comply.

As noted above, however, across UKAuto there was a clear feeling that if performance was not raised as high as it could possibly be, or that costs were not controlled, then there would always be the threat of plant closure and relocation. Interestingly, we were told that it was not hard to move these plants. Despite a $465 million investment to upgrade the plant, so that it can manufacture a new range of engines for four of Auto's models, the HR manager explained that this does not necessarily safeguard the workplace's future:

We were in competition with lots of plants for this, but particularly with Sweden, because it's their design. We'll take on another 600 people for this. We've had 7,000 applications and the books are closed. Does this secure the plant? Sort of. It would have with the older technologies. But with the new flexible machinery centres, they are relatively easy to move. (Plant HR Manager)

This story resonated with much of the academic literature on the fragility of manufacturing jobs in the UK and USA (Thompson 2003; Sallaz 2004). When we asked one middle manager about her take on job security, the response was revealing. She noted not only the severity of competition within the Auto group and the domestic market, but also the wider nature of international competition:

Q   *What are your expectations in terms of a career and job security and …?*
If you look at what's happening in manufacturing within the UK then personally there's a lot of fear about low-cost producers. At the moment in this plant, say in the last year, and into manufacturing the engine that we make here, we've seen a lot of components now starting to be sourced from China. In that respect then it's quite worrying and it's not just, say, affecting [USAuto] and the automotive industry but it's a lot of industries.
Q   *How do you personally deal with that?*
For me just to try and keep doing what I do, which is about meeting the business objectives for this plant. My personal view is if we can increase our volume, improve our quality, reduce our costs then we have a chance to survive. If we don't do that then we're basically looking at the plant closing. Now I'll play my part in that, which is basically making the shop floor aware of that. (Middle Manager)

Managers and workers at UKAuto were very much at the receiving end of restructuring pressures, as major shifts in the international car industry were directly impacting on their workplace. The case reinforces the sacrifices that middle managers make to their employers, and reveals how much the company depends on continual goodwill and working well over contracted hours. The very high gearing of staff levels, in theory, should make the company vulnerable to a withdrawal of effort from staff, but there appeared to be little sign that employee resentment would turn into conflict and resistance. There appeared several reasons for this. Firstly, the staff appeared to have internalised the company narrative about the intensity of international competition and the need for total commitment to avoid closure. Indeed, in this respect, the UKAuto managers sounded similar to the stylised conception of the traditional Japanese employee, in that they were proud to be a part of the company, wanted it to be a success and would be prepared to make sacrifices for it. Secondly, the middle managers at UKAuto were either not unionised or were very inert members. This also appeared to apply to the hourly workers, and was enshrined in the partnership agreement. White- or blue-collar workers had no real platform upon which collectively to resist or influence senior management. Middle managers mentioned how the union could actually assist in the running of the plant (again somewhat reminiscent of the Japanese situation). Thirdly, Auto top management in the UK and the USA appeared to be in a position of strength, meaning that disruption or resistance at any local plant would rupture relations with the centre and probably hasten its demise (as we have seen in several cases, where unions have had little choice but to reach concession after concession, see Dudley 1994; Sallaz 2004). The end result is that middle managers in the company, although motivated and committed to their work, are likely to remain under considerable duress. If they wish to stay in these well-paid and relatively high-status jobs, they simply have to put up with the long hours, the stress and the pressure.

A similar story is found at our next case study, UKUtilities, a company which is also going through changes that have hit middle managers hard. This is true even though this organisation is currently in far less economic distress than UKAuto.

UKUtilities: 'We are here to make money for shareholders'

UKUtilities is a PLC providing, primarily, water and electricity services and employing around 15,000 staff. The company has an asset base of £30 billion and 3 million customers. Its origins were two English regional state-owned monopoly providers privatised in 1989 and 1991, and merged in 1996. Water and electricity remain its core business (approximately 95 per cent of turnover), but it also provides asset management facilities for two water distributors in two other UK regions. Most of the company's operations take place in quite heavily regulated utilities sectors, yet it is also attempting to build a reputation in other, less- or non-regulated, sectors such as telecoms or consulting. The 1996 merger of the two former organisations resulted in considerable redundancies at both. In common with several of the UK firms in this study, the company embarked on a major culture change programme. This attempted to turn the company away from its technical, engineering focus, to one of 'customer focus'. Cost control has had a heavy presence, even though this company is currently quite successful, with a high share price at the time of our field research. It had also delivered some important improvements in the technical side of the business, such as more reliable, uninterrupted delivery of power, and improved quality of water supply. Compared to UKAuto, workforce morale appeared generally high. This is perhaps understandable given the company's recent history of success, and the fact that it effectively enjoyed monopoly positions in several markets. Nevertheless, UKUtilities was also described as a 'demanding' workplace, and some quite severe work-life balance problems were reported. In particular, some middle managers often experienced discomfort with the 'robust' approach to decision-making taken by some of the senior managers.

During our research visits to UKUtilities, we interviewed an HR director plus eight middle managers. Five of the managers had joined the organisation in the 1990s, one in 2000, one in 1976 and one in 1983. In general, the workforce is fairly long established, with many having between twenty and forty years' service, and is heavily unionised. The organisation had undergone a period of rapid change in recent times, with privatisation followed by merger, acquisitions, a public listing, several major restructurings and a culture change programme. The rapidity of change inevitably had impacted on certain employees' quality of working life. As a female middle manager explained:

I think almost certainly the utilities, which are seen as stable organisations traditionally by the outside world, I think you almost need that rapid change towards a senior level. Because you're getting fresh thinking in all the time, because you're having to respond to an environment that is starting to change in terms of being more competitive. Whether you like it or not you're being besieged by the regulator, and other utility companies. You have to move up the league tables. How are you going to do it? And so you're looking at new ways of working, smarter ways of working, how can you be more efficient, how can you be more effective all the time? [...] What you do find though is a lot of people underneath are a little bit vulnerable because they always feel that things are changing. And I don't know whether people lower down the organisation, [but] certainly the feedback that I've had in the past [is we] want a little bit more continuity. And yet at this level that we're at it's kind of, well it's great because it's another opportunity, I'll go on and do something else. So there's different perceptions depending on what you're looking for. Whether you're one of the persons who it's being done to or you're making the change yourself, it generally happens at a senior level. (Commercial Manager)

The Director of Facilities Management concurred:

There is a lot of pressure in terms of work and time, particularly in terms of meetings and appointments and meeting deadlines. You know, there are occasions where I'll work from seven in the morning till midnight and do that for five days and feel completely knackered at the end of it. There are other occasions where it's quiet and things are happening and I'll finish early, at lunchtime, and go fishing. It really is, it's down to me very much to drive myself and to make sure I take whatever time I need, time to relax and get the balance right. And I think the only person I blame is myself, you know, I commit to what I want to commit to. [...] I've no doubt that I won't be here in twelve months if I don't secure new business. (Director of Facilities Management)

Indeed, the Director of HR, who was our first contact in UKUtilities, and who provided our access to middle managers, noted early in our discussions the heavy pressure on managerial employees:

Yes, we've been working with them on a particular organisation change that we made around this new structure that our new chief exec brought in. And I would say that a lot of our middle managers are quite under siege. I think the culture change, we did it so that we trained everybody simultaneously, and I think that was quite hard for our managers. [...] I feel like they've got a bit of a pincer movement because there's these people at the senior levels of the organisation who say, you know, 'we've got to do all these things' and it is like raining down on people. If you think about the different initiatives, the culture change, the need to perform, and you know we've got very demanding targets on the regulated business for investment and capital improvement projects. I would shudder to think how some managers come into work some days and think 'well, how do I prioritise all of this?' Culturally I'm being told I've got to talk to my people more, I've got to get out more. (Director of HR)

Organisational change has had far-reaching implications. The Director of Facilities Management described this in detail:

It's probably not as bad a picture as I'm perhaps painting. [...] But, yeah, the general approach was that the electricity industry was a captive market, people could not go anywhere else for their electricity service. And when businesses wanted new electricity supplies so that they could operate their business they always wanted electrical services to start up new developments and there were repairs required to the network. Then the right attention wasn't given to the customer, it was very much a 'we'll get round to it when we can get round to it' type of approach. The priority really wasn't thinking about [whether] the customer could have a choice and if you don't provide the right level of service they'll go somewhere else. The background was that they couldn't go anywhere else. The privatisation brought the opportunity for the customer to be selective about who they bought their electricity from. And therefore [there was] the need for a complete change of mindset in respect of how we provide levels of service to the customer. If you go and buy a suit you can choose where you buy it from, and a lot of things you go for the quality and also the service that's provided. If the shop assistant is helpful then you're more likely to go back there again. And I think that's where particularly in electricity there needed to be a complete change of culture. [...] There was a need for quite considerable downsizing in terms of the organisation structures, which meant that a lot of people would be leaving the organisation. The trade unions had campaigned for many years against compulsory redundancies and to my knowledge nobody was going to be made compulsorily redundant, it was all being done through natural wastage and voluntary severance. To that extent we've had no disputes over people leaving the organisation, but that's been handled in a fairly consistent way. I think I would say the main area of work that's changed is the general workforce's attitude to the new requirements in the privatised industry, and therefore there's no point in talking with the trade unions; most of the work has to be done with the grass roots, with the general workforce. And that is where most of the effort has been placed in terms of the culture change. (Director of Facilities Management)

All of the managers reported work intensification and many of them described the stress that went with it. We asked whether tight deadlines existed. A senior manager replied:

Some of the time, some of the time it is. [...] If we're delivering things to the regulator, for example, we normally are working to a specific deadline. And then as you close things, you know, they will get fairly frenetic, and it is fairly tight. [...] Sometimes it is very stressful, sometimes, you know, I've got day-to-day things that I need to manage and then specific projects. So there's very much peaks and troughs, you know, it can be very difficult managing it. (Head of Group Strategic Planning)

Work intensification resulted in long working hours. A female manager noted that meetings consumed most of her time, and that these were increasingly taking up most of the working day. It was difficult to complete her personal workload, as it could only be tackled outside of meeting times. Meetings tended to run from:

[E]ight in the morning till five, half past five at night, and you really do have to be disciplined about how you do it. And most people, and I was the same, you know, if you go in at seven in the morning you've got an hour to do some work before your meetings start, and then you've got a couple of hours when you finish meetings at half past five. So you do have ten- or twelve-hour days. (Commercial Manager)

Although all of our managers reported similarly long working hours, they differed in their explanation of how much difficulty this presented to them. The Group Financial Controller reported very long work hours, but he was much more sanguine about this:

Well, I suppose my normal work hours [are] I leave home about eight in the morning and I probably get home seven, seven at night. And I do try and stick to that [but] if I have to take work home with me, I do. Writing and reading and then do a bit of work later, so yeah. So even if I'm on a project, that project can run on, I mean it's not unusual to be here at eight or nine with a project. I try not to do that, I try and break off and say do it from home if I can, and working weekends as well can happen, and more, as much for people that work for me as much as for me. (Group Financial Controller)

A female HR manager described the impact on her home life, and the personal strategies she has negotiated between herself and her husband who was also a manager at UKUtilities. Although there are obvious signs of strain, at least it demonstrates that a working compromise is possible and that, in this case at least, the husband can contribute more (unlike the deep pessimism shown by most of Hochschild's (2003) working couples). Nevertheless, this is still a very demanding juggling act:

So you've got to sit and listen and the same at home, you know, the kids will come up to me, you know, I got home at seven o'clock and 'cos I don't want to talk to them and they're telling me about school. And sometimes you've had a tetchy day or doing a bit of work or something like that, and I'm trying now to focus on giving them the attention. So I do take work home but I won't do it until they've gone to bed, like sometimes that might be doing something at ten o'clock at night, but I want to make sure that while I've got that time at home

I'm with them. Yeah, I'm married, I've got two children, a little girl of seven and a boy of ten, that's about it, my husband works in here as well, he works down there, he's a project manager. We have an excellent child minder who's looked after the kids since they were born so we just manage it between us, we both work full-time. He tends to do less hours than I do and that's the balance we've got between us, he's comfortable with that, that's what he wants to do. And I couldn't do what I do without him supporting me in that area. He's the one who goes home to pick the kids up from the childminders' at five o'clock, gives them their tea, does the homework, all that, you know. I tend to time it really well to stroll in at seven o'clock when all the jobs are done and I can spend time with the kids then. (HR Manager)

The Head of Employee Communications had a lot of interesting points to make about work-life balance and organisational demands. Like many other informants in this study, she noted that the long hours (and 'presenteeism') were not coerced out of staff by heavy-handed management surveillance. In keeping with many other middle managers we interviewed, she described her long hours as her 'own choice'. However, we would suggest that personal choice plays a minor role here. Rather, the sheer volume of the workload necessitates long hours or it will simply never be completed. Managerial staff regularly faced the stress of being behind with their work and hardly ever feeling 'on top of it all'. This manager mentioned being available to answer queries even when on holiday, yet rationalises this away as not too serious a problem. A lot of stress seemed to emanate from a feeling of not being sufficiently in control of work and its demands. Some managers felt the need to be contactable at all times, especially if unexpected problems arose. This perhaps is the result of an overindividualised workplace, with insufficient support or collegiality to cover absent workers:

What I do find is I've not got anybody on my back watching and checking [me] out, so I'm treated as a responsible human being, and I have been in this organisation. It's different to [nationally owned electricity board, one of UKUtilities' predecessor companies] which was very bureaucratic and institutionalised as a company. My contract says I work the hours required to do the job and yes I do; sometimes they vary, sometimes they're OK, sometimes I put a lot of hours in. [...] I count in the work the time spent thinking, I spend time outside work thinking. I choose to do that 'cos I actually like my job. I suppose that's what is required ultimately. I spend a lot of time thinking about what needs to be done, planning stuff, thinking, a lot of stuff which you'd expect any good manager to do. I have my mobile phone on all the time, twenty-four hours a day. [...] I don't feel I need to, nobody tells me I have to, but if there's a crisis, heaven forbid. I know our newsroom deals with a lot of that, but we would be required to be part of that process to inform employees, so we would automatically be called in. But I feel I want to be, unless I'm on holiday or going away to Lanzarote or whatever, but even then I've given my number to some of the suppliers I deal with and say 'if there's an issue talk to me'. Because it's not going to be a big deal for me to say 'do this or do that', so I don't feel like some people must feel: 'I can't ever switch the phone off, it's a nightmare, it's horrible.' I don't feel stressed out by it or hounded or harassed; it's my choice. (Head of Employee Communications)

In an organisation previously characterised by stability and job security, privatisation and consolidation had heightened fears of future insecurity. A more senior manager reported that restructuring is:

[A] fact of life for business today, and it does increase stress, but it's something that people have got to learn to live with. And the biggest worry for me I guess, the biggest concern would be that increasingly businesses are getting taken over. And if we got taken over then it is possible for people to survive, you know, and it might be a big German competitor, for example. [...] So even if they thought that I was a good person it might be that the opportunities were in Berlin and not in Manchester, or opportunities in London and not in Manchester. [...] Change is happening more and more, and it's likely to happen in this organisation as well. I think there will be, you know, we've been through this enormous restructuring three years ago now and I suspect we are likely to do another restructuring. And I guess my goal is to, my goal would be to get involved in it so therefore I can. It's control isn't it? So, you know, so that I can have some sort of control over what happens. But for people who haven't got that control I guess, you know, people need to be better, I think definitely people need to be better these days, people need to have skills, more flexible skills. (Head of Group Strategic Planning)

The reorganisation had impacted on career structures. Another female manager, this time in HR, reflected:

I think with every reorganisation we moan and it's a little bit pessimistic, 'jobs are going and restructuring, all the change', or you can be optimistic and say 'hey ho, there's another ten jobs I can have a look at now'. And, you know, do I want to try my hand over there? Plus the experience of going to interviews and things like that just to keep yourself better on that kind of thing. So I think there are more opportunities with the different [...], it is a lean structure and there's not as many jobs for jobs' sake as maybe there were fifteen years ago if I'm honest about it now. So in that respect you could say, yes, there's less opportunities, but I think they're still there for those who want to go and find them. (HR Manager)

Other managers were accepting of the change. For example, a senior financial accountant described a much more settled work life:

I feel fine. I don't believe it's a job for life any more, and take chances and take responsibility for your own career and your own life and it's not from cradle to grave. I'm happy working here now. I think it's completely in my hands when I choose not to work here, so I hope I do a good enough job to make sure that the decision stays in my hands; it isn't taken by somebody else. Yeah, so I'm quite comfortable that it's in my own hands. [...] And if I probably do a rubbish job then I probably deserve to go, so yeah I'd expect that. And that's the standard I expect from people these days; they do a good job and you expect that commitment from them. (Group Financial Controller)

The Head of Employee Communications observed that change and insecurity was:

[T]rue of most organisations, I think, that's not just [UKUtilities], and people often find it difficult. And I think major restructuring people find it difficult again 'cos I think the sense is you're always trying to stay ahead of the game. I think it puts a lot of stress on people in their everyday life and I think that's true across, well, everywhere, it's just how it is. And some people go down and other people kind of keep their heads above water, and I think in all of that it's very difficult to hang onto some of the values. (Head of Employee Communications)

She went on to add that organisational change had altered the culture of the workplace, demonstrating deleterious effects on worker dignity:

I found it very challenging, I felt at one stage that I was changed out, that I didn't think I could cope with another change yet again. But you always find you've got something to pull out of the bag I think, and I think it is challenging, I have found it quite stressful. I think we have to be careful about how we use the word 'change', because for some people change means doing more for less, and for other people it's about, yes, I've got an opportunity to grow here. And a lot depends on how you personally perceive that but also what history, what understanding history is carried from the way the organisation behaves, so it's different for different people and people will say different things about it. So I personally found it on occasions very challenging, the types of change have been very challenging, a lot of changes of director, and a lot of physical moves, and I think you get to the point where you think 'well, yes, this isn't going to stay the same'. It would be good if it could just stay the same for a year so you can build on what you've got. But you're lucky if it stays the same – you're constantly having to reinvent yourself, and I think that's not a bad idea but it requires a particular mindset to be able to adjust. And what's key is how a company behaves if people can't adjust, how they behave with people. Are they a compassionate employer? Or are you just out if you can't hack it? [...] Depending on which business you're in, the perception I think is that it's, if you can't hack it you're out of the door. Again we're not uncommon in this, I think it's true of a lot of businesses, I think it would be nice if we were to be known, if people talked about this company, our employees, our ex-employees said, 'well, [UKUtilities] they really were good with me after my husband died' or whatever. I'm not sure they'd say that about it; we tend to do it by the book with a lot of processes in place, but we are trying to change that, I think. So there are lots of those issues going on for people and there's certainly been issues for me. Having said that, it's one of the, out of all the places I've worked it's the place I enjoyed working in most, and I've actually had quite a few different jobs. And I think it's the organisation where we have an extremely good chief exec who's leading the culture change programme, and that makes my job a lot easier. But we are here to make money for shareholders and all we talk about, I know we talk about our different stakeholders groups, but at the end of the day it's about money, it's about growing the company, it's about making a profit. And sometimes it's, I have to be careful about how I present messages 'cos it can look like spin if you're not careful, but at the base of it all, around all of it is we're here to make this company a viable concern, that comes above all else, and we're not going to say that, which the company is, and that's what's difficult. (Head of Employee Communications)

At a personal level, this demanding culture had given her some causes for concern. Some feelings of self-doubt certainly emerged in the course of the interview:

My director said I wasn't ruthless enough. I found that quite hard to deal with, I don't know what that means. [...] I know emotionally what it means. I don't think I have that within me so maybe I'm not right for here, I don't know, those are the struggles I've had. To what extent do you bring people out, develop them if you're stressed out, and I'm not saying the organisation actually does that, so I'm wondering what challenges are coming my way, and I'm not process-focused as much as some people as well. I'll begin the process or end it. I like to think I'm more intuitive and people-focused. So I've found that quite difficult in the utility environment. [...] It's a very, very macho organisation and it's a very racist organisation, and diversity isn't yet, and it should be, at the top of our agendas. And I think with all those things comes other things from aggressive behaviour and bullying as well, and that doesn't sit comfortably with me either. It's not right for our organisation. By macho I define it as quite, it can be a bit thuggish in parts, there's a lot of effing and blinding you get in here. And the stress levels are high. So I define that as macho. So that's a difficult one to deal with. [...] I think women do get promoted now, I think they do get promoted, I'd like to see more, I don't think it's going to happen for a while, I'd like to see more on our exec and on the board either coming from a utility background and maybe engineers and [...] more black people, disabled or whatever, we need to reflect that diversity; we don't, we don't. But then we're not uncommon. (Head of Employee Communications)

On the other hand, it is important to note that restructuring had positive consequences for certain middle managers. Despite all of the pressure, many managerial employees stated they enjoyed their work. One noted that restructuring:

[C]reated a lot of opportunities for particularly the younger people to progress a bit more in the organisation – it became a much more dynamic organisation, much more customer-focused. So I think that was the main difficulty, a lot of the older people who had worked for the public, in the public sector for many, many years faced changing from being a service provision, that the customer could take it leave it type of attitude to one being very much customer-focused, and the customer could make choices as to where they went for their electricity service. And a lot of people struggled with that change of culture. It was very much a culture shock, a load of people, many, many people in the organisation left to pursue other opportunities or retire. With that went a lot of experience, unfortunately, at the same time because of the drive to reduce costs. (Director of Facilities Management)

In the final analysis, the UKUtilities case demonstrates how the demands for profitability and high performance at the macro level are translated into personal pressures. This is true even in a successful firm that was, at the time of writing, enjoying a comfortable financial position, and profited from a lack of competition in some monopolised markets. The descriptions of the company as macho and uncompromising are disappointing for a well-regarded FTSE 100 firm. However, more positive appraisals about working life did surface at times, in that much of the work was engaging and some of it had intrinsic value. There were some (limited) elements of a public service ethos that had survived privatisation. The company had a no-redundancy policy and job insecurity was not a major problem. But in general, the complaints around work overload, a lack of upwards movement and of increased demands without increased rewards were reminiscent of other organisations in this study. A similar story can be told at UKInsurance, a firm which has been fundamentally challenged by the contemporary pressures of financialisation and hyper-competition.

UKInsurance: 'Managing in a "one per cent environment"'

UKInsurance had undergone a considerable restructuring process set within a context of two developments typical of the UK financial services industry. First, the company had demutualised and, second, there had been considerable acquisition activity. Much of the UK home mortgage and insurance market had, until the 1990s, been operated by mutual societies owned essentially by either the mortgage or insurance policy holders. However, this had changed, with many of the building societies and insurance companies being converted to PLCs. As a consequence of this, and also the internationalisation of the financial services industry, there was considerable consolidation across the financial services through merger and acquisition activity. At UKInsurance we interviewed the Director of Business Services plus eight middle managers, many of whom were long-serving. The longest-serving manager had started in 1974, five others had started pre-1990 and the newest in 1998.

At the time of our research, UKInsurance employed 4,000 staff in the UK. As a result of growth through acquisition the company had not downsized as such, although a number of the acquired companies had undergone redundancies subsequent to takeover. The company operated in a mature, competitive and heavily saturated environment. Moreover, a prominent comment throughout the research interviews was the major change in culture from a somewhat old-fashioned 'mutual society' to a PLC. The pressures of financialisation were obvious: now the focus was on shareholder value, entailing constant pressures to 'manage' (i.e. cut) costs alongside ones to increase business activity and diversify the products on offer. Work intensification posed serious challenges for middle managers. The organisation had engaged heavily in outsourcing, with all direct sales activities offshored to India (with 300 redundancies) and many ex-direct sales staff becoming self-employed. It had also undergone seven mergers or acquisitions in the nine years prior to our research. The firm had recently de-layered, taking out what were called the 'head of' managerial positions. Middle managers now reported directly to senior managers, known as 'directors'.

The demutualisation and conversion to a PLC (in 2000) had a profound impact on the organisation. As the Director of Business Services (a senior manager responsible for HR) noted, there was a series of complex issues to resolve. Floatation on the stock market had brought certain advantages, but also major pressures for cost control. Moreover, the new regulatory environment had changed the way the company could make profits on writing new insurance work. The emerging regulatory regime meant that traditional, front-loaded products could no longer operate, meaning an extremely narrow profit margin on each new product sold. This, in turn, generated more pressure to write more, and higher-value, insurance rather than simply looking after the existing insurance 'book' (which would have already secured the front-end income). The Director of Business Services described this as the 'one per cent environment':

Listing on the stock exchange had some very positive impacts in terms of access to capital and our ability to drive the business forward. It had some not so positive impacts in terms that we were much more, if you like, exposed to market discipline, and so there was a need to start to change the culture of the organisation from that pretty cosy paternalistic environment. I mean, I wouldn't want to overstate because as an organisation in a competitive environment we still had to behave as though we had investors in the form of shareholders. I mean, our investors were policyholders, but I think there was probably much more of an arm's-length relationship with them than shareholders. Shareholders demand returns in a different way from the way in which policyholders demand returns. So the demutualisation created a lot of challenges for us as an organisation, and that overlaid by increasing regulation of the industry, both from a financial control perspective through the Financial Services Authority, but also from a product control environment through the government which was introducing stakeholder pensions. You've probably heard of those, the stakeholder pensions were really created to, if you like, engage with the masses of people who had not got pension provision beyond state provision. And I think there was a recognition by government, and to a degree driven by government – both this government and the previous one – that the state was going to be pulling back to a degree from the provision that had been introduced, say, during the 1970s. And part of that stakeholder environment was what we call 'one per cent charging', which is that effectively all our charges could only be accommodated within a one per cent management charge annually going forward. Whereas hitherto we'd been able to sell products on the basis of what we might call 'front-end loading'. So in other words we took quite a hefty chunk of charge upfront and had much lower charges going through the life of the policy. And that reflected very much the fact that to put business on the books was the expensive part of the business, because you had advice, you had people selling products et cetera, et cetera. And so clearly we have to pay those, we have to incentivise those, and actually to have a front-end loaded type of product probably matched the way in which we sold products much more effectively than a sort of fund management charge, an annual fund management charge, which are quite low. (Director of Business Services)

He went on to explain the process by which the organisation has changed in order to 'manage' cost reduction within the 'one per cent environment' and the effects this had on staff:

So as an organisation we've had to change the way in which we do business and identified that we need to cut out a huge amount of cost from the business in order to be able to manage within that one per cent environment. And a lot of that has been around service automation, there's been outsourcing, there's been offshoring, there's been a significant focus on cost. And clearly that has a potential to damage the relationship you have with your staff if they see you all the time cutting cost out of the business. Now clearly what we're trying to do is make the business much fitter going forward, so that for the staff who remain with us, you know, they have a much greater opportunity to grow with the company than if we actually were to stay where we were, because effectively the company would become unviable. So cost has been a big issue for us over the last couple of years. (Director of Business Services)

He continued by explaining the major cultural change in the organisation associated with the recent reorganisation of business, that based on the 'Achieving Customer Excellence' programme, a vehicle for 'empowering ourselves':

I suppose the other thing that's been a big issue for us is identifying, you know, what is our key differentiator as an organisation, and that, we believe, is customer service. Now I'm sure a lot of service-orientated organisations say that, but one of the features of increasing regulation, the one per cent environment, is that it's very difficult to differentiate on product. So actually what we can do is differentiate on service, so one of the big culture changes that we've introduced, and it's been running for the last two years, is what we call Achieving Customer Excellence, a phased programme. Which has been about getting all our staff to understand what it is, what it looks like to give excellent customer service, and that's about doing the right thing but doing it in the right way as well. I think as an organisation we tended to concentrate very much on doing the right thing in the past, but we've not really focused too much on doing it in the right way. So it's actually having that sort of what we call empathy with the customer, and so the phased programme was really all about empowering ourselves and giving them the opportunity to empathise, understand what the customer needs, and support what the customer needs by service delivery. But in an environment where cost is critical, because it would be very easy to say, 'OK, well, customer is king, therefore we do everything the customer wants.' Now clearly we can't do that, we have to do it in the context of the cost restraints, and that's been a big challenge for staff. (Director of Business Services)

The culture change programme and the cost-cutting measures implied some major problems for middle managers' career progression. In fact, the tactics of flattening the hierarchy and introducing culture change programmes were hard to differentiate from what we saw at other UK firms. The language of flatter, less bureaucratic and paternalistic firms, and of customer excellence and empowerment, and individualised performance management systems dominates many of the organisations featured in this book:

I don't know if we're alone in this, I mean we've developed quite a flat management structure. You know, again if I go back say five years we had lots of grades of managers, but now we have quite a flat structure, so effectively there are three management roles, management layers. There's the directors, there's a 'head of' and then there's a 'manager', so actually the opportunities for upward movement are relatively limited. So for middle managers what we're encouraging is actually people to move across the business rather than up in the business. So yes there are opportunities but they're probably becoming more limited and we would actually seek to get people to develop their skills within the current roles and maybe take on bigger roles. (Director of Business Services)

A male middle manager in the Finance department, who had been with the organisation for nine years, reflected on the magnitude of the changes that had taken place. He emphasised the significant impacts of financialisation and regulatory changes:

I mean when I first joined [UKInsurance], as I say I'd been working in a lot of businesses, I joined [UKInsurance] and it was very much a sleepy sort of mutual insurance company. I was amazed when I got here in terms of the urgency to do things was not as great as you'd think, it was quite a sort of sleepy place. It was a very nice place to work, the reason why I came here was because, you know, you can look out at the settings, and it was a lovely company albeit very sort of old-fashioned and quite paternalistic. But people definitely, people stayed here for a long time: on my very first day I met someone who'd been here for sort of twenty-six years I think, I think I was sort of twenty-eight at the time and it blew you away, that. But, I mean, I've been here now nine years and I can see why people stay here, albeit that it has changed a huge amount since then. I think the first biggest change was when we demutualised and really that happened pretty soon after I joined I think, I think it was about one or two years, something like that. And really since then every year there's been deals in terms of mergers with other companies, takeovers, ultimately culminating in the listing of [UKInsurance] in 2001. And obviously since that as well there's been even, you know, if anything the activity has really run, 'cos being a public limited company certainly from working in the finance side of things, the finance function has been absolutely transformed in terms of the work ethic and just the pressure and the interest on the numbers. Because it used to be the case that the accounts were published in May and you had six months to do the FSA returns, so it was a very sort of leisurely six months to do the work and then six months to be planning for the next year end sort of thing. And now it's obviously the pressure is working for the PLC. (Manager, Finance Department)

He noted some important changes in the organisation:

But certainly in the Finance section it's changed a lot, and I think in terms of the quality of people's lives and what they've, you know, people have had to put the hours in or want to work here, the nature of the organisation has definitely changed. There's been a lot of things that would have been unthinkable when I first joined, that have started to affect people in a real way. Such as they've got a very good pension scheme here and we didn't have to contribute to it, but now we're a listed company and the stock market has had three years' bad returns, you know, so that's something that the staff have all seen. And while we can tell people that it's a very good scheme, which it is, it's just that thought of, you know, perhaps in the old days people didn't have to pay for your pension. (Manager, Finance Department)

A long-serving female manager noted that most staff had no option but to accept the changes. Although it took time for employees to accept this new situation, they tended to suggest that it was useless to resist:

It was very much more paternal in the old days, there was a feeling of there being jobs for life and we look after our workforce. I think a lot of that has had to go, sort of the reality of modern business, and I think we struggled a little bit in getting to grips with some of that early on. But I feel now that the organisation has got to that point of understanding that, you know, sort of another world and the difference that it needs in its managers in taking that forward. (Network Services Manager)

Another female middle manager echoed similar sentiments:

When I first joined it was a very different organisation, it was very nice, very friendly, you know, it was brilliant, absolutely fantastic, you were looked after. The organisation was smaller as well, which is worth considering. It was just this site when I first joined. And as the years have progressed obviously we've acquired more and more organisations, the organisation's grown, the pace of change has got a lot quicker as it has in almost every industry. Also demutualisation, so you can no longer be as paternalistic as we were; there's the shareholder value, pressure on cost, and you could say, well, it's not such a nice place. But I think because we've got corporate values, that we introduced back in '98, they still do hold those values. And it is actually a good, it is still a good place to work because we hold true to those values. So although, you know, change is quicker, we're not as tolerant, we want to performance manage a bit more closer, yeah, we are becoming a bit more focused on the bottom line. And inevitably there's going to be casualties, people that don't like that, and also people's roles are changing, so no longer have you got a regiment of filing ladies that go round with their trolleys or, you know, you don't have secretaries. (Manager of HR Consultancy Services)

The transformation of UKInsurance from a mutual society to a PLC, together with a number of acquisitions, had led to a series of restructurings which, perhaps inevitably, had an unsettling effect on staff. A marketing manager noted that some of the restructurings, especially the latest one, were not handled well, creating a lot of anxiety. In fact, her own story was particularly interesting, as she had experienced more than her fair share of organisational trauma. She secured her first management job at the insurance division of a major UK retail bank. She reflected on her previous experience of redundancy, which had been announced with no warning or consultation. She described it as:

Absolutely devastating, absolutely devastating. Because my husband is retired, and so I'm the only earner in the family, and suddenly literally with no warning I had to find another job. And then, of course, trying to cope with a team, at that time I had a team of twelve people who were all, you know, there was one that was newly married, one that had just moved house. And all of these people are trying to cope with the tremendous emotional impact of 'I haven't got a job anymore, what do I do now?' [...] We've been through changes here and redundancies, and it's a bit of a lottery. [But this] was all of us, it was 200 marketing people went in a day. And so it was very difficult, but it focuses the mind. [...] I got a phone call on my mobile driving into work from my boss saying, 'Make sure you're here by nine o'clock, and there's a managers' briefing', and of course by that time it had hit the press, because the stock market had been told. And that's why they hadn't, they couldn't say anything beforehand because of the stock market, so we got in and there it was on the news that [insurance division] had been closed by [UK retail bank]. (Manager, Strategic Partner Marketing Team)

This experience had coloured her judgement on job security, as had several organisation restructurings at UK Insurance. Appearing to be a well-liked figure among the more junior members of her marketing team, she spoke at length about the importance of treating her team well, focusing on them as individuals and giving constructive feedback. The background threat of restructuring and the prospect of having her team taken from her, just as it was at her previous employer, were major concerns:

Job security is a really big issue with me. My husband and I have quite big conversations of 'what ifs', and every time things get a little bit shaky here we do have the conversations of 'what if I were made redundant, what would we do?' I don't take it for granted at all, I think having gone through [redundancy at her previous employer] and having been through several restructures here where, and particularly last year when I was up against somebody and it could have gone either way, I was absolutely convinced it was going to go against me. It didn't as it happened, but I think any manager who is complacent is a fool, because we're the easiest level to chop and this would make big savings for the company in one fell swoop. And while I think it's a mistake, I mean, several of my team have said to me on occasions: 'We couldn't manage without you, you're what holds us together.' I like managing a team, I do the job well, but, you know, I manage a team, I motivate them and bring them together and advise them, counsel them, mentor them with their studying. You know and they say that it's me holding them together, so if the company just decided well we're going to take out that tier 'cos it will save us a lot of money I think they'd lose more people not having that kind of skill and that kind of mentoring role. But we can't take anything for granted and I do have one eye on if I was out of work next month what would I do? (Manager, Strategic Partner Marketing Team)

She expanded on the nature of the recent restructuring exercises at UKInsurance, and notably on the most recent, which 'wasn't handled very well':

There's been a lot of change at [UKInsurance]. I think it's more settled now than it's been for quite a long time. I hope they don't go headlong into another restructure in marketing, because things are just starting to kind of bed down a bit. And I think sometimes certainly in [UKInsurance] over the last sort of four years there's almost been a bit of a joke that, oh well, it's been twelve months since the last restructure, there's bound to be another one, and there was. And I think sometimes you need a bit of time to bed things in, you need a bit of time for people to have a little bit of a comfort zone, otherwise people are on edge all the time and you're always wondering when the next bombshell's going to be. And I think the last restructure fifteen months ago wasn't handled very well and I think the managers at the top would acknowledge the fact it wasn't done very well and it wasn't communicated very well. And I think the impact on morale was appalling, we had lots of redundancies, there were a lot of people left in the aftermath of it, an awful lot of people were feeling very unsettled and I don't know where I go from here and I'm going to move on. So we've seen a lot of change and I think now is the time to leave it alone, let it settle, and you know there's a sort of look just let me get two years settled down to get people embedded in a role before you then start thinking about changing it again. It's almost like in the marketing department, it's historical that you have to have a restructure every year otherwise you're not a real marketing department. (Manager, Strategic Partner Marketing Team)

This manager then offered insights into the human impact of both redundancy and the threat of redundancy:

You almost felt like there's someone eyeing my job. Am I going to get, am I going to be back in a selection process and having to fight for my own job? And that uncertainty was appalling, I think people would have rather known from day one you're in a job or you're not, that's it, you know. And it was worse than at [previous employer], at least we were all in the same boat and we knew we wouldn't have a job, that was it, end of story you know. Once I got over the shock I knew exactly where I was and exactly what I had to do, you know, whereas this it was 'am I going to have a job, is it going to be a job I like, is it, you know, where do I go?' you know? [...] And it was just before Christmas, which was terrible, and then there were some people that were even worse off than me and my team, and their announcement got delayed by another week. So I think they needed to learn a lot of lessons, I think they acknowledged the fact that they didn't do it very well. But that kind of change, that kind of uncertainty really can be very destructive for people. (Manager, Strategic Partner Marketing Team)

Another manager discussed how organisational restructuring had led to longer working hours:

Yeah, I'm one of the ones that do silly hours, I'd probably be doing, I don't know, I work at home in the evenings, yeah, I'll probably be doing fifty hours a week.

Q *Does that sometimes cause stress for you?*

It is at home, yes, there is a conflict, yes, yes big time yes, yes. But the way I balance that is, you know, I always make sure that I take holidays 'cos I've got two daughters. And so it's, yeah, I don't mind working very long hours but as long as you know my holidays are sacrosanct and they're the times that we spend time with the family. (Manager, HR Consultancy)

Other managers worked similarly long hours:

I'd be surprised if I did much less than about ten, twelve hours a day, and I don't see that as being unusual within [UKInsurance], but I'd say the UK is like that, you know. (Corporate Projects Manager)

I'm in the office at seven thirty most mornings and I will leave here about six o'clock, we will probably take about thirty minutes for lunch, so and on top of that I would say I will probably do three hours over the weekend. (Head of Business Change)

All of the middle managers we interviewed at UKInsurance reported considerable and increasing work intensification:

I think the challenges of being a manager are about delivering more with less budgets, less people, but motivating people at the same time. The pressure is more intense than I've ever known it, because there's pressure on reduced cost, 'do more, deliver more', there's perpetual discussions where I'm saying 'right, well, we need to prioritise'. I mean I'm quite lucky that I've got a good relationship with my 'head of' and with the director, but if there's something that I'm really not happy with I can challenge it. But there is no doubt that the work pressures are considerable, I mean I'm very often working in the evenings, and I do try not to but you know there are things. If I've promised one of my team that I'll check something over for them, if I don't have time in the day, I'll do it in the evening. And I think, well, really I shouldn't be doing that because you know my job is my job, my family is my family, but the work-life balance is hard, and you do get, again, you do get squashed from both directions. (Manager, Strategic Partner Marketing Team)

A long-serving manager observed how the pace rarely lets up; that work matters rarely seem to settle into a manageable routine:

I think the pace of change and the amount of work that's coming through is just growing. Originally it used to be sort of spikes of effort, and then you'd see things settle out and drop back, and you'd have almost a sort of a stable period before you had another spark, a bit like a sort of heartbeat pattern. I think now you're not seeing the drop back after many of these activities, it's just the next thing comes along that sets it a bit higher again, sets it a bit higher again. So I think the demand on middle management is getting much, much stronger. (Network Services Manager)

An older middle manager agreed that job security was a major issue for many staff (although fortunately not for himself):

Well, I'm in the lucky position now that I don't care, what I mean by that is that I've been with the organisation a long time, I'm now of an age where if I was made redundant it would not be a disaster from a financial perspective. And I think I'd be willing to add that I really don't worry about job security any more, you know I'm happy doing this job, I enjoy what I do, but if it wasn't around it wouldn't be the end of the world. So I'm not sure that my personal take is relevant 'cos there aren't that many people of my age now with [UKInsurance]. I think there are some people in the organisation who have got some very real fears about their job security. (Corporate Projects Manager)

While de-layering and downsizing had not been as extensive as in other organisations, cost reductions meant that vacant positions were often not filled. Promotions were difficult to come by, causing motivational problems. Fair treatment issues were also starting to come to the fore:

At the moment it's all one way, and it is building up to pressure time I think, and certainly the feedback from the staff survey is about pay and about recognition. And they'll measure how we've done against them, and we get to the end of the year and they're measured on their performance. And I seem to be having the conversation more and more with [my team] that I want them to be doing something that's about personal development, that is something that they can feel that they can add to their CV, this is a skill I've developed or a qualification I've added that I can feel like I've grown as a person and as a marketer at the end of that twelve-month period. But that's the thing that goes, that's the thing that gets sacrificed to deliver objectives, because it's delivering the objectives that then determine the bonus, not delivering against your personal development. So you get to the end of the year and you've delivered against your personal, you know, your own objectives business wise, but at the cost of actually developing yourself as a professional. And I think that's where we're going to run into problems, because people will do that for two or three years, but then they will feel actually they're not growing as individuals any more. And that they may need to be fulfilled by moving outside the organisation. There's somebody at a very senior level one grade down from me who's just handed in his notice because of that very reason. 'Cos he's reached a point of 'where do I go from here', and I think we're not as an organisation putting enough emphasis on people progressing and developing. I don't think it all comes down to pay, I think people realise that there isn't a limitless pot, that we are a PLC, that we do have stakeholders, that we do have shareholders and we have to maintain that cost, and we have to be realistic. I think people do understand that, but I think it's about the position and about recognising the right people, and you've only got to have discrepancy of somebody talking about the fact that someone's got this added bonus and actually they've not delivered very much. And then it's the dissatisfaction starts to spread and people think 'well, that's not fair', you know, I think that's probably the most destructive thing, it's not a fair thing that I'm working my guts out and I'm doing all this. (Manager, Strategic Partner Marketing Team)

She went on to describe how much top management depends on continual spending of middle managers' time, effort and goodwill. She noted how, ultimately, middle managers will give up in an unfair environment in which they are not valued. This amounts to a reversal of the 'Hochschild syndrome'; employees once again start to escape work by retreating back into family life:

I think there's a tendency in the company at the moment that they are cashing in on a lot of goodwill, and I think that's going to run out at some point. At the moment they're calling in a lot of goodwill of people who are prepared to put that extra in, they're prepared to put the hours in, they're prepared to put the devotion in because they want the company to succeed. But they will hit a point where you think 'I'm not doing this any more', you know, where something will give, whether it's your time with your family or other choices. (Manager, Strategic Partner Marketing Team)

In a similar fashion to Graham's work (2005) on Japanese insurance workers, employees at UKInsurance engaged in personal strategising in their attempts to survive and prosper. These focus around how much more effort a person is prepared to keep giving, when to resist and refuse work overload, how to prioritise the various kinds of work, and how to manage family commitments. Given the persistence of traditional gender roles, women managers tend to sacrifice more of their work life for family commitments. In this case, a female manager is in the 'lucky' position of having a retired husband who can take the pressure off; the implication being that this is an unusual arrangement (see Hochschild 2003):

It is extremely hard, I mean I'm probably luckier than most that when I got the first promotion to direct proposition manager in [UKInsurance] my husband was given the opportunity to take early retirement. And we actually made a sort of definitive decision to say this job is going to be a lot more demanding, let's take some of the pressure off you by him not working, which meant that he can take our daughter to the school and pick her up. And it sort of takes that bit of pressure off in the day time, so I don't have that issue of if my daughter's at home sick that I've got to be at home, you know? And so I'm probably luckier than most in that respect, but it does, it does intrude on family life, and you have to be juggling and it's very difficult. And it tends to be that I'll end up working late when she's in bed rather than intruding on the time with her, which is a juggling act. (Manager, Strategic Partner Marketing Team)

Another middle manager noted the impact of IT on work life:

So email now, you can't get away from it, and you know always being in contact is not necessarily a good thing from a work-life balance perspective. So personal impact has been huge, the impact on the business has been incredible in terms of the volumes that we deal with, you know, processing over the Internet now, customer enquiry over the Internet, customers changing their addresses and making fund switches in their own home. You know, I dread to think where it's going to go in the next ten, fifteen, twenty years. (Corporate Projects Manager)

Given that UKInsurance, in common with many other corporations we researched, had a long-hours culture, some middle managers were not motivated to career advancement:

Until this role was created I was pretty much thinking 'well, where am I going to go next' really. And I was also thinking, you know, 'my boss works even longer hours than I work, do I really want his job?' But yeah I mean I think I've been fortunate since I've been at [UKInsurance] because I've been promoted a number of times and I've done a lot of different jobs over that whole period; I think I've done a different job every eighteen months to two years. (Manager, Business Services)

Although many managers complained about the long and hard nature of their work, there was also a sense of pride and enjoyment. For many highly trained workers in the insurance industry, long hours on the road were common (as was homeworking). One manager explained how the pressure was very intense, and that staff were basically left alone to 'sink or swim'. He had also given up on the next promotion up the scale, but noted that this didn't matter so much as long as the work remained financially, and personally, rewarding:

There's 500 or 600 of us on the road. There's a huge amount of responsibility. As regional sales agents we're managing the business back into the organisation. Responsibility for managing IT, compliance, new business, regulation, this all falls onto the regionals. This has added about 50 per cent to my workload. We had a report round last week about email usage. Regional managers receive over a hundred emails a day on average! My PA is full-time screening emails. Regional managers work about three times what the average person does, and twice as much as the next person below me. As an organisation, the problem we have is that we operate on tighter and tighter margins. There are lot of people out there looking at the top ten companies in the sector, looking for an Achilles' heel. If we show an Achilles' heel we are potentially a target. A potential issue was cost control – everyone has become very stretched. We are new to market, and people say when you're new to market 'will they survive?' You're always treated as the next target. But you're only a target if you've got a weakness.

Q   *A target for takeover, you mean?*

Oh yes. […] Any company needs to demonstrate to the City or its shareholders that it knows what it's doing. The last thing you want to do is put your money somewhere where the company doesn't know what it's doing. […] I'm paid on results, so if I don't get my results I miss out. My director doesn't give a stuff about my hours. All he cares about is am I bringing more business, more profitable business, that's relatively risk-free? I really couldn't guess how many hours a week I work. I'm away from home two or three nights a week. I must work at least fifty to sixty hours. My basic [salary] is seventy grand, but with bonuses I can get more. I made over a hundred grand last year. I do feel responsibilities, there's a number of degrees in the mix. I do feel I've got the ability to influence and that's key. If you feel you've got no influence, then it's time to give it up and go home. They have to trust us to carve out a business, to raise the opportunity for us to create business. The darkest moments are when you feel that some management things have to go through committees, this is the most frustrating and difficult thing. Any large company can be slow to change and slow to react. But then I get absolute support from my director. To some degree the hours and workloads are self-inflicting. The work is exciting and you want to be getting on with it. [UKInsurance] is a good employer. It's very open, very honest, a fair and good employer. They have loyal staff, and the firm is loyal in return. […] In my father's day you'd work for a bank and you'd stay there all your life. I can't conceive now of any job for life. I personally wouldn't want a job for life. Where I've seen it change in the last seven or eight years is that the job title is set in stone, but the responsibilities and package has changed quite a bit. The trick is not promotion to job title, it's 'what am I doing?' It's a business that's growing and expanding. In effect, you're making your own business and make your own promotion. The loss of jobs for life has forced people to become more entrepreneurial. But I've had the support of a big company behind me. If it all went tits up for [UKInsurance] I think I'd get out, set up on my own. Maybe I'm different. Once I've been in a job for two to three years and everything's running swimmingly that gets dull. I'd rather have it that all the cards are up in the air! Others are quite different, they want stability, the status quo.

Q   *How do you see things working out for you in the next five to ten years?* I've no desire to look at the next move upwards, which is probably director level. It's more likely that I'd have to go to another organisation. I've been at [UKInsurance] twelve years. I know how it thinks. How to get things done. I've never really planned my career, I've not been thinking how to move, or 'who's next to retire?' It doesn't work that way for me. The way I see it is we've got a big task on with the last restructuring. We've lost the 'head of' positions, and the director, who, not being rude, but he hasn't got time to say, 'What's going on, lads? What are you up to?' We've gotta develop the business. We've been able to do that without interference, which has been great for us. Where that leads I don't know, but I hope to still be here at [UKInsurance]. Whether I'm still a regional manager, I don't know, whether I'm called 'manager', 'head of', I'm not so bothered by that. (Regional Manager, UK Distribution)

To summarise, the UKInsurance case had gone though considerable change. In a similar fashion to UKUtilities, it closely reflected the wider transformation taking place in the UK economy, away from the stability, predictability and public-sector ethos of nationalised providers (in the case of UKUtilities) or the traditionalism and paternalism of a mutual, policyholder-owned insurer (in the case of UKInsurance). The two cases provide vivid evidence of how financialisation and increased competition impact on workplaces. Although the work in many cases had become more interesting and engaging, employment security has been sacrificed, upwards mobility had stalled and heavier demands were made on the effort and quality of work. Managers frequently felt isolated, lacking the 'face time' with seniors that they used to have access to. Crucially, time-scales were radically reduced, placing severe pressure on many employees. A wide variety of complaints was raised at UKInsurance, although it appeared to be a relatively open and enlightened employer. As we shall see below, employees elsewhere in the UK financial services industry were less fortunate.

UKBank: 'There is life beyond it, but you don't think that at the time'

To end this chapter we include excerpts from an interview with a former manager of what we call UKBank, a major player in British high-street banking. We chose to include this interview, even though it fell outside of our established case profiles, precisely because it was one of the few interviews we conducted with a manager who had left a large corporation. This former bank manager now works for a UK City Council, where he is a middle manager. The focus of our interview, however, was exclusively on his experiences as a branch manager at UKBank. As the interview unfolded, the level of indignity this former bank manager was forced to endure made his a compelling story of the human costs of organisational restructuring. It is one that probably resonates strongly with managers who have received similar treatment in other corporations undergoing 'radical' change. It perhaps represents a cautionary tale; i.e. for senior managers to consider the damage their performance-enhancing strategies and policies can cause. The narrative explains how the corporation's incessant demand for higher profits causes work intensification which in turn can lead to personal difficulties for employees. In the process, the narrative serves to unmask the emptiness of many corporate 'values' and the ruthlessness of performance management regimes. Although the information provided by this former bank manager is largely retrospective and the viewpoint expressed clearly influenced by hindsight, our informant nevertheless produced an exceptionally clear and compelling story of restructuring.

UKBank is a household name in UK and international banking. Its operations cover most of the financial services spectrum: from savings and investments, through corporate banking, to high-end, client-based services for 'high net worth individuals'. The firm had been through numerous change programes in the 1990s, with the most severe taking place in 1996–7, involving widespread branch closure and redundancies. Fundamental to this restructuring was a shift from servicing its existing customers in a traditional fashion, towards chasing ever more clients and selling ever more products. Branches became high-street retail outlets. New IT systems had facilitated enormous centralisation, involving root and branch rationalisation of employment and work systems. All managers were given aggressive sales targets to hit which caused increased stress for front-line retail staff and branch managers.

The branch manager we interviewed was hugely critical of the new regime.

He began by describing the nature of the firm he first joined. Since leaving school he found work in:

[A] small retail branch and there were in the region of about twenty to twenty-five staff at the time. There was a very senior manager there and below him an office manager and then myself so that is where I fitted into the structure. Over the next four to five years the branch became subsumed within the [wider geographical area] group of branches, both managers were taken out and I was left running the branch. So that really was where the costs started to bite and the axe fell, really.

Q   *So managers were just let go?*

Yes, just let go, and a lot of the work and responsibility was centralised and it left a relatively junior manager then responsible for the branch and security in a market town. It was viewed at the time as an excellent career opportunity for me and development, but where do you go after that? That was the next question.

A new performance management system was introduced, along with a major culture change programme. These were described by our ex-UKBank manager as unimaginative and heavy handed, and they clearly represented a major attempt to rationalise and intensify the labour process of all staff, including bank branch managers. He went on to describe the increasingly tough sales demands being made on his staff, and a managerial climate where concerns could not be raised or discussed:

Previously we had a system of appraisals. Then performance management was introduced and changed all this and we then became very much more results, targets, objectives focused. I think that change was one of the reasons for me reconsidering my position and looking elsewhere. [...] It then became very heavily target driven. And the targets from the Performance Management, when it was sold to staff, it was very much, 'They are your personal targets for you to agree with your manager, something that you are able to commit to and achieve.' The reality over the three years [was that] it changed very much to something heavily sales orientated. Well, the bank was in business to make a profit so you would accept that. However, you would be set a target at the beginning of the year within your region of branches.

At this point he produced a box file containing a series of documents. These documents contained masses of detailed numbers broken down by department, branch and task, showing where different parts of the business had met or exceeded expectations. There were many other similar documents, taking performance management measures down to a personal level. What was remarkable about these documents was how consistently high the numbers were. On a monthly basis practically all of the branches in the geographical region were hitting between 96 and 107 per cent of their customer service index targets. Yet this performance was never enough. At a personal level, the comments made about this manager in his performance review were highly positive, yet none of the boxes marked 'Excellent' had been ticked by his reviewer. The final verdict was a 'B' – 'Consistently high level of performance'. He was clearly a hard working and respected manager. Comments read, 'The branch runs as a "well-oiled", well-organised team, rising to meet challenges and opportunities. [Name] is an experienced team leader and a high level of teamwork and cooperation is very evident in [branch].' But in reality UKBank top management could never be satisfied, as the targets kept increasing. Pointing to one of these sheets, the former bank manager continued:

So this is the target that you were set to achieve ... the target you were set was 94.7 per cent. Now this is customer service index for the counter, so this was based on mystery shopping and customer responses to questionnaires and that was all factored in and number-crunched centrally, which then produced your actual percentages. So you can see there the branch was meeting 98.9 per cent. So if you met 100 per cent then you were obviously personally speaking doing very well. However, with these things, if everybody, or if the majority of branches had hit their target and some were, say, performing at 102 per cent, if they were exceeding their target, your target then moved partway through the year. So you were then asked to at least meet the average and that became very, very frustrating because you never actually were able to say 'this is how we are doing against our target'. What you were able to say was that is what the target was at the beginning of the year and then it starts moving and the performance of all the other branches in sales or customer service then moved and the average moves, so therefore you had to chase something that you didn't know what you were chasing because it wasn't apparent where the target actually was.

Unsurprisingly, the costs of this target-driven sales culture on staff were severe, with the branch manager caught in the middle as he attempted to drive more and more effort from those below, while enduring heavy monitoring from those above. He very candidly described how tough this was, using some of the most emotive language we came across in the whole research project:

So the target changed, more or less it was a moving feast, it changed daily as one branch was increasing their sales in, for example, say mortgages and did exceptionally well, every other branch would then have its target changed right away to actually try and achieve the same level. So I became very very disillusioned at this point. The performance plans are still showing that performance was still good, under the old system I think the last appraisal out of six ratings gave an excellent performance rating. But when these things were factored in to the performance management it became more and more difficult to achieve targets and therefore 20 per cent of your salary became bonus related and I decided that I didn't want to have much more of that because the size of the bonus was getting more and your fixed salary was getting less. That wasn't what I had joined really. So I then sort of took a view and decided I would look around and see what else there was.

Q   *When you first started I assume there was none of this; your contract*
      back then would have been a lot more basic.

No, none at all. A forty-year contract, which, up until the time I left the bank, the bank was trying to get around the forty-year contract issue, a contract for life, but hadn't found a way through. But I think they may well have since then, I think they reached a new agreement where people's contracts have changed beyond recognition. So as far as I was concerned I had a job for life, that job security was important for me, still is, I have got a couple of children and a mortgage and what have you, so those things to me are important and I wished to maintain that. That was then gradually being eroded and I felt that really it was time to go. The performance management did cause an awful lot of problems. […] When targets were set staff were put under quite a lot of pressure to actually achieve the sales and the pressure was increased because as the targets changed as I said throughout the year the targets to the individual staff had to change. Therefore I was being asked to put them under extreme pressure to achieve the sales targets because otherwise I didn't get my bonus. You try and do it as gently as you can with people and behind this there was a coaching programme put in place so that you can daily coach your staff. There was also the issue where observation was key to that and then the sales technique and I was daily required to sit behind each member of staff in a sales role, a confidential sales role, monitoring their performance and then discussing it with them afterwards and agreeing an action plan for improvement. Which again was very uncomfortable for them and for the customer.

He offered some further anecdotes to make the point:

I was at a Novotel in Hammersmith [London] the night before last, when I was checking out yesterday morning there was somebody doing it to the member of staff on the desk. I knew exactly what she was doing and this poor guy was trying to just deal with my bill and he felt totally overshadowed by this person standing behind him and from a customer point of view it was a bit off-putting as well. One day I found a member of staff underneath a desk upstairs in a disused part of the building; because obviously you can imagine the accommodation was far greater than was needed in my reduced bank. One of the sales staff just couldn't cope and I had to coax her out from underneath the desk. She had a breakdown and ended up going out sick. [...] I didn't see her return to work. Two other staff were off on periods of long-term sick and they were sales staff under the same pressures.

As the targets were not tailored to individual branches and their different customer bases, this led to staff being forced to sell products either to uninterested customers, or to customers for whom these products were not ideally suited:

Each branch has its individual quirk. So you are having to put staff under pressure to meet targets to sell products that really aren't suitable for your market. There then came the pressure of the telephone. I don't know what you are like, whether your bank phones you, but weekly telesales was a requirement for staff that have already worked the working week to then stay behind until 9 o'clock at night to phone customers to achieve sales. Which again you come back to profitability. It can produce sales, however, if staff don't want to do it then you have to make them or you have to put pressure on other people to do it who didn't necessarily want to do it. So there was a telephone issue which again I think that was really why a couple of staff actually just blew a gasket in the end because they just could not give any more.

Q   *And they had no downtime?*

No, none at all and we weren't able to do that because the staffing numbers were run to such a low level that you barely had sufficient staff to manage it. In fact the office was a full service outlet with every member of staff at the customer interface, except for one member of staff who just happened to be the manager. And the manager was given the responsibility for ensuring the security of the contents of the waste paper bins – so I had to actually empty the waste paper bin at the end of the day, make a cup of tea if it needed making. It was the manager that made a cup of tea because there was nobody else that could be released from a customer service position to do it. So you were just trying to manage an organisation that had run itself down to the core.

This interviewee presented a depressing account in which the whole series of changes was driven by cost-cutting, technological determinism and profit-seeking. There appeared a sense of inevitability about the increasing pressures and their degrading effects on staff. Equally worrying was the lack of openness to discussion, and the way in which concerns bubbling up from middle management were ignored by seniors. Our ex-bank manager went on to describe how he was forced to look for work elsewhere secretly, because of the threat of being sidelined:

It is interesting there was a monthly breakfast meeting, which was the area managers' meeting, but obviously you weren't encouraged to be negative in those meetings. It may sound as though I am being very bitter and twisted but I am not, I had a great time working for the bank at the beginning, actually. I thoroughly enjoyed the time I had there, I made some good contacts with people and friends and colleagues and the organisation developed me to enable me to go into a position that I am really comfortable in, so I have a lot to thank it for from that point of view. But when you are working there you think you can only do this job because you have been trained the [UKBank] way and therefore you are no good to anybody else. That was quite interesting actually, having been released from that. Turning back to the issue of being able to express yourself, well, you couldn't really. If you had concerns you could raise them, if you had something a bit stronger than that it would need to be on a one-to-one basis with your manager. But another issue was the two managers, they had a 'good cop, bad cop' regime. It was very uncomfortable for a lot of managers because these managers had their [own] targets to meet and reported directly to the national sales manager. And so it was: 'That's the job, get on and do it, if you don't like it we can put somebody else in your position.' That was actually said to me. I reconsidered my position when I was standing outside the office in the morning waiting to get in. And my stomach would turn over and I would really think, 'I should be doing something else, there has got to be something better than this', and that is why I decided to leave.

Q   *So basically you had pressures from above and pressures from below?*
We did, yes, because you could only get the staff to do a certain amount and you were managing that dissatisfaction while trying to maintain a very high customer service index. So everybody has got to be smiles for the customers. You were in a no-win situation really and there was no clear route for progression. [...] At one stage when I first took over it was [manageable] but then the targets were increased to something beyond what could be managed. You do burn out very quickly, I was thirty-five when I left and I felt that by the time I was forty, allowing for them wanting me there, I would have been too bitter and twisted and I had wanted to leave before then.

The interview with this ex-manager then focused more directly on one of the major organisational change programmes devised by the bank:

Q   *In the literature about organisational change one of the things that is
     emphasised a great deal is trying to keep people informed about change,
     keeping those further down informed, those who are going to be
     impacted on. When this came in obviously you felt unhappy about its
     subsequent effects on the organisation. How well communicated was it
     to you, the need to introduce it and what it was all about?*
I think pretty well actually, I have to say that. This was badged under 'The
Power of One' and every manager came together at a conference and there
was an enormous conference where the chief executive launched 'The Power
of One', which was the branch change programme, a huge fanfare. Through
workshops and through the training that followed, yes, you were kept very
well informed.

This manager had kept hold of his copy of the 'The Power of One'
performance management manual. Its cover depicts what we assume is
meant to be staff (and possibly customers) skipping around in a circle,
childishly holding hands. Sitting alongside the strict, top-down imperatives and prescriptions around the new performance management system were several passages about dignity and fair treatment, such as '1:
We approach every aspect of our work with the highest standards of
integrity' or '4: We treat each other as we wish to be treated ourselves.'
(UKBank 'The Power of One' documentation, page 4.) He went on to
describe the emptiness of this rhetoric:

There was a lot of difficulties with staff and staff leaving and redundancies,
but I wasn't affected by that directly because I was in one of the modern jobs.
If you weren't in one of the modern jobs, one of the sales jobs, it was quite
ruthless, previous colleagues of mine were axed quite viciously. You just
checked to make sure you were in one of the modern jobs, because if you
weren't you then would try to position yourself so that you were. I was
fortunate in that I had adapted throughout the process and those staff that
hadn't adapted or had gone into centralised units that were then subsequently chopped on a regional basis and centralised even further, the only
option was for them to go. So yes, there is life beyond it, but you don't think
that at the time.
Q   *It seems that the strategy of the bank would have been quite similar to
     those undergoing similar transformations elsewhere in terms of
     centralisation. I assume one of the reasons or motivations behind that
     would have been the introduction of more advanced IT?*
Yes, IT was a major impact, it enabled lending decisions to be delivered on a
customer credit scoring basis. So in actual fact when I joined the bank, when I

first went to [town] as a lending officer with a lending discretion of in those days £5,000 per personal customer, that was withdrawn and replaced by the decision being made centrally through the computer system, and we then had to deliver the decision that was made. [...] You couldn't interpret it because you don't know the details of the credit score but yes you were just delivering decisions.

You have been accepted or you haven't. Then obviously for customers that weren't accepted for a loan or whatever, an overdraft increase, you then had to manage that situation and try and ease that problem. But of course that doesn't go on your sales targets, so you are driven to not be spending too long with these people. Because if there is a major problem, it's off to the Citizen's Advice Bureau for them, whereas previously you would support a customer, build a relationship and get them through a financial difficulty. Whereas currently now it is just 'you can apply across the Internet can't you?' [...] The support mechanism wasn't there at all, it was profit, profit, profit and if you are not happy with this you are out. I know people that it has happened to in the same area. They are on their fourth or fifth manager since I had left. So I think my feelings and my opinion at the time have been proved right.

The interview then moved on to discuss issues of cultural change in the banking industry more widely:

Q   *Can I take you back a bit further in time. [...] The banking industry and working in a banking sector would, at the time you joined, would have been seen as certainly a prestigious, good job.*
Absolutely, yes.
Q   *Certainly one with good prospects and obvious stepwise progression.*
That was one of the major factors in me joining it, yes.
Q   *How would you then characterise what has happened to that image? Has it gone away completely?*
Yes, I think it has. 'The Power of One' introduced performance management and the salaries were then pegged within the industry. I suppose it is difficult to say within the industry, but it was then pegged at a level for a branch manager, for a sales assistant and we were compared among a lot of other organisations. But one of the factors was the managers of branches salary as being compared with the same type as a supermarket manager in Tesco's. So you were purely into retail, the professional side of banking disappeared and it was purely a retail outlet.
Q   *So the whole culture of the thing changed.*
It did, it was purely a sales outlet and customers are sales fodder. That sounds derogatory on the staff who generally are very, very nice people but it was just 'what can I get out of this person sitting in front of me?' [That is] as a manager monitoring what that person is doing, what have they missed, what sales

opportunities were missed? It is not necessarily what is the need of that customer that is being missed, it was 'what else could have been sold?' That is the way the bank chooses to drive its profitability, [...] you either say, 'yes, I am going to go with that' or you get out, and I decided to get out.

Q *Why do companies suddenly start changing their whole ethos towards retail?*

It is bottom-line profit, that is purely what it comes down to – the share price and bottom-line profit. That was the story we were given and it is believable, totally believable, everything became cost-focused. Training budgets went and travelling budgets, overtime budgets, it was all cut. So it was purely profit-focused.

Q *And this was made fairly explicit to staff, was it?*

Perfectly clear.

Q *If changes aren't made then the future of the company is going to be in doubt, that sort of thing?*

Yes, that's right. [...] Because of the sickness issue and lack of staff morale in the place, because of the pressure I ended up being shadowed by my manager for two days, constantly. He just actually watched what I did, when I did it, how I dealt with various issues across the branch and then tore me apart basically. From that point I thought, 'I don't want to be a part of this organisation any more.'

Towards the end of the interview our former UKBank Branch Manager presented to us the reply to his letter of resignation:

I wrote to the bank actually, I didn't write to Personnel, I wrote to the head sales manager and I said, 'If this is the way you are treating people, that is exactly the reason why I am leaving.' He wrote back, accepted the comment, and said, 'It will change.' I felt a bit sad about that, but there you go.

Amid the performance reviews and performance management documents, our former UKBank manager had also kept hold of some more personal letters from others in the organisation. One sympathetic employee had written to him on hearing of his decision to leave. It read: 'Congratulations for having the courage to do what many of us would like to do.'

Interestingly, his decision to resign was not all about departing a bullying environment, for at the city council both the tangible and intangible rewards would be greater:

So job security is good, I am working for a local authority, the pension is second to none, better than the bank's. So those things that are important to me I have improved on but the job satisfaction overall is the most fantastic thing. I have never worked so hard, a fifty-hour week is common, but I don't mind doing it.

Ultimately this manager found career satisfaction by simply changing careers, a not uncommon strategy for escaping bullying climates (see Rayner *et al.* 2001). The case reported here is by no means an unusual one of when senior management push too hard with little regard for the well-being of their staff. The intensification of managerial labour in the name of increased efficiency and performance can have far-reaching effects, as employees (and customers) become drawn increasingly into the maelstrom of higher returns and greater profits.

Conclusions

In this chapter we have given a lot of space for the UK managers interviewed to describe their working lives and the organisational changes they have experienced. Such is the consistency of the picture that there is little reason to offer a lengthy summary of what we have found. Many of the managers were able not only to describe in detail the new corporate environment, but to offer convincing explanations of the reasons why it has come into being. Overwhelmingly, this included reference to drives for profitability and higher performance in an increasingly competitive situation when firms are pushing equally hard. Organisations and their staff were struggling to keep up amidst the ever-increasing pressure for better results. This explanation is in keeping with the neo-Bravermanian critique of contemporary capitalism that forms the theoretical crux of this book. However, there is a danger of oversimplification and fatalism in this picture, and we have barely touched on the topic of resistance to this new system (see Chapter 6). Many of the middle managers interviewed described their own systems of 'personal strategising' in order to cope with the heavy demands of work and family (see Hochschild 2003). But the new systems introduced were generally described as 'inevitable' developments, in a tougher climate which was understood simply as 'the new way of the world'. Rarely if ever did our middle managers describe the possibility, or even the desirability, of a response that might rebalance the system in their favour. As we shall see in the next chapter, a similar degree of resigned compliance was visible in our Japanese case studies.

5 | New world of the salaryman: Management restructuring in Japan

The ultimate question is [...] whether corporations can please capital markets and simultaneously maintain their characteristic commitments to employees.

(Jackson, 2002: 123)

Amid the claims and counterclaims surrounding the subject of large firm restructuring, Japan is a particularly interesting case. Japanese firms are renowned across the world for the high levels of quality and competitiveness of their products. The country has received great praise as a developmental model for other societies to follow given its enormously impressive recovery post-1945. During the high-growth phase from the 1950s to around 1990, Japan and its flagship firms such as Toyota and Sony were highly regarded, with Japan famously predicted to overtake the USA itself as the world's largest economy (Vogel 1980). Concepts such as 'Japan Inc', 'coordinated capitalism', 'stakeholder' capitalism, along with lean manufacturing, total quality management and *kaizen* rose to prominence in the West. Many of these ideas were, to a greater or lesser extent, emulated by Anglo-Saxon firms attempting to improve their own competitiveness in response (Best 2001; Milkman 1997; Starkey and McKinlay 1994), and they were widely imported into foreign environments in Japanese overseas transplants (Adler 1992; Danford 1998; Delbridge 1998; Kenney and Florida 1993; Morris *et al.* 1993). Analysts frequently claimed that the Japanese variety of capitalism was superior in many ways to the liberal and high-risk American and British versions (Abegglen 1958; Dore 1987; Hutton 1995). This view stemmed from the argument that 'patient capital' and the long-term, trust-based relationships between firms and their suppliers, overseen by some degree of state coordination, was able to deliver high-quality and competitive goods and services, whereas the necessity to deliver short-term returns to the stock market prevented Western firms from adopting a long-term and strategic view. In the

1980s and early 1990s highly respected and influential Western analysts subscribed to this view, as the moribund US economy lagged behind the pace set by Japan (and the other main 'coordinated' economy of Germany). Porter, for example (1990: 731), argued that what was needed in the USA was:

[A] new approach to corporate governance in which the long-term prosperity of the company is made a central concern. Relaxation of the limits on bank ownership of equity shares, for example, represents one potential way to promote a more constructive role by capital providers who could develop deeper long-term relationships with companies.

Such long-termism in Japan both supported and was supported by 'employee-favouring' personnel policies (Dore 2000) in that staff served under systems of implicit lifetime employment and explicit seniority-based pay and promotion. Moreover, traditional views in Japan about the nature of the firm's socio-economic purpose differ substantially from those in Anglo-Saxon economies. Rather than the firm as a tool for delivering shareholder value, the Japanese firm's purpose has to focus on a much wider group of stakeholders, notably its core employees. In much of the literature, Japanese employers are described as much more effectively attuned to the needs of employees than US firms, especially in the way they typically focus on high wages and job security. For example, once a staff member makes it to *kachō* (department chief), he is suddenly a big stakeholder in the firm. Conversely, if a Japanese company resorts to layoffs, not only are its staff hurt more dramatically than they might be in less stable Anglo-Saxon contexts, but the firm's public profile also suffers more than it might in a Western setting. It loses its public standing – all of a sudden a large company is not 'treating people as it should'.[1]

It is not just the organisational forms and long-term perspectives that were lauded. Perhaps more notably, Japanese management systems and lean production methods have received (and continue to receive today) significant praise as flexible, high-trust, high-performance systems that promote strong worker commitment, industrial relations harmony and quality goods and services (Jaikumar 1986; Liker and Morgan 2006; Womack *et al.* 1990, 2007). On the other hand, this optimistic picture

---

[1] We would like to thank Dr Peter Matanle of the Department of East Asian Studies, University of Sheffield, for making this point to us.

of a production system that produces large benefits for both management and labour has for some time been challenged as unrealistic (Kamata 1973; Morris *et al.* 1993; Williams *et al.* 1994; L. Graham 1995; Danford 1998; Delbridge 1998; F. Graham 2003, 2005; Mehri 2005, 2006). From a critical perspective, working life in Japan is simply a more efficient, but no less authoritarian, form of Taylorism. Moreover Japanese workers have even fewer possibilities to challenge management's prerogative. Japanese 'high-commitment' or 'Toyotaist' methods have always masked bullying and management by fear cultures – cultures that are at least as authoritarian as those traditionally found at, for example, Ford and GM (as documented, for example, by Beynon 1986; Starkey and McKinlay 1992). The authoritarian streak in Japanese companies is well expressed in the popular phrase 'the nail that sticks up will be hammered down'.

A large number of critical accounts have expressed reservations about the highly controlling and exploitative nature of Japanese workplaces. Writers such as Morris *et al.* (1993), Graham (1995), Danford (1998), Delbridge (1998) and Milkman (1997) have demonstrated from the beginning that Japanese transplants in the UK and the USA do not reflect the high-road, high-quality vision associated with domestic Japanese production. Ethnographic analyses from Kamata (1973) to Mehri (2005, 2006) have also been damning in uncovering similarly problematic working environments in Japan itself. Rather than describing a world of employee involvement, high skills and innovation – i.e. the received philosophy of a world-class company such as Toyota – Mehri (2005, 2006) found the managers at Nizumi (a Toyota group subsidiary) to be extremely disciplinarian. Company safety policy, for example, was a 'smokescreen' which forced the responsibility for safety onto the individual worker's shoulders. White-collar engineers and managers were enmeshed in a culture of intimidation, overwork and secrecy, whereas blue-collar workers became involved in industrial accidents as they struggled with unmanageably high line speeds.[2] Software and mechanical engineers, rather than 'innovating' in a genuine and honest fashion, frequently copied the designs of competitors (and also co-workers). Managers shunned individuals who did not belong to their

---

[2] Mehri's interpretation may appear extreme, but reports of deaths from overwork are far from uncommon in the media. See, for example, 'Court rules Toyota employee worked to death', Reuters UK Online, 30 November 2007.

in-group of favourites, regularly ignoring what little creativity or initiative that did happen to bubble up. Although Mehri was impressed by the sharp focus on product quality and market share, rather than on short-term share price fluctuations or meretricious marketing, he lamented the degree to which individuality was stifled and creativity stunted – making precisely the same kinds of criticism that were frequently made of traditional US workplaces. Mehri (2005: 10) is equally unstinting in his criticism of how Japanese 'familial ideology', rather than a benign cultural aspect of corporate welfarism, is actually:

[U]sed to bind workers to the culture of rules. [...] [T]he reason the Japanese are diligent and disciplined workers is not because they feel an obligation toward a company that provides them with many benefits, but because they are working within rules that tightly control every aspect of behaviour. Workers acquiesce to the demands of management simply because they have no choice.

Mehri's view of Japan's vaunted production systems has much in common with the realities of Japanese white-collar life. There is a major dichotomy in the literature on Japan between the widely held view of strong blue-collar autonomy and trust at shop-floor level, and the rigid hierarchies with few dissenting voices at white-collar level. Overbearing paternalism is still very much an abiding characteristic of Japanese workplaces. Contrary to so much of the literature that claims lean manufacturing and associated concepts provide the opportunity for genuine worker involvement (Liker and Morgan 2006), Japanese workplaces are in fact highly authoritarian at all levels. Seniors tend to brook little or no opposition from juniors. The need to demonstrate humility and respect for authority is drilled into new recruits (Graham 2003) and the open expression of alternative viewpoints is strongly discouraged (Mehri 2005, 2006). Opportunities for self-directed careers are very limited, with the Personnel division taking the important decisions regarding employee development and the assignment of staff to areas within the firm (Graham 2003; Jacoby 2005). Women are still expected to leave the firm upon marriage and hence are rarely treated as genuine core employees (Mehri 2005; Ogasawara 1998). Senior management remains dominated by a 'boys' club' of male company 'lifers'. This literature suggests that it is extremely important to insert a degree of perspective into discussions of the Japanese 'miracle', in that Japanese firms have always been authoritarian, strict and extremely demanding.

Some sections of the literature have attributed Japan's 'culture' as a major part of its economic success. Respect for authority, strong loyalty and unquestioned commitment probably did play a part in Japan's postwar growth, particularly if the patriotic national mission of rebuilding is considered. On the other hand, national culture is an elastic concept and is often used in an essentialist manner that offers little genuine insight. It is difficult to see where culture ends and where administrative heritage begins. In other words, national culture goes hand-in-hand with organisational traditions, many of which we have seen in other times and places. Moreover, times change, and younger generations of Japanese are often described as less willing to toe the traditional authoritarian line (Dore 2000: 57–59; Hatano 1995/2005). According to Hatano the values of the younger generation of workers are moving away from the self-sacrifice associated with post-war national recovery towards more personal quests for self-realisation, including the need for more meaningful and rewarding careers, rather than personal capture within an authoritarian firm, the Personnel division of which has the power to determine a person's future (Graham 2003; Jacoby 2005).

Moreover, Japan's differences from the West in terms of workplace culture are frequently exaggerated. It wasn't so long ago that US and UK firms resembled Japanese in terms of the absence of open speaking, entrenched sexism and ritual respect for those in authority positions, not to mention the more defensible concepts of long-term employment, seniority-based pay and internal career ladders. If the reference to 'first-name informality' was deleted, a passage from Jackall's *Moral Mazes*, which describes the USA in the 1980s, reads much like the caricatured Japanese firm still rooted in a stifling pecking order and obsessed with 'not losing face'. Jackall (1988: 19) portrays:

[A] patrimonial authority arrangement that is crucial to defining both the immediate experiences and the long-run career chances of individual managers. In this world, a subordinate owes fealty principally to his immediate boss. This means that a subordinate must not overcommit his boss, lest his boss 'get on the hook' for promises that cannot be kept. He must keep his boss from making mistakes, particularly public ones; he must keep his boss informed, less his boss get 'blindsided'. [...] A subordinate must not circumvent his boss nor ever give the appearance of doing so. He must never contradict his boss's judgment in public. To violate the last admonition is thought to constitute a kind of death wish in business, and one who does so should practice what one executive calls 'flexibility drills', an exercise 'where you put your head between your legs and kiss your ass goodbye'. On a social level, even though an easy, breezy, first-name informality is a prevalent style of American business, [...] the subordinate must extend to the boss a certain ritual deference. For instance, he must follow the boss's lead in conversation, must not speak out of turn in meetings, must laugh at his boss's jokes while not making jokes of his own that upstage his boss, must not rib the boss for his foibles. The shrewd subordinate learns how to efface himself, so that his boss's face might shine more clearly.

The hierarchal, authoritarian, sexist and closed nature of old-fashioned US corporations has a lot in common with Kanter's (1977: 37) famous description of 'IndsCo', in which:

The number of people at each level got thinner and thinner, of course, as grades increased; the corporation resembled not so much a pyramid as the Eiffel Tower. The number of women above grade 10 anywhere in the corporation could be counted on one hand.

Bullying and sexism have long been part of North American and European as well as Japanese organisational culture. Starkey and McKinlay (1994: 981), for example, describe white-collar managers who 'walked in fear' of their bosses at Ford. The sexism so vividly described in Japanese workplaces by Ogasawara (1998) in the 1990s is very similar to that observed by Kanter (1977) in the USA in the 1970s.

Culture notwithstanding, historically we have seen quite similar behaviours and organisational traditions in UK and US workplaces (although the authoritarianism seems somewhat more extreme in Japan than elsewhere). The tall hierarchies, lifetime employment and seniority-based pay systems of Japan are also quite similar to previous practice in Anglo-Saxon systems (Jacoby 1997, 2005: 78–100). These systems were substantially eroded in the 1980s in the West, but went mostly unreformed in Japan until around the mid-1990s. It is probably wrong, therefore, to attribute much of Japan's post-war success to cultural factors, as much of these manifestations of culture are difficult to distinguish from some fairly widespread organisational systems that have existed in many other countries, possibly in earlier historical periods.

Regardless of the roots of its success, few would disagree that the Japanese economy and its firms were performing extremely positively in the post-war decades, and the work, organisational and financial systems of Japan were widely admired. However, by the mid-1990s, the enthusiasm for Japanese firms had evaporated (Amable 2003: 1–2;

Dore 2000). Prescriptions for the revival of Anglo-Saxon models based on long-term, Japanese-style thinking began to sound hopelessly outdated in the new era of shareholder value logic, radical restructuring and increased speed to market of new products and services. The collapse of Japan's asset bubble in 1991, weak domestic demand and a proliferation of bad loans led to a major slowdown that lasted from 1991 to around 2003. From being lauded as a superior version of capitalism, suddenly it became a 'basket case' in need of drastic reform. Western analysts turned, with a degree of *schadenfreude*, against the long-term focus of Japanese systems of labour management, patient finance, insider governance and incremental innovation, and argued strongly that Japan was doomed to failure and stagnation if it failed to push through 'tough but necessary' and 'radical' corporate and political reforms (Porter *et al.* 2000; Katz 1998). Widespread job cuts and plant closures took place in the 1990s and early 2000s. These cuts were traumatic, especially at world-renowned firms such as Mitsubishi Motors, Fujitsu, NEC, Toshiba and Matsushita, which laid off thousands of workers (Mouer and Kawanishi 2005: 104). The electronics firm, Sanyo, cut over 15,000 jobs over four years amid poor trading conditions and an accounting scandal.[3] Less widely reported were the travails of thousands of small- and medium-sized firms, which were harder hit by recession. Bankruptcies suddenly became commonplace.

In general, large Japanese firms took a slow and conservative approach to change. They were widely criticised for this in the West, and the tardiness of transformation is often regarded as symbolic of their short-sightedness and defensive nature. Senior management, schooled in 'patient capital' and long-termism, seemed extremely wary of changing course. Interestingly, Japan's gradual economic recovery from 2003 to the global recession of 2008 began to suggest that the incremental and patient legal changes and firm restructurings were finally having positive effects, and that the slower, less radical approach to change in Japan may have worked better than the fundamental shake-up many Westerners advocated. Interest rates finally climbed in July 2006, which was symbolically important after virtually zero inflation and interest rates since the early 1990s. The government's privatisation of Japan Post in October 2007 was also

---

[3] 'Struggling Sanyo wields axe', *The Guardian*, 24 November 2006; 'Sanyo threatened with de-listing in accounting scandal', *The Guardian*, 27 December 2007.

highly significant, as it represented a major shift of domestic savings from low-risk deposit accounts into higher-risk securities.

Although still in recession when we first visited our Japanese case study firms in 2003, in the years that followed, the country's economic fortunes seemed slowly to be changing for the better. Until the global economic downturn of 2008, Japan once again began to be cast in a positive light, and as back on the road to sustainable economic growth, with analysts once more promoting portfolio investment into Japanese securities.[4] Optimistic Western commentators suggested that Japan, after a decade of vacillation and delay, had finally started to reform its firms along US-style 'shareholder value' lines, unwinding defensive corporate cross-shareholdings, and abandoning its commitment to outdated and parochial lifetime employment and seniority-based pay systems.[5]

The real picture of recent Japanese corporate change, however, is somewhat more complex. We found that Japanese firms have indeed initiated significant changes, but this has occurred alongside major continuities. Change has been rather limited in the case of 'top-end' corporate governance, but there have been some significant restructurings of organisational hierarchies at the middle level of employment. The macroeconomic recovery of Japan is probably more a result of the serious and prolonged surgery performed on the country's woefully underperforming financial sector, than on any internal corporate restructuring. Bad debts have been written off, new laws have been passed, and the Financial Services Agency has been granted wide powers of regulation and reform. In July 2006, it announced concerted attempts to converge with international standards of accounting, declaring that:

[I]n order to make our economy more dynamic and competitive, the country needs to have fair and transparent markets, which could maintain and foster market vitalities. The importance of investors' viewpoint[s] needs to be reaffirmed, and the confidence in our capital markets needs to be enhanced.[6]

---

[4] See, for example, the lead article in the February 2006 issue of *Money Observer*, issue 307: 18–24, 'All eyes on a new dawn in the East'.

[5] See *The Economist* special report on business in Japan, 1 December 2007, for arguments in this vein. Typically of mainstream Western business media, the report approves any Japanese moves towards American-style corporate governance but expresses concern with the overall slowness of Japanese reforms.

[6] Japanese Financial Services Agency: 'Towards the Internationalization of Accounting Standards', 31 July 2006, available at: www.fsa.go.jp/en/news/2006/20060731.pdf

Clearly there is the possibility that statements such as these are essentially symbolic, and that there is little genuine reason to expect Japanese firms and government agencies to implement change. However, in an excellent overview of legislative changes, Dore (2000: 95–104) suggests that they are not to be dismissed lightly. Indeed, a body of literature has emerged that suggests Japan has been quietly undergoing a major, although slow and considered, restructuring (Dore 2000, 2004; Gedajlovic *et al.* 2005; Graham 2003, 2005; Hasegawa and Hook 1997; Inagami 2001; Matanle 2003; McCann *et al.* 2004). Although substantial corporate governance reforms have not taken place thus far (Witt 2006), there have been some meaningful changes. Dore (2004) claims that the number of people describing themselves as 'market analysts' has exploded in recent years, and that the business press is far more concerned with 'shareholder value logic'. Several accounting scandals have led to significant increases in financial and managerial transparency. Japanese companies are less likely to use the 'ten-minute AGM' and AGMs are less open to *yakuza* disruption. Legal changes have also been significant – in 1994 a law was introduced to allow shareholders to bring derivative lawsuits against managers at little expense, and holding companies are now legal entities for the first time since the *zaibatsu* era (pre-1945). As a result of the recession, many key financial and real estate assets have been purchased by US companies, this being a change that Witt (2006) regards as significant. Furthermore, many employment changes have taken place: labour unions are weakening, lifetime employment and seniority-based pay are being reformed, and companies are increasing their use of outsourcing, 'mid-career' hiring, contract labour and early retirement. Perhaps crucially, employee attitudes and behaviour may well be changing, with certain stigmas and taboos about open speaking and the decline of company loyalty being slowly removed.

In short, Japanese firms and Japanese government policy have attempted to emulate some Anglo-Saxon forms of corporate restructuring, but the changes, while similar in many of their effects on managerial work, have not gone as far as in the UK and the USA. The limited execution of change is in part deliberate on the behalf of top management, and in part a result of forces beyond their control, and notably the long-standing social structures into which the economy is embedded. This is an almost exact inversion of the debate about Japanisation in the 1980s. US and UK firms were sold on the concept of lean

manufacturing, but were unwilling and unable to implement it wholesale (Danford 1998; Delbridge 1998; Jaikumar 1986; Milkman 1997;
Morris *et al.* 1993). The same now applies to Japan – its firms cannot
fully embrace Anglo-Saxon flexibility and shareholder value logic even
if senior management would wish to. Japanese firms will adopt which-
ever elements of the new organisational ideology it feels are relevant,
and will ignore the rest, adapting and tinkering with core Japanese
organisational features rather than dumping them.

Having said that, change is clearly afoot. A significant slice of the
Tokyo stock exchange is now under overseas ownership – as much as
18 per cent, up from 4 per cent in 1990 (Jacoby 2005: 38). A number of
blue-chip Japanese firms fell into serious financial difficulties in the mid-
1990s, and could only be rescued by overseas takeover (such as
Ripplewood of Long-term Credit Bank, Ford of Mazda and Artemis
of Aoba Life Insurance) or strategic alliances (such as Nissan-Renault).
More generally, firms have responded to poor trading conditions by
undergoing restructuring, flattening their hierarchies, releasing staff on
early retirements and being more open to external recruitment. This
updated picture of Japan as a more open economy and its firms having
gone through change is at odds with the traditional view of a highly
stable Japan as depicted by the early works of Dore (1973, 1987),
Rohlen (1974) and Abbeglen and Stalk (1988), or the more recent
literature that claims Japan cannot change because of institutional
rigidities (Witt 2006). Institutional theory, in the mould of that developed by widely cited authors such as DiMaggio and Powell (1991), has
for some time suggested that radical change in a variety of settings is
extremely difficult to bring about, not least because of the embeddedness of firms within broader social structures. This is true to a certain
extent in a country such as Japan with strong embeddedness effects
(certainly stronger than the highly open US or UK economies).
However, although Japanese firms have not gone for radical liberalisation or restructuring, the combined weight of smaller, more piecemeal changes over time are significant and, at the level of middle
management work, the consequences are very similar to those in the
USA and the UK. While we would not wish to suggest that national
institutions are irrelevant, it seems from the findings of this study that
they are less important than many authors have argued (Hall and
Soskice 2001; Whitley *et al.* 2003; Witt 2006). The problem with the
varieties of capitalism and institutional theory literature is that it

downplays the transformatory power of capitalism and, in doing so, diverts attention away from the often harmful effects of restructuring on staff well-being and organisational performance.

Moreover, the sub-prime crisis of 2007 onwards has clearly affected Japan, just as it has all OECD nations. The Tokyo stock exchange lost 20 per cent of its value in one week in October shortly after the collapse of Lehman Brothers on 15 September which triggered the latest round of financial panic.[7] Japan's government, in common with many other OECD nations, introduced fiscal stimulus packages to the tune of $30 billion in its attempts to ward off recessionary pressures. Despite the differences in institutional practice from the Anglo-Saxon model, many of Japan's firms have been affected by the sub-prime crisis. For example in December 2008, Toyota, widely regarded as the best-run car company in the world, announced that it expected to make an annual operating loss of over one billion UK pounds – its first ever annual loss in over seventy years of trading.[8]

Several recent studies of Japan have highlighted significant changes to large firms, including traumatic and in some cases shambolic restructuring efforts (Graham 2005: 55–90; Matanle 2003: 86–96; Mehri 2005: 123–5). As we shall see below, our case studies also reveal significant changes at the level of employees' quality of working life. If the literature continues to focus on institutional adjustment or the societal coordination of Japan – in which we see little change (Witt 2006) – it will continue to miss the human angle, which points to a rather different picture.

Our research evidence strongly supports the more critical view of the tough reality of Japanese workplaces. Although we did not come across some of the most extreme forms of management behaviour described in insider accounts, such as those of Graham (2005) and Mehri (2005), all of our case study Japanese firms had undergone changes, with the universal result of white-collar work intensification with little or no gains in the way of increased compensation or promotion. Moreover, many of the restructuring measures (such as de-layering and culture change programmes) and the underlying philosophies about 'global best practice' were essentially the same as those used in the USA and

---

[7] 'Asian Stock Markets Crash Again', *The Guardian*, 27 October 2008.
[8] 'Toyota expects £1.1 billion loss a year after record profits', *The Independent*, 23 December 2008.

the UK. Baumol *et al.*'s 'dirty little secret' of downsizing (2003: 262) – that it squeezes out more output per dollar of labour cost – appears equally applicable in the coordinated economy of Japan as it does in the liberal economy of the USA. The overall findings of Green's quantitative study of employment figures, showing major increases in work intensification along with up-skilling in Europe, the USA and Australia, would also seem to fit the Japanese picture. As Green notes (2006: xvi): 'the phenomenon was not confined to the liberal market economies: an intensification of work effort and its consequences were being bemoaned almost everywhere I looked across the industrialised world'.

However, although Japanese white-collar work had certainly been 'sweated' by reforms, Japanese employment systems had not been radically transformed. The firms in our Japanese sample were at pains to demonstrate that they were keen to maintain the tradition of long-term, internal career ladders. Moreover, shareholder value logic (SVL) did not seem to have taken hold in our case study firms (Jacoby 2005). On the other hand, the concept of SVL was hugely relevant to respondents in the UK and the USA; to middle managers as well as senior HR managers or heads of department. The rhetoric of SVL had clearly been strongly and regularly impressed on these employees, so much so that the idea was regularly raised as important by our interviewees in the West, before we had even mentioned it or used the terminology, but it was never used by any of our Japanese interviewees.

The pressures for organisational reform are very similar across Japan, the USA and the UK. But in Japan it is not restructuring for shareholder value – despite some decline in recent years, shares of large firms are still heavily tied up in cross-shareholdings and defensive, mutual holdings, and there is still no market for corporate control (Witt 2006: 45–7). Therefore the story of Japanese change is not really compatible with the Lazonick and O'Sullivan (2000) 'downsize and distribute' model. Nor has it much to do with value skimming (Froud *et al.* 2006), or value extraction. Senior management does not appear to have made such massive financial gains from restructuring as it has done in the USA and the UK. Instead, we believe Japanese firm restructuring is more directly connected with slow sales, the impact of Chinese low-cost competition and weak product market performance. The impacts of restructuring, however, in terms of organisational forms and work practices at the level of managerial work, are very similar to what has gone on in the West. The fundamental rationale for restructuring is cutting costs, even though shareholder value is not the stated motivation in Japan. In this context labour still bears the full force of restructuring measures.

Having introduced the debates on Japanese restructuring, we now turn to our analysis of case study companies. We focus on six cases from a range of sectors, revealing the various successes and failures of different parts of the Japanese economy, as well as the difficulties they share and the similar, general restructuring measures they have implemented. The first two cases explore organisational change in the auto industry, in a parts supplier and in one of Japan's largest automotive parent companies. Subsequently, we explore an electronics company, followed by an engineering firm. Both are struggling with declining market share for their core products. These cases are followed by a discussion of a major steel manufacturer, which had undergone many decades of employment shrinkage; and, finally, issues of globalisation in JUSBank, the Tokyo office of a major US investment bank, and notably how restructuring has affected the lives of two younger managers. We provide a lot of space for these final two respondents, as they had directly experienced Japanese and American management styles, and were able to comment on both, and on how the former may now be influenced by the latter, in a significant, yet not uncritical way.

We begin our analysis, however, with a discussion of two case study firms operating in Japan's highly competitive automotive sector.

JAutoComps and JAutoGroup: 'Managing the cost-down strategy'

During the time of our research visits to Japan (2003–7) the country appeared to be slowly starting to haul itself out of long-term economic stagnation. While a great many large firms still faced considerable difficulties, many had managed to emerge fairly strongly from a decade or more of recession. One of Japan's most successful industries is cars, and until the global economic downturn of 2008 the main Japanese carmakers appeared once again to be dominating their US and European rivals (Maxton and Wormald 2004: 220, 248–54). Honda, Toyota and Nissan were regularly beating US or European firms when it came to reliability, customer satisfaction and safety.[9]

---

[9] 'Honda leads, Land Rover trails miles behind in reliability survey', *The Guardian*, 3 July 2007.

Two of our case study firms are JAutoComps and JAutoGroup. JAuto-Comps was (until quite recently) an important part of JAutoGroup's *keiretsu* supplier network, but recent restructuring and new strategic plans at the top of JAutoGroup have meant a concerted shift toward more arm's-length contracting. This has seen a more conflictual relationship between parent and supplier than the more mutually supportive relationship one finds in earlier times (Gerlach 1992).

In common with steel, automotive manufacturing is an industry characterised by fierce international competition, overcapacity, high fixed costs and reduced margins. JAutoComps is a first-tier supplier to one of the major Japanese auto firms. It employs over 6,000 people and specialises in designing and manufacturing cockpit systems, dashboard instruments, radiators, mufflers and air-conditioning units for a range of the parent company's models. Our research visits were to JAutoComps headquarters, where we interviewed the Head of the Personnel and General Affairs division as well as a number of middle managers.

Unusually for Japan (but now fairly common in the auto supplier industry), the firm is the result of a recent merger of two previously separate companies that employed between them around 7,000 staff. This was a rationalisation measure forced upon the two companies by the cost-cutting demands of the parent auto group. Since the merger in 2002, a number of changes have been made to the personnel system, including cutting the number of management levels. One of the former separate companies had seven layers of management, the other had six. The new, post-merger entity had only three layers, *buchō*, *jichō* and *kachō* (division head, deputy division head and section chief, respectively). This meant a major regrading of pay scales and a large number of early retirements. Employment numbers have come down by around 300 per year since the merger, as retirees have not been replaced. For example, the numbers of white-collar staff in the Accounting and Finance division were reduced from seventy-five to forty-eight because of role duplication following the merger. The Head of the Personnel division was clear about when the trouble began for both the economy and the firm:

So the milestone should be '91 or '92. Before that day, the Japanese economy was prosperous, but it was a boom, the so-called 'bubble economy'. But the end of '90 or '91 was the burst of the bubble. At that moment they get to be cautious, you have to change. So probably '91 or '92. So the rapid growth, and after '91 or '92 the volume has reduced after that. So at the beginning of the 1990s it was the beginning of the transformation of the organisation shape. (*Buchō*, General Affairs and Personnel Division, JAutoComps)

As he continues, one can detect a degree of resentment in his description of how the firm has been treated by the parent. Much like case companies in earlier chapters, however, this situation was seen as inevitable given the wider economic scenario. Resistance, therefore, appeared pointless:

Q   *Does [Head of HR] have meetings or correspondence with his equivalents in [JAutoGroup]?*
Yes. Of course up to now they have organised such meetings.
Q   *Would they be regular?*
No, no more regular meetings. Because all the [JAutoGroup's] strategy, the philosophy has changed. So [...] not regular meetings.
Q   *How has the philosophy changed?*
The *keiretsu* group Chief Executive Officer [name], has declared clearly that only three suppliers still remain with the group, and to dissolve the *keiretsu*.
Q   *Why has that been the strategy for suppliers? Were they forced to be more responsible for their own costs?*
After the arrival of [CEO], he showed the main policy with three items, three poles. One is lower costs, the cost-down strategy. This has dissolved the *keiretsu*. The second pole is the world, global purchasing. And the third one is modularisation. In Japan there are eleven automobile makers. Toyota, Honda, Nissan, these are the three major groups. Now in the end of March 2002, the final annual data, the annual report, Honda Group was best. It means the Japanese automobile suppliers are not homogeneous in terms of prosperity. It's a very zigzag way. So three years ago [CEO] has declared, has asked suppliers to cost down 20 per cent in three years. [CEO] has declared to sell all the shares of suppliers except four companies. That announcement of [CEO] to declare to sell all the shares except four shocked the suppliers.
Q   *So who were the four companies? Was [JAutoComps] one of them?*
Yes, not included in the four companies. [JAutoComps] has expected to be included in the four companies.
Q   *But they still have a 30 per cent stake, will they sell that?*
[JAutoGroup] keeps 33 per cent.
Q   *Has that declined?*
It keeps the same. So after the declaration of [CEO], all the Japanese makers followed and imitated this strategy, this cost-down strategy. So Toyota, for instance, asked the suppliers to reduce the cost 30 per cent to 2003. So [JAutoComps] now regard the situation as a challenge, because, of course,

all the suppliers are affecting their cost-down efforts. But with the request for the very harsh requirement for customers, if they overcome their requirement, they will compete in the world. (*Buchō*, General Affairs and Personnel Division, JAutoComps)

Alongside the disruption to the *keiretsu*, however, there appeared to be considerable survival prospects for the system. Other automotive parent companies were much less happy to dismantle these relationships:

Q   *There's a lot of history here, yes? Can you imagine a situation in Japan*
     where [JAutoComps] could perhaps supply to Toyota or to companies
     other than [JAutoGroup]?
Yes, I wish to have a chance. Japanese car makers require 20 per cent of costs down because [this is] the basis of global benchmarking. So it means that Japanese suppliers, if they don't respond, don't achieve the requirements of the Japanese carmakers, it means the decline of the whole Japanese industrial automobile industry. So [JAutoComps] belonging to [JAutoGroup] should present more cost-effective products to Toyota, because in Toyota Group they have for instance Denso[10] et cetera. You have to compete to overcome Denso in order to supply the products to Toyota Group. So it is very harsh competition between Japanese suppliers, [...] it is inevitable, it is unavoidable. So I wish the Japanese automobile industry will have a very good day if they overcome this very harsh situation. So the three poles of the company is the [first] enlarging of sales volume. And the second one is cost reduction, and the third one is new product. So these are the three poles, the three targets of the company. (*Buchō*, General Affairs and Personnel Division, JAutoComps)

He continued his argument by noting how the development of new technologies could signal that 'indirect' workers, such as middle managers, can be potentially bypassed:

With the development of IT, the importance of indirect workers, we call it indirect workers in Japan, has less importance. We can say it is less important, but the volume of personnel, former personnel is 3,000 – they can [now] do with 2,000 or 1,500. But we have to point out that there are two functions that we require from middle management, one is the management, and also

---

[10] Denso Corporation (formerly known as Nippondenso) is a powerful first-tier supplier to Toyota, employing around 34,000 staff, which was originally a wholly owned member of the Toyota Group before being hived off as a separate entity, of which Toyota retains a 25 per cent stake (see Sako 2006: 106). Denso works extremely closely with Toyota Group and has long been one of their most trusted partners.

the expertise, which cannot be substituted by information technology. So the role of middle management still remains.

The Head of the Personnel and General Affairs division also noted how Japan was 'notorious' for its long-hours culture:

Japan is very famous for notorious longer-hours working, it still remains this way. In headquarters they begin to work at 9 o'clock and legally it is eight hours' work. Well, some, the longest one [is] from 9 o'clock to 9 o'clock, but the average should be [...] probably nine to ten hours' on average, and eight hours work is the legal one. So, the argument was for years in the 1980s, the working hours of Japanese people exceeded 2,000 hours a year; it was notorious, it was very criticised. So from that day on, Japan, they tried to reduce the working hours from 2,000 to 1,800. It was rejected. So in reality the working hours of direct workers have reduced due to the volume-down reduction of production. But for the indirect workers, for the managers and middle managers, they keep the same, the long hours. Probably exceeding 2,000 hours a year. (*Buchō*, General Affairs and Personnel Division, JAutoComps)

Restructuring seemed to entail making use of technologies and new organisational forms that enabled 'doing more with less'. In the wake of the JAutoComps merger, this meant that larger workloads were being shared among fewer middle managers, just as we had seen in the UK and USA:

So, the volume of work task, for personnel, for each middle manager has grown in comparison with the former volume of work before the merger. Because the volume of work from both companies has merged. The volume of work still remains, but the people were duplicated in certain parts of the company, like in Finance. And they reduced the number of the people to forty-five in the Finance department. (*Buchō*, General Affairs and Personnel Division, JAutoComps)

JAutoComps was also experiencing downward pressure on promotion prospects. The senior personnel managers we interviewed suggested upwards mobility was now much harder to achieve, and that it would generally only apply to the very best staff:

Twenty years ago when I was recruited by the company, at that moment everyone had expectations to be promoted to *kachō* level. It was, roughly speaking, automatic. So it was connected with the rapid growth of the company itself. And nowadays only 40 per cent of newly recruited university graduates have chance to be promoted to *kachō*. [...] In contrast to roughly twenty years ago, today only 40 per cent of freshmen have expectation to be promoted to a higher grade manager. This it is a little bit disappointing, less motivating for the freshmen. But twenty years ago, for example, in my freshman age, everyone had expectation to be a manager, they were very happy, and sustained the motivation. So there is a lack of candidates for next *kachō*, but only 40 per cent can be promoted to *kachō*. The rest, 60 per cent, how to motivate them is very important. And it is a task for [the Personnel division], how to motivate them? (*Buchō*, General Affairs and Personnel Division, JAutoComps)

Middle managers at *kachō* level also reported this problem, albeit in a slightly more critical tone. When we asked about workloads, a *kachō* in the General Affairs and Personnel division replied:

You picked a very tough question, that's a big question for us because in the past everybody got promoted so you had something to look forward to. But these days [with regard to the] *buchō*'s position [there are] not so many [posts], so it's really the point that we are troubled and we are thinking about how to deal with the motivation issue. And these days more and more people are left behind sort of in the bottom level, and the bottom level is becoming big. So the way we cope with the motivation and incentive issue is for example we give certain people for what they have done in the job, a reward of [more] money. And besides bonus, besides the traditional bonus we give certain people a special bonus for their work, and in that way we are coping with the incentivisation. But still it's not a perfect solution. So we are still figuring out how to cope with this situation. (*Kachō*, General Affairs and Personnel Department, JAutoComps)

Despite the generally reserved and guarded nature of the Japanese interviews, the management at JAutoComps made it clear that the competitive pressures being felt by the company were urgent and serious, and that this context was a difficult one in terms of managers' quality of working life:

The next pressure for us is the cost-reduction pressure. So right now we are working on how low the costs can be. So we're in the process of determining the minimum costs. So as a manager we have a very big question. [...] That's the current situation. (*Kachō*, General Affairs and Personnel Department, JAutoComps)

The Personnel managers also explained to us that JAutoComps had a mandatory retirement age, now set as low as fifty-three. *Kachō*s would then either retire or stay on in an 'expert' role on much-reduced pay.

Despite the widely held belief of large Japanese firms as employee-favouring environments, what we saw here and in subsequent cases was an intense management focus on cost control. Although the corporate governance and meso-level institutional features of Japan's corporate environment were not transformed significantly, this has not insulated managerial workers from change. Cost control was clearly significant in the minds of top management, and this pressure was cascading down the organisation. As we shall see below, similar cost pressures were described in all our Japanese case companies, and represented a feature consistent with the interpretation of the motive force behind modern corporate restructuring being the progressive extraction of ever more labour from middle management employees.

While the automotive industry is atypical in a number of ways, the intense pressures on JAutoComps and its staff were similar to those described by Mehri (2005: 185–6) as Nizumi became 'the dog of Toyota'. The 'squeeze' applied by parent companies to their suppliers is widely criticised by industry analysts such as Maxton and Wormald, who tend to regard US and European companies as the most notorious users of bullying tactics on suppliers (2004: 158–63). According to data from this case, Japanese *keiretsu* suppliers appear just as threatened by top-down, cost-reduction pressures and aggressive micro-management by auto parents as Western suppliers. In general Japanese auto firms are highly competitive and successful, but they have been far from immune from restructuring. The managers we interviewed spoke of the 'harsh requirements of our customers' – yet another symptom of the broad context of the uncompromising demands of international competition. This intense pressure tends to be met with resigned compliance by managerial staff, as they interpret this new context as 'simply the way things are'.

These pressures have short- and long-term effects on staff. In the immediate context, middle managers face increased workloads and intensification of work. In the longer term, their career structures are also affected. We asked how these top-level restructuring measures have affected white-collar careers in JAutoComps. The response of the Head of Personnel at the firm, although somewhat guarded, suggested significant impacts on career development:

Nowadays the very harsh restructuring is regarded as unavoidable in Japan. So, to adapt to the new situation, middle management probably can be divided into two. One regards it as a challenging situation, because you will be promoted with your effort, with your merit, et cetera. But the other part of middle management will be disappointed. Because before 1991 or '92, they had some expectations of roughly automatic promotions with the growth of the company. But that is ending. (*Buchō*, General Affairs and Personnel Division, JAutoComps)

A similar situation was described by middle managers (at *kachō* level) of JAutoComps. Having outlined to us the increased use of performance-based pay in an effort to move beyond traditional seniority-based pay (albeit with the maintenance of minimum seniority qualifications), the discussion moved to the interesting issue of generational change, and the declining importance of corporate loyalty:

I think there are two types of young people. These days there are many people who don't want a regular job, they work from one job to another like part-time working. They are called *furītā* in Japanese. On the other hand there are some young people who want to get a regular job – like get employed by a company. But the people are changing, I think. There are many young people who are not so concerned about getting promoted to *kachō* or *buchō* and to manage people. As long as they can do what they are good at, or as long as they can do what they want to do, they are satisfied. [...] They are more centred on their job, what they want to do. So as a personnel manager what we have to think about is how to reward those kind of people, professional people. [...] We need to diversify the reward system, not just promotion but reward them in other ways. [...] For example there is a man, Japanese man, Mr Tanaka who got awarded a Nobel Prize, and he is just an employee, he's not a manager and still he gets the Nobel Prize.[11] But he's not concerned about becoming promoted, he was just satisfied being just an employee, a regular employee, a common employee as long as he can concentrate on such reward schemes. So the company has to think about rewarding that kind of people. Their orientation is changing. (*Kachō*, General Affairs and Personnel Group, JAutoComps)

While the example of the Nobel Prize winner is, of course, exceptional, the trend for highly skilled workers to focus their minds increasingly on work, rather than on promotions and their positions in the hierarchy is a major issue (which we have also noted in the US and UK cases). It appears that many middle managers have effectively given up on upwards promotion

---

[11] Koichi Tanaka won the 2002 Nobel Prize for Chemistry for his development of a mass spectrometry technique known as 'soft laser desorption' while working at Shimadzu Corporation. Aged forty-three at the time of the award, he is the second-youngest-ever winner of the prize, and the first without a post-bachelor degree to be awarded a science Nobel Prize.

following cost-pressure driven restructuring and de-layering. In the Japanese case, the impact of this can be even harder to bear given how difficult it is to leave large employers and take one's chances on the (highly underdeveloped) labour market for management talent. The maintenance of internal career ladders in many large companies makes it extremely risky for staff to quit and search for a new job in mid-career.

The need to diversify the reward structure to take into account the collapse of upwards mobility expectation was a very common response across the Japanese case studies. Partly this could be explained by the increased demands made of managers along with the removal of layers and cutting or merging of divisions, and partly by the need to find a new category of employment in which to place the slowly growing number of mid-career hires. Many mid-level management staff were not expecting to be promoted in this leaner structure. Demands on mid-level managers had definitely grown. Not only were staff expected to carry out their usual duties, they were also encouraged to 'go that extra mile' and act more independently. Of course, this was not encouraged to the extent that one might act above one's station or openly question hierarchical authority:

Q   *Is it true that you've got this need to think a bit more differently, be more creative, maybe more independent-thinking in a Japanese company to be successful, whereas in the past you just followed the line and climbed up slowly, now you have to be more creative and independent, is that true?*
I think that is half true, recently the society is changing very quickly so you have to catch up with changes, so in that sense like in the past you just had to do the routine work and you get promoted automatically. But these days if you do just the routine work it's not enough for you to be successful, the company expects you to give them some added value. So you have to be creative and give ideas, but at the same time if you are very independent and sort of like you don't care about everybody that's not so good. So half true, half true, and you also have to be cooperating with other people so you need both aspects, both characters. (*Kachō*, General Affairs and Personnel Group, JAutoComps)

Even though one of our *buchō*s mentioned that 'Japanese people keep their emotions under control', he went on to complain fairly openly about his working hours:

So first I'd like to talk about the work hours. When I joined the company the *kachō* and *buchō* they come to company very late and they leave company very early, so their work hours were short and I looked at them and thought 'I want to be like that'. But when I became a *kachō* I didn't get to come late and leave early, I had the same hours of working, I had to work the same hours. And when I became *buchō* that was the same, I had to work the same hours, so that's changed. And [another *kachō*'s name] is the same, he has the same experience. So the member of the Board of Directors even, for example, nowadays he comes to company like eight in the morning and leaves around at least at the earliest like ten o'clock.

Q   *At night?*

Yeah, at night at the earliest, so even the President works that long. So the employees feel they must work as hard as he is working. So it's much, much longer hours than before. [...]

Q   *That must be tough with trying to combine that with some sort of life at home as well?*

That's true, I rarely meet my family now. I was in the United States, I was stationed in the United States last year for a year, I went there all by myself and so I didn't see my family. But even so the situation hasn't changed. Even though I'm back in Japan it's not changed, I rarely meet my family now. I don't like that situation.

Q   *And presumably that's got worse by the sound of it, the working hours have got longer and it must have got worse than it was ten years ago maybe?*

Yes, yes. Yes compared to like for example ten years [ago] the company also is growing so the company itself is becoming bigger and that the broadness, the width of the content of the work is increasing. And now we have the relations with foreign companies and so the job itself has widened, but the personnel numbers have not increased. So in that sense we have much more work. Personally speaking I used to have a lot of miscellaneous work so personally I don't feel that different compared to before, but I was used to doing different kinds of work at the same time. But in terms of the whole company the width and the depth of each individual's work has increased. For example in the past you only had to do your work, your division, but now we have cross-functional work as well as foreign relations. So the width and the depth has increased for each employee. (*Buchō*, General Affairs and Personnel Group, JAutoComps)

A *kachō* spoke of decreased employment security, and more discussion around the workplace about the possibility of moving between jobs:

Personally I don't feel insecure about my life and also in addition society itself, not just the company, is changing. Because in the past the lifetime employment was commonplace and to appoint a person in middle of their age, I mean the middle of their work age is very, very rare. But in that time, in those days [...] for example the company may appoint a person in the middle of their careers, the reason is because that person is very, very good, very, very good in their work or the company needs to fill that position.

Q   *Yeah, a specialist perhaps.*

Yeah, or someone left or something, at that time the company didn't promote that person in the same speed as the rest of the employees who has been working from their graduation from college and things like that. So they had the handcuff kind of if they haven't been employed from the beginning, but in those days it was OK because there are lots of babies, there are lots of population, the population was growing so there was no problem. If the company wants to employ someone they could easily find someone, but these days the population is not growing so fast, in Japan the babies, nowa-days decreasing very, very quickly. So in the future we don't have many workers, and at the same time there will be more older people, elder people. So but still the company needs to employ people, so in these days and from now on they have to employ people even in the middle of their career. And if the company keeps giving handicap to those people the people won't come, so the company is treating those people on the same level, in the same way as the people they employ from the beginning. So in other words people, the employ-ees are, their mobility has increased and the environment is favourable for the mobility of these employees. Because the company treats those kind of people in a better way than in the past. And so in that sense even if you quit the company in the middle of your career it's easier for you to find a good job. So the environment has become favourable for [a] more mobile labour market. (*Kachō*, General Affairs and Personnel Group, JAutoComps)

The broader social science literature on the Japanese labour market does not generally support this view, but several of our respondents noted this change. One interpretation could be that this widely dis-cussed idea of increased labour market mobility (especially for those aged under thirty-five) is simply an impression in wide currency, but it is largely a surface-level, symbolic change. In our company visits we met very few workers who had joined mid-career. One of these was a former police officer who then ended up working in the Personnel department of JElectronics (see below). Mid-career hiring seemed in general to remain rare in Japan, except for the parent company JAutoGroup itself, where it was reported to account for as many as 50 per cent of new managers.

Although the hypothesised increase in mid-career quitting and hiring was rather debatable, as was the repeated suggestion that more able younger staff 'can get promoted faster' (given that most of our firms had very few *kachō*s under the age of forty) the claims around the intensi-fication of work seemed much more credible, and were often expressed with force by our interviewees. In fact, there were striking similarities with the US and UK cases as regards middle management role expansion. In general, and especially in Japan, the increase in performance pressure had not been compensated for by higher pay levels.

The competitive pressures in the auto industry are particularly severe, and much of this pressure is applied down the supply chain. The traditional *keiretsu*[12] structure was certainly threatened in the JAutoComps case (although there was much less evidence of this structure being so directly threatened in our other private sector firms). This trend is common throughout the international car industry, as the complexity, overcapacity and overdiversification of models are being combated by further contraction and rationalisation. Auto firms are starting to narrow the product range and rationalise the number of platforms. This will probably lead to more cost-cutting and job removals (Maxton and Wormald 2004). On the other hand, and as with JSteel below, Chinese growth was highly relevant. Import demand in China at the time of writing was very substantial, and all of the Japanese carmakers were benefiting from their proximity to this market. Sluggish domestic sales, however, remained a major cause for concern.

At the parent company, JAutoGroup, we conducted interviews with two *kachō*s, both from the Personnel Administration section. This was not in the head office, but in a major production facility located in southern Japan. They described an even stronger degree of change than that experienced by their supplier, JAutoComps. The impression they created was one of fairly significant change and severe overwork, but also of a generally successful company whose future was a great deal more secure than that of JAutoComps (or indeed USAuto or UKAuto, Chapters 3–4). De-layering was even more radical than many of the Western firms. One area that did buck the trend, however, was that the numbers of managerial staff at JAutoGroup had grown despite de-layering. This was due to an increase in the number of departments set up recently in an attempt to tackle new industry challenges.

Our middle managers opened the discussion by outlining how the pay system at JAutoGroup had been changed significantly:

---

[12] Confusion surrounds the correct translation of the term *keiretsu* in the English-language literature. For our purposes, we define *keiretsu*s as hierarchically organised groups of manufacturing firms that traditionally supply one much larger parent firm.

And so our pay system has changed and traditionally there used to be a kind of position allowance, but that's been abolished and now we have the pay band. So we have two bands – for example for *kachōs*, *kachōs*' pay band is called N2 pay band, so *buchō* and *jichō* share the same pay band in one, but in each pay band there's a maximum and minimum amount decided. Within the pay band their salary or annual pay is decided according to their performance. [...] And so the pay, or the annual pay, is decided according to the person's contribution to the company or performance that the person has shown in the previous year. So if the person makes a larger contribution he surely gets the top band pay, but then if the person was sick or something and could not contribute much to the company it's possible that the person's position in the pay band will be gone. [...] Compared with a person's pay at the top of the pay band, the person would get 20 per cent more than the person at the bottom of the pay band.

Q   *And so age does not contribute, or seniority does not contribute?*
Zero. (*Kachō*, Personnel Administration Section, JAutoGroup)

Although in general the number of management roles had gone up in recent years, cuts had been made to managerial posts in administrative areas, such as Personnel, as in JAutoComps. This suggests, in line with the analysis of Jacoby (2005) on the USA, that personnel functions may be losing some of their power and influence in such an engineering-focused firm as JAutoGroup. Much like at JAutoComps, cuts were being made to indirect workers, meaning that administrative middle managers were especially at risk. JAutoGroup was similarly focusing more tightly on cost control in areas (such as Personnel) where top management believes savings can be made:

The number of managers or managing positions has actually slightly increased. And because the company's practice has become, or the work has become, quite specialised. And the company's organisations have been divided into smaller sections. Therefore the number of managerial positions have increased accordingly. However, when I look at the content of the increase, actually the administration-related sections, the number of managerial posts has actually been declining. While [in] the engineering-related or development-related sections the number of managerial positions has increased. (*Kachō*, Personnel Administration Section, JAutoGroup)

It was easy to sympathise with these personnel *kachōs* who have felt the squeeze. This middle manager went on to describe his frustrations at some length. We asked:

Q   *In administration has there been a big decrease [of posts]?*

I do not have a specific number, but then in my case the managerial position, compared with the past I now feel I am doing the work of three *kachōs* by myself. [...] I think overall there has been a 20 per cent decrease in the number of managerial positions in administrative sections.

Q   *And have the working hours increased, or ...?*

Yes, we are working longer hours now.

Q   *What would be the typical working day for a manager?*

I will give you the figure of our annual total. So an average worker works for 244 days a year, and about eight hours per day is 1,952 hours per year. And the average overtime worked is fifty hours per month and that's multiplied by twelve months of the year, so that comes to 600 hours' overtime per year. And then so 1,952 plus 600 overtime hours and the total average working hours of managers is 2,552 hours a year.

Q   *But managers will not get overtime [pay] will they?*

No, they're not, because their pay is based on annual payments, they are not paid for their overtime hours.

Q   *So how many hours a day would you work on average?*

An average of ten to eleven hours a day.

Q   *And weekends too?*

No.

Q   *The reason I ask is that typically in the United States or Britain, and particularly in the car industry, people are, managers are, working very long, increasingly long hours, sometimes crazy hours.*

So people work long hours in the States and the UK also?

Q   *What we're finding in Britain and the United States is that some of the routine work that managers did has gone because of email, internet, technology change, but that sometimes managers are doing a wider range of tasks and jobs than they previously did.*

Yes, at the same time we're seeing at [JAutoGroup] email is available for us and then even teleconferences [are] available for us. So in that regard some routine works that we used to do have been reduced. But on the other hand, the scope of our responsibility has been extended, because [of] the change that [JAutoGroup] has undertaken in the past five years. So accordingly our work hours have increased.

Q   *So do you have some examples of that?*

I have two examples of the expanding scope of responsibilities, especially in terms of people in a management position in administrative sections. And so previously I worked [...] in Yokohama, there was an engine plant with 2,000 employees, and next to Yokohama there was another plant called [town] plant with 300 employees. And at [town] there's exclusive work for [AutoGroup], so there used to be a personnel manager for each of the plants, both at Yokohama and [town]. However, now with the new change the one personnel manager has to oversee the personnel affairs at both Yokohama and [town]. And the same can be said about other positions, like our company has a position of manager who oversees the use of utilities like water, electricity, gas and other energy in the Energy section. And there used to be that kind of manager in each plant, but then now the manager has to oversee several plants in the same area. So these are just two of the examples. (*Kachō*, Personnel Administration Section, JAutoGroup)

This experience of role expansion resonates with that of many other middle managers across the countries studied. Those in administrative roles in particular, such as HR professionals, have regularly felt the force of such cost reductions. On the other hand, Japanese managers in such important companies as JAutoGroup, although subjected to very similar kinds of role expansion and work intensification, have perhaps not felt quite the same pressures of insecurity as their Western, especially American, counterparts. Responding to our questions about a perceived sense of job insecurity, one *kachō* replied: 'In that regard I should say there's no change in our company. Twenty years ago people took the job for life as granted, and that has not really changed among our managers.' Although blue-collar workers were not part of our research, it is probably reasonable to assume that many of them do not share these feelings. When we asked one of the JAutoGroup *kachō*s to describe some of the biggest changes he has seen in his thirty years with the company, this was his response:

First of all the major change was the closure of some of our factories, and mainly the [...] plant and the [...] plant in Tokyo. So these were both off-line plants but those have been closed. With the closure of those two plants, some were shifted to [this] plant, and while others where shifted to [other] plant, another plant in another prefecture.
Q   *But presumably overall the workforce has declined?*
Yes. [...] However, the cost reduction was brought about in a different way. Also, for example, one of the important points is to raise the operation rate of the existing facilities in order to cut the cost of production. And at that time [JAutoGroup]'s facility operation was 50 to 55 per cent. By raising the operation rate to 75 per cent a further cost reduction became possible. [...] Now the number of vertically affiliated companies has come down to only 10 per cent of what we used to have. And those who have remained as affiliated companies are the ones that have the [JAutoGroup] core technologies, both in terms of manufacturing and development, such as the electronics components or the control, transmissions, things like that. (*Kachō*, Personnel Administration Section, JAutoGroup)

At the end of the interview, the two *kachō*s started to ask questions of their own. They wanted to know how managers are paid in the UK and the USA, what percentage of US or UK automotive industry would be made up of female workers, and whether there are daycare centres at work. We responded by saying:

[They] have long working hours and that is not family friendly, it's not, you know? I was interviewing a female engineer manager at a car company, a car manufacturer in Britain, and I said to her, 'my wife would not do your job'. The hours were just, fourteen hours a day, weekends, not with children. So they want more women, but they don't make it easy, you know.

Q   *So the automobile industry may have to change the working environment?*
Yeah, I think it does.

Because half of our customers are women so we have to develop our cars that are reflecting the voices of the customers' wishes. And [JAutoGroup] has a policy to make the working environment friendly for female workers, and as of April this year [JAutoGroup] opened a daycare centre for female workers at [another plant]. Our factory may also have to set up a daycare centre because at this plant there are strong calls for a daycare centre. (Kachō, Personnel Administration Section, JAutoGroup)

Both JAutoGroup and JAutoComps have experience of significant organisational and managerial restructuring. JAutoComps was a good example of both change and continuity. The merger of two previously separate units represented a radical and troubling process, and substantial changes were subsequently made to middle managers' work tasks and pay systems. However, radical employment cuts were not undertaken. JAutoComps was very reluctant to make compulsory redundancies or to abandon seniority-based pay. Instead it made gradual alterations to both systems. Middle managers' concerns over job enlargement and work intensification were serious, as were their complaints regarding diminished promotion prospects. What had substantially changed, however, was the company's position with relation to the parent, for *keiretsu* ties appeared to have become much more competitive and market-based. This is partly the result of large foreign shareholdings in the parent group, forcing firms within its orbit to go further down the 'stock-market capitalism' route of change.

As for the parent company, JAutoGroup itself, similar changes were afoot. Even though the company was enjoying much greater success than many of its competitors (especially in the States) and its market position was much healthier than the smaller *keiretsu* suppliers, white-collar workloads seemed to be just as heavy as they were at JAutoComps.

The JAutoGroup factory closures were described as 'shocking', albeit rare, events and were part of the broader and more intense process of rationalisation, capacity utilisation and effort drives, all of which were placing pressures on middle managers. In both companies, managerial work had been upskilled and responsibilities widened. While this had some positive implications as regards the intrinsic content of the job, such benefits were probably outweighed by disadvantages relating to fewer promotion opportunities (even as managerial roles were growing at JAutoGroup) and responsibility overstretch (such as overseeing personnel matters across two plants). As we have seen, even though organisational reforms were carried out in a more measured way in Japan than in the USA and the UK (i.e. no redundancies and the maintenance of internal career ladders) the combined result of these workplace changes for middle managers in Japan were remarkably similar to those experienced in the studies of the other countries.

JElectronics: 'A difficult economic scenario'

Electronics was a major part of Japan's post-war success story, but recent performance has not been encouraging. Major firms such as Sony, Sanyo and Matsushita (owner of the Panasonic brand) have faced major sales problems, especially given the massive price competition associated with the sector, involving substantial amounts of Chinese outsourcing. The troubles of the large firms are well known. Our case study is a smaller firm that nevertheless has played an important role in Japan's electronics industry in the past. Today, however, it faces an uncertain future. JElectronics is a major producer of IC lead frames, precision stamping dies and machine tools for the semiconductor industry. Its main customers are the large consumer electronics firms of Japan, America and Europe. It has five production plants in Japan, five in mainland China and five across South East Asia. The company is relatively small, employing 1,663 staff in Japan and about 1,500 overseas. JElectronics is clearly feeling the pressure of heightened international competition. In the mid-1990s it possessed about 30 per cent of the global market for lead frames. This share has now dropped to around 10 per cent. Sales income had fallen steadily over the five years prior to our research.

To combat these competitive pressures, the company has made several important changes to its work and payment systems for middle managers. It has reduced its management layers from five to four, by merging two levels of middle management (traditionally called deputy section chief – *kakarichō* – and section chief – *kachō*) into the new title of group chief – *gurūpuchō*. This has led to considerable task expansion for middle managers, although they claimed that working hours had not changed significantly. Working days for *gurūpuchō* were already very long, with the figure of twelve hours per day given as quite normal. Sometimes, however, staff experienced the very extremes of overwork, as hours climbed to as many as fifteen to sixteen per day. We questioned a middle manager in the Personnel group about the expanded role of *gurūpuchō*s in recent times:

Q   *What we're finding in other companies in other countries and Japan is that gurūpuchōs have to have a much greater awareness of maybe financial issues and business issues than they used to, would that be true here?*
Yes, because the *gurūpuchō* are more and more expected to be part of the management of the company, therefore they become quite aware of the financial and business aspects of the activities. And the company still tries to raise the awareness among the *gurūpuchō* by providing them with the training to manage company affairs. (*Gurūpuchō*, General Affairs and Personnel Group)

JElectronics had responded to competitive pressures by moving much of its lower precision production overseas, while keeping the highest skilled and research and development or design work in Japan. We asked one of the *gurūpuchō*s (a lifetime JElectronics employee) to provide us with his view on why these changes are being made. His comments emphasised the realities of hollowing-out:

My personal view is that we have all entered a very difficult era, and the Japanese production bases are more and more shifted towards China. And so this kind of thing was not quite expected when we enjoyed the economic bubble because we could keep employing new hires because every year we could have the expansion of our businesses and we could always expand new stations and hire new people and so that kind of thing was quite easy in those days. However, we have now entered the era of changes, and so we have to seek ways to motivate younger people so that they can give full flight to their abilities. And therefore we have set up the evaluation system for engineers so that they are given a due position depending on their experience and skills that they acquired, and so that the company can support them in their activities to pass on their skills to the next generation of engineers; although there are arguments within the company whether to introduce the more

American style of hiring system based on annual contract and annual pay or giving more emphasis on merit- or performance-based pay. However, we still do not know how we can define performance, how we can evaluate people fairly, so I don't think things are that easy. (*Gurūpuchō*, General Affairs and Personnel Group)

Given this pressure on costs, graduate recruitment at JElectronics had slowed dramatically from a high point of 200 staff in 1997 to a low of just fifteen in 2001. They also claimed to hire only about three to four mid-career recruits at *gurūpuchō* level per year. Senior staff based in Japan were not being replaced as they retired, at age sixty (about ten staff per year retire), so cost pressures were reduced without having to undergo the trauma of making employees redundant. Having said that, JElectronics valued highly the skills of senior staff, with around 40 per cent of retirees being rehired on 60 per cent of their pay until they retired for good, aged sixty-five. The company was also increasing its use of temporary staff.

We asked managers to explain the motivations for the recruitment cuts and organisational changes. The 'difficult economic scenario' was given as the main reason for the cuts. A *gurūpuchō* explained that many skilled engineering staff are no longer expecting or seeking promotion into management positions, and are happy to stay in the newly developed 'engineering-only' track. However, JElectronics management was unwilling to abandon the minimum seniority for promotion to *gurūpuchō* of twelve to thirteen years. It seems that the concepts of internal skills development and the fostering of strong employee loyalty were both important to JElectronics. Having said that, concepts of loyalty were declining in importance on both sides of the employment relationship (company and staff):

Q   *We never had in Britain lifetime job security as you have in Japan, but we nevertheless had long-term jobs, and if people joined big organisations such as in the auto industry or the steel industry you expected more or less a job for life. I think that that has very much changed if you talk to young people now. Regarding young people in Japan, has there been a change in mentality?*

The loyalty in the company per se has declined actually for a while. When we had the lifetime employment system people used to stick to the company rather than to get jobs or particular skills or professions. But that has changed. Instead of being loyal to the company people nowadays are becoming more loyal to their jobs or skills or occupations that they choose. So [a graduate] does not really care which company he works for but what he wants to do on the job. So therefore in the past people tended to stick to big name brands and thought that their life was assured once they got into a big company. However, that kind of thing has changed. So that trend is quite obvious, especially for people younger than thirty-five, because in Japan people younger than thirty-five have many opportunities to change jobs. (*Gurūpuchō*, General Affairs and Personnel Group)

The case of JElectronics reflects how Japanese companies are making significant changes to their managerial employment systems. Such changes have led to employees experiencing a worsening perception of their occupational status, conditions and prospects, and notably so with regard to the perceived decline of company loyalty to staff and staff loyalty to the company. Whereas over the years the firm's domestic headcount had progressively shrunk, its production presence in China and South East Asia had expanded significantly. These are all symptoms of the wider cost-control demands of global competition and as such are inherent features of long-term industrial restructuring in mature economies. Clearly Japanese middle managers are as vulnerable as those in the UK or the USA to such restructuring measures, despite the resilience of lifetime employment, seniority-based pay and institutional structures.

JEngineering: 'Increas(ing) the per capita activity'

Another firm with an uncertain future was JEngineering. This company, employing roughly 6,500 staff in Japan and 2,500 elsewhere (including the USA, the UK, Sweden and increasingly China), manufactures a number of specialised industrial products, notably production-line robots, industrial motors and chip-mounters. Its main customers are firms in the automotive and food processing sectors. In recent years high costs of labour and materials have created substantial pressures to shift production to China, in common with so many other industrial firms. The reality of competition in this area of manufacturing is that even highly sophisticated and technically specialised production lines, such as those at JEngineering, can be dismantled from domestic plants and rebuilt in new, lower-cost overseas sites, with surprising ease.

The cost pressures on JEngineering were severe, meaning that the firm had to redouble its efforts to reduce costs and increase staff productivity.

The managers that we interviewed indicated that significant human resource changes had been made (starting in 2001), including several of the measures (plus associated managerialist rhetoric) identified above. As one senior manager commented, 'instead of the traditional Japanese seniority-based promotion system we have been shifting to a merit system in that young people who are talented and show good performance can get promoted earlier than they used to'. Performance-related pay has also become a much larger part of the remuneration package for salaried staff.

In terms of formal restructuring exercises, the company went through a change programme known as 'WIN21', which, as the name suggests, was designed to improve performance in the new century. In a way similar to many of our sample US and UK firms, however, WIN21 was swiftly followed by another change programme (which in turn apparently will be the launch pad for additional restructuring schemes):

In 2002 we were about to finish our mid-term programme called WIN21. The target year for the programme was 1999 to 2002. [...] And we are now into the successor programme called WIN21 Plus with the target fiscal years from 2003 to 2005. And now we're in the process of establishing the system, of a kind of new system based on slimmed down personnel, increased production and performance, and flattened management systems. So [...] by the end of WIN21 Plus target period we are going to strengthen those new systems by carrying out several projects. (*Kachō*, General Affairs and Personnel Division)

He went on to describe the nature and goals of these systems in terms of their potential impact on personnel and performance:

The board sets the company-wide target in terms of the slimming down of personnel. And based on the company-wide target each business unit has its own target, and in order to support these targets we provide the more efficient information infrastructure, because that is the infrastructure to support individual's performance so that each employee can raise their activities. So one of the goals is to increase the per capita activity. [...] And at the same time we are reviewing our personnel system in order to draw out the best of each employee and to motivate them, so these are our long-term goals. [...] Suppose there is a person in the position of *kachō*, the *kachō*'s salary itself consists of three parts, and the first part is the role-based pay and so the role in this case means responsibility or scope of responsibility, so there are six grades of the scope of responsibility so which means the heavier the responsibility the more he gets paid for that role. And secondly, the second part is the performance-based pay, and that performance-based pay is reviewed every year and that pay is calculated based on a person's performance in the last fiscal year. And the third part is the position-based pay, so if the person is *kachō*, there is a base payment for a *kachō*. So for example there are two gentlemen [both] with the position of *kachō* and those *kachō*s [receive] number three *kachō* [level] position-based pay. However, if they have a different scope of responsibility or [display] different performance [levels] in the last fiscal year their pay may be different because of the two parts of the pay. So in an extreme case there is going to be a difference of one hundred thousand Japanese yen per month between a best performing *kachō* and a least performing *kachō*. [...] The average salary, monthly salary of a *kachō* is half a million Japanese yen – five hundred thousand Japanese yen. So the difference of one hundred thousand that means 20 per cent. (*Kachō*, General Affairs and Personnel Division)

Changes to the payment and promotion systems had ramifications for the motivation and morale of white-collar staff. The *kachō*s we interviewed described the need for a new employment relationship, involving possibly a more proactive HR department, able to provide educational and developmental opportunities to middle managers whereby 'in order to give full play to their ability inside the company we have to keep reviewing [the] human resources system so that each individual can have a vision for themselves'. However, the provision of such 'developmental opportunities' was likely to be affected by contextual factors both inside and outside the firm, notably the poor trading conditions, financial weakness, wider spans of control, tougher workloads and stricter performance evaluation:

In the last several years we have seen the scope of responsibility for each manager has dramatically increased or expanded. [...] As the project team increases so there's no doubt that the manager's volume of work increases.
Q   *And so does that mean they're working harder or longer hours?*
Yes, to tell you the truth, managers work longer hours than before, and including myself, I work longer hours than before. And our systems have been under scrutiny and under a lot of change, so these two or three years are going to be very tough for all of us. And so some companies are shifting their production base overseas and our company is also dividing some manufacturing units into separate companies. Therefore our work itself is increasing in its complexity and we have to seek ways to do our work more effectively and efficiently. So we are still in the process, on the inner process of trial and error, so the coming two or three years' time is going to be very difficult for us. (*Kachō*, General Affairs and Personnel Division)

The above extracts from our interview with a manager from the General Affairs and Personnel division reflect the various problems facing

Japanese managerial employees in an era of new organisational forms. Although we were unable to get firm figures on this aspect of the restructuring story, the interviews at JEngineering gave a strong sense that wages and bonuses had not grown significantly to compensate for the greatly ratcheted hours, effort and responsibilities. Although the Japanese salarymen in our study generally agreed that job security still exists, this was one of the few beneficial facets of their working lives in this era of cost control and entitlement cuts (see Iida and Morris 2008). Given the very limited exit options for mid-career managers, the impact of restructuring was possibly felt in an even more acute form for Japanese middle managers than for their UK or US counterparts. Moreover, it is clear from our interviews just how much personal sacrifice salarymen make to their firms (which in general is probably more than that made by Westerners to their companies). The flipside to this situation is that once restructuring is broached and the psychological contract is altered, the possibilities for anxiety and resentment among Japanese staff are possibly greater than those in less intense employment relationships. It can be dangerous therefore for Japanese companies to ignore these commitments, for restructuring can lead to the potential loss of personal identity for salarymen. This is possibly one of the reasons why suicide is such a serious problem in Japan, and why middle managers are particularly at risk of it (see Chapter 6).

JSteel: 'Many ranks and layers just flattened'

JSteel is a very large steel corporation with six major production and treatment works across Japan and one in China. The particular works that we visited was built in 1901 and is a major part of Japan's industrial heritage. Over the years the JSteel group has been through several changes of ownership structure through mergers and reorganisations. In keeping with trends in the steel industry elsewhere, employment numbers at the steelworks we visited have dropped steadily, from a high point of 50,000 staff in 1940, to 42,000 in 1966, to 10,000 in 1991, to 3,400 when we first visited the corporation in 2004. Output volumes of crude steel and finished steel products have also slowly decreased until recent times. In 1940 the works produced just 2.1 million tonnes of crude steel. The works' role in the post-war reconstruction of Japan is shown by the spectacular growth in output, peaking at 9 million tonnes in 1967 before slowly falling (particularly after 1973) to just under 6 million tonnes in 1984, bottoming-out at just 2.7 million tonnes in 1987 before rising to today's level of just under 4 million tonnes. Given this output, the huge reduction in headcount indicates an enormous increase in productivity. For the JSteel group as a whole, employment across all sites stands today at around 23,000, with this also representing a dramatic decrease since the post-war era.

In its heyday the JSteel works we visited was organised in an almost military fashion. Managers and workers were arranged into a very rigid bureaucracy with a tall management structure, large divisional staffing numbers and little or nothing in the way of cross-functional cooperation. The growth in productivity in the process of steelmaking inevitably placed pressures on both the number of employees and the way they are organised.

The discussion with managers at JSteel revealed how the company had reduced its layers of management from five to just three in 1997, and the number of divisions from sixteen to eleven in 2001, making cuts to managerial employment as part of both reorganisations. Both these changes are very much in keeping with the picture for large firms in the UK and the USA. In common with the experiences of Anglo-Saxon firms which have been through similar reorganisations, removing these layers has made promotion much tougher than before. As positions are taken out of the hierarchy, fewer managers can be promoted into these positions. It could be argued that this competition is even tougher in Japan than in Western countries. The Japanese peculiarity of seniority-based pay and promotion, despite some significant modifications (Matanle 2003; Watanabe 2000), remains a major element in firms' human resource decision-making. Even in JSteel, one of the most extensively reorganised firms in our study, new staff still had to fulfil seniority-based criteria before even being considered for promotion. Again, cuts were made in particular to the administration management track, while many of the production management positions were less affected. We asked a JSteel middle manager:

Q   *If somebody joins [JSteel] at twenty-two as a university graduate, how long would it take them to become [a] first level manager?*
Seven years.
Q   *And group manager?*
Double – fourteen to fifteen years. [...] It depends on the person. It's a very difficult question. More than ten years. [A group manager would be] twenty-seven, twenty-six years of age. Not all the newly employed workers are

promoted to this level. This organisation chart shows the challenge to be a general manager, a long way. [...] If you compare the number of divisions they are drastically reduced. The number of divisions [was] sixteen in 1994. [In] 2001 – eleven. The number of production divisions is constant, unchanged. So the staff department divisions have reduced dramatically. (Group Manager, General Administration Division)

On top of these cuts, recruitment has also been severely curtailed and over 150 managers had left the business in the five years prior to our first research visit, mostly through early retirement, and with some through transfer to other 'external' business units in the JSteel group. These external units are typically engaged in consultancy and environmental clean-up activities. We met a middle manager in one of these units during a return visit to JSteel in 2006. He had served in the steel-making side of the business since 1977, but now found himself in charge of a subsidiary environmental research division. He provided his views on the main changes to the employment system during his career. Once again, the similarities between his experiences and others in mature industries in the UK and the USA were obvious, particularly the reference to the speed at which new graduates are expected to 'mature' even when the options available for promotion are not so widespread. He practically replicated the view of a UKAuto HR manager, quoted in Chapter 4, when he suggested:

As far as the graduate is concerned, once upon a time maybe 80 per cent could get that very high level. But nowadays, as far as I know, really just 40 per cent or so. So in that sense the competition is getting very intense. [...] [New graduate intake staff] are expected to mature very quickly, and that's a very sad fact. (Vice-President, Environment Research Centre)

A crucial difference from the UKAuto situation, however, is that despite the rhetoric of flattening layers in order to speed up promotion for the most able staff members, younger staff are generally not rising up the ranks quickly:

Q   *So the kachōs are younger than they used to be?*
Yes, but the *kachō*, you know, it's very complicated – this *kachō* is just a manager, not a senior manager for the payment level. And as for the staff there's only group leader and managers and [staff ...]. So you can see many ranks and layers just flattened.
Q   *But does that mean people can get promoted quicker now, in quicker time?*
I don't think so, no.

Q   *So OK that's one potential thing, the other potential thing is that promotion becomes more difficult?*

Yeah, you can say that, because the position itself, the number has decreased. [...] For the general manager, once upon a time there was almost twenty or something when I entered this company. But nowadays maybe ten or something like that, that's all merged. (Vice-President, Environment Research Centre)

JSteel has obviously been strongly affected by the cost pressures associated with increased competition and the traditional problem of overcapacity in the sector. Some relief is being provided by China's seemingly insatiable demand for steel, but JSteel also faces competition there. JSteel had moved some of its production to a new plant in China, although it kept a very significant manufacturing presence in Japan, which is hardly surprising given the massive sunk costs in the physical infrastructure and employee skills of its several Japanese operations. In short, JSteel had made major alterations to its managerial employment structure, with these alterations suggesting substantial 'Americanisation'; although the company certainly continued with the policy of long-term employment and internal skills development.

Of all our Japanese case companies JSteel was the firm where the pressures to reorganise appeared the greatest, and management's concern to deal with the crisis the most obvious. Although when researching in the Far East it can sometimes be difficult to ascertain just how conversant are interviewees with the goals of the research, in the case of JSteel, however, managers were very familiar with the issues we wished to explore. On arrival for one meeting at JSteel we were presented with a five-page English-language document that had been prepared for us, entitled 'Measures for Strengthening International Competitiveness'. The outline steps on the first page read:

1. *Downsizing the Multilayered Management System*
2. *Revamping the Salary Package*

In the JSteel case, the reduction of employment numbers has taken place over a long period and is intimately linked with broader structural and technological changes in the industry (which necessitate upgrading of capacity while also reducing headcount):

When I entered this company, [JSteel] had 25,000 employees in those days. So including operators and staff and management, about 25,000. But today just 2,600, so one tenth [of the headcount].

Q   *Are they producing similar output?*
Same yeah, almost the same number, the same tonnage. [...] Fifteen years ago
or something you know, we had two blast furnaces but now we have only one.
In that sense the amount of the pig iron was reduced, not to say in half, but to
say 60 or 70 per cent compared to once upon a time. [...] So we are now
having approximately four million metric tonnes of products and that is
almost the same. Once upon a time maybe five million metric tonnes a year,
or such kind of thing, so not so much difference. (Vice-President, Environment
Research Centre)

Against this broader, long-term background of shrinking numbers, a
more direct set of changes had occurred, involving de-layering in particular. This manager, a lifetime JSteel employee, spoke of the major
changes that took place around 1995:

What was the trigger, you know, the reason for the change? So from our eyes
it's a kind of restructuring. In those days the American style of restructuring
was very, very popular within Japanese large companies. And in addition the
Internet and such kind of IT, information technology, with this progress, they
gain the information as quickly as possible. And so the flattening is very good
they thought in that way. So in addition, even today it's said that the productivity in Japan, the productivity of white-collar workers is not so good. So
maybe this is part of top management thought, that by reducing the position
or making it flat then they can improve the productivity. (Vice-President,
Environment Research Centre)

However, in describing some of the impacts of employment reductions
and de-layering, some reservations were raised by this senior manager
amid a spirited defence of the *kachō* and his role and expertise. He
suggested that the middle manager ought to remain a highly valued
member of staff – one who can perform specialist tasks and conduct
problem-solving investigations that are largely beyond the capacity of
blue-collar workers. He suggested further that cutbacks can result in
harmful losses of skill and expertise:

My view [of] the *kachō* or manager, senior manager or manager, [is that] the
numbers are reduced greatly because many departments are gathered together
or sections gathered together. [...] Mainly they are the graduate of the
university, say electrical or in my case metallurgy or say construction or
such kind of things. My point is they have the, not so much experience, but
they have the logical way of thinking or specialised education. So I think that's
very important, it's very important they have the experience in case of an

emergency if this happens. Or they were lucky enough to have the chance to start up some equipment, say modernisation. [...] So in that case they have to think about the design, original design or construction itself or have a chance to know about the newest machine or such kind of things. So such kind of experience is very, very important. [...] Also middle management from time to time change their position [and] by doing it they have the network of other divisions or other departments, people, or how to make the management to achieve some project, or how to get more money from the Financial division. And so that kind of experience is also very, very important I think. (Vice-President, Environment Research Centre)

Our experienced JSteel manager suggested that, over the years, the increased use of IT systems led to the circumvention of traditional, bureaucratic line management, meaning that the expertise of middle management was not always sought. Our informant was rather disappointed with this development:

But the one thing I am concerned about is something to do with the development of the Internet, or you know, email system. But once upon a time when we submit some document to a different department our management chief must make check, or in your country maybe signature, or making seal in Japanese case. But in the Internet or email this can, you know, see just the cc or such kind of things, so [it is] very quick. [...] So sometimes it goes very directly to the other department, so in that sense the experience of such kind of middle management value cannot be cultivated or cannot be used in such case. (Vice-President, Environment Research Centre)

Heavy workloads have always been a part of white-collar life in JSteel. Looking back over his career, this senior manager did not see an increase in hours of work, even though there was a definite widening of responsibility in recent years:

When we got to management we were told you are paid not by the hours but by the achievements. Or when [promoted to a] production line manager we were asked to act twenty-four hours [a day]. Because if something happened at midnight we'd have to do [something]. [...] I mean we've changed now. [...] Even the middle management should work just eight or ten hours, but I don't know that's very correct or not, I don't know. But basically we can say eight, ten hours. But in the case of the starting of the time, or say when the business is very, very difficult, or [meeting] a deadline for the project achievements, maybe not say twenty-four hours, but certainly twelve hours, or even Saturday, Sunday, that's very usual. (Vice-President, Environment Research Centre)

The steel industry has always been a very demanding and uncompromising sector (Bacon *et al.* 1995). The outsourcing of production to China noted by JSteel respondents would seem to support a traditional labour process interpretation of changes to working life in that the incessant drive for rationalisation and cost-cutting makes lower-skilled employees vulnerable to work degradation (Thompson 2003). Higher-skilled middle managers are also threatened by efficiency and cost-cutting drives, especially in white-collar administrative work. Once again, in many respects the story is similar to that reported in interviews we conducted at the matched case company in the UK, UKSteel. Industrial firms are responding to pressures by cutting high-cost labour and increasingly turning to lower-cost regions. The widespread movement of industry to China builds on the development reported some time ago in Ikeda's research into the auto industry: 'The low-wage economies of South East Asia and China are being integrated as part of an international subcontracting network, supplanting the rigid stratified structure within Japan.' (Ikeda 1998: 126; Morris *et al.* 2008). More recently Sako (2006: 71, 228) has noted how Matsushita has subcontracted large swathes of supply chain manufacturing to China and has used the threat of further offshoring to achieve union concessions in Japan.

In other words, Japanese companies' long-termist traditions in employment, finance and corporate governance, cannot insulate managerial or manual labour from changes associated with the transition of the country to a high-cost, mature economy. Macro changes in the global economy, notably the entry of millions of new, lower-cost workers from later-industrialising nations such as China and India onto world labour markets, place major pressures on Japan's traditional domestic manufacturing. In this longer-term context it is almost inevitable that Japanese workplaces will be forced to adapt to global restructuring pressures.

JUSBank: 'In Japanese companies they've got boys' jobs and girls' jobs'

There is, however, another source of change taking place which might have more immediate effects on the economy. Following the collapse of the 'bubble economy', the degree of foreign ownership of Japanese equities has soared to almost a fifth of the total traded on the Tokyo stock exchange (Witt 2006: 45). One might expect this heightened degree of Western ownership to lead to the exertion of greater Western influence over traditional Japanese practice. Moreover, as real estate prices have shrunk, Western, notably US, investors have flooded into the Japanese property market, and the Tokyo offices of US investment banks have been extremely busy in recent years. With this in mind, we conclude this chapter with a discussion of US-style employment in Japan, illuminated by the employment histories of two younger Japanese employees working in this sector.

We have so far concentrated on large-scale manufacturing and heavy industry sectors in Japan. Such cases have demonstrated many of the problems one might expect in mature, highly competitive industries affected for some time by overcapacity. Restructuring pressures have existed since at least the early 1990s (and considerably earlier in the case of JSteel) and the responses have mostly included early retirement, work intensification of middle managers and de-layering. Having said that, Japanese firms did not abandon their commitment to long-term employment, and, although career ladders were considerably tougher to climb than they once were, internal career development certainly still exists. Few *kachō*s or *gurūpuchō*s were seriously contemplating leaving their firms. This suggests continuity with traditional Japanese practice, in line with the findings of Jacoby (2005) and Witt (2006). The continuation of traditional career policies in large, traditional Japanese workplaces is understandable and broadly in line with our expectations.

However, there is an increasing diversity of employment in Japan, particularly as foreign firms and investors have increased their presence following the collapse of the bubble economy. Staff employed in the offices of US multinationals might well have a quite different view of restructuring and middle management work in large corporations. Such was the case with the final study we present here. We were fortunate to have the opportunity to interview two younger Japanese employees (both aged twenty-nine), one male and one female, who worked for JUSBank, the Tokyo office of a major US investment bank. Unlike most other case studies in this book, access to this organisation was not arranged via official intermediaries or direct contact with the company's HR department; both of these employees were instead introduced to us by a fellow graduate of the university attended by one of the authors. This was a fortunate occurrence as we had only one other female interviewee in our Japanese sample (at the City Government), very few younger managers, and were unable to secure access to any other financial services companies in Japan. We were also interested to see how the employment systems in place in a paradigmatic example of a firm from the highly liberal US environment, such as JUSBank, might differ from what we had seen at the other, far more conventional, Japanese firms. This final interview was conducted off company premises and outside of company time. During the interview the two employees frequently interjected and spoke over each other (n.b. overlapping speech is indicated by /). The first subject of conversation was the pair's career aspirations:

Q   *When you left university what were your ideas about getting a job and working for maybe a large company? Was it something you wanted to do?*

[...] My aspiration was, yeah, my career ideally was in a financial industry, as I studied economics, and also to be a translator. For me, the size of the company didn't really matter.

Q   *Why is that?*

Because I really think the size of the company doesn't mean anything. Actually, in fact, I wanted to work for a very small company because they can pay more attention to you. And, also, I really wanted to work for a company that I could build a relationship with. But, my first job was with the investment bank Nomura and they had about 10,000 people there and, yeah, they were very nice but I think the working environment was, yeah, I didn't have a good impression of an investment bank. I don't know why I'm working for an investment bank now. Then I worked for a very small research company and that was my ideal job, I think. Afterwards, I worked as a translator in a publishing company [abroad] and then I came back to Japan. Ever since, I have worked for [JUSBank].

Q   *So, you don't have the impression when you start working for a large company of wanting to stay there for the rest of your life?*

No. In large companies, you are usually assigned to one specific work [area], but in smaller companies you can do more. You are given more responsibility for many things and can choose the way that you want to work. But in a large company you have to be part of the machine.

Q   *So there's not much autonomy if you worked for a large company, Sumitomo or somebody? [...]*

There is to some degree. I'm sure that you can do what you like, but it's more restricted. [...] Usually in Japan what happens is [...] the company only take on new graduates and they don't take those people who worked previously. They don't want to train [them]. [...] I think that Japanese companies want to brainwash new graduates because they pay so much money, it's like their investment. So they want to make sure you're very clean, no background with other companies. Another thing is that in Japanese companies they've got boys' jobs and girls' jobs. Boys' jobs are real work, what you'd think of as a job. A girls' job is just administration. Paper work! Paper work, yeah. I mean the salary to start with is totally different. And also, the second thing is that you can't choose what job you want to apply for. You can choose which company to work for, but then you can't choose which department you want, because the human resources [department] control [that]. I found the system very strange, because someone who'd studied, I don't know, a financial background, may start doing something totally different, like human resources or receptionist. It's strange, very strange.

Q   *So, the Personnel department has a lot of power and tells you what to do. Is that right?*

Oh yeah, definitely.

Q   *And they basically pick the career they want you to do. Right?*

Yeah, definitely, particularly for women. But it's changing now though I think. But then, I interviewed a couple of new graduates, I was quite surprised, they didn't have a clue what to do or what they wanted to do. Many people just wanted to work for a big company; they didn't really care about what they would do.

Although there had been some recent change in employment systems and practices, the two young employees, both with considerable over-seas experience (one had a degree from a British university) still identi-fied plenty of 'traditional' Japanese features at JUSBank, and expressed their frustration with these. This was especially true with respect to sexism, authoritarianism and slowness of promotion. One of the main reasons the female employee quit her previous job at a highly presti-gious Japanese financial company was because of her 'unfair treatment as a woman'. She changed jobs because she hoped to be treated with greater respect in a US-owned bank (see Dore 2000: 62–3 for similar case scenarios). As she explains:

My previous company, the men do all the deals and the negotiation work, and the ladies just prepare the negotiation work. And also, calculations, taking phone calls …

Q   *So, women aren't considered to be people that could make deals or really work with clients, and really males do the serious work. Is that really true?*

It's changing a little bit.

Q   *In what way is it changing?*

It seems like paperwork is also important [laughter]. And many learn from paperwork, so sometimes, they know better than the men. Gradually the percentages change, and the ladies are able to go up a bit more than men and slowly the percentage gets stronger. [But] usually, in many Japanese companies they want to hire girls with a good figure and [who are] good looking, you know, what they call good looking because they know, or rather, they put pressure on these girls after thirty years. When they hit thirty they force them to leave, because they want to have a new girl, under thirty!/

Yeah, because these guys are spending, like, I don't know how many hours, like, fourteen hours a day in the company, they don't meet girls. So, in Japan, it's pretty common to meet and get married to someone who's in the same company./

But all these guys put pressure on girls. […] But then what happens is the girls might quit the job but then they still work in a different company and they're more independent, they don't get married straight away. Yeah, it's really changing.

Q   *So, when a woman reaches thirty, it is just assumed they will get married and leave their job, just not work? Is that still the assumption for women?*

It's changing, but yeah, it's still a conservative area. Definitely, in conservative companies.

Our interviewees both commented on the slowness of promotion in traditional Japanese companies, criticising senior managers who were perceived as self-serving, comfortable with their success and frequently unwilling to either support, or give way to, juniors:

Q   *So, in the large, old-fashioned Japanese companies, is it hard for young people to move upwards?*

That's true. There are many older people that are holding the positions already. And they already have the rights to order the young people. And also Japanese, maybe you know this, but for Japanese if you are one year older, you have to speak in a respectful manner. And that gives the older people authority too. So in any company, it's the same. If they are one year older, you have to show respect. You have to listen to that person, whatever the older person says.

Q   *And, so you have to be there a long time if you are going to move up in a company?*

Yes. Especially in the governmental company, if you are young. If you want to do something, you have to wait twenty, thirty or forty years.

Q   *But now, you're getting lots of people who don't want to do that anymore, who want to move around different companies, smaller companies, like yourself?*

Yes.

Q   *Is that more common now? Not to want to apply to work for these companies?*

Of course, especially people who have some kind of skill. They don't mind moving. And also, you are not worried that you might be unemployed.

Q   *So, we've seen it from the perspective of the older people in the larger companies, and they tell us that the old-fashioned lifetime employment system is still in place, but is struggling. They're reducing its importance. They say they want to sometimes allow skilled, talented people to move up the hierarchy quicker, but they are not really doing it.*

The problem is that the older people have already made money and they have all individual money. They don't have to change. Even if they're losing money, they don't care. Even if the company goes bankrupt, they already have enough money to live their life. But for young people, we don't have such assets, so many young people are trying to force them to change. There is a conflict between the older and the younger people.

Q   *So, would it be common among yourself and people of your age to have already had four or five employers? How many jobs might you have had when you get to the age of thirty? How many different companies have you worked for?*

For me, I've worked for four companies already.

Q   *And, that's quite common among your friends?*

Two is common. [...] Because many of my friends are afraid of moving. Because, quite often, younger people, twenty to thirty, are not experienced and if you move, your salary will go down. Also, you don't have the confidence that you can do another job …

Q   *Is it true, also, that company loyalty is seen as very important in Japan? If you move too often, or move at all, people think that you are disloyal?*

I heard that in Western companies, or in the States, HR look at how many companies you have had, and you are such a great person! But, in Japan, if you move too many times then the person is suspicious.

Q   *[…] So, where you are working now, obviously, it's an American-owned company, right? How different is this from a traditional Japanese company?*

Very different. One thing is that, if you are capable, the American company will give you full responsibility. But, if you are unsuccessful about what you are given, then you will be easily fired. In Japan, you won't be given any responsibility soon, even if you have the capability.

Q   *So, it's more competitive, more risky?*

We see more risk in working for a foreign company. More chance of being fired, but more chance of being successful, too. Because if you are in a Japanese company, many of the things you can't experience when you are young.

Q   *Do they have Western-style job titles, or do you have Japanese job titles – kachō, kakarichō, at [JUSBank]?*

No, no, no, no. It's like, 'consultant'.

Q   *[So] it's not like a Japanese company?*

No. Our group is doing quite good, so many people are coming in. Right now, real estate in Japan is quite hot, because interest rates are really low. Many foreign customers are trying to buy here. That's why a lot of people are going into the real estate business, probably almost double.

Q   *What is the working environment, the atmosphere like? Can you tell me about it?*

If you look at our group, everybody is really independent. They don't really care about what other people are doing. Whatever you are working on, you just do.

Q   *So, no teamwork?*

Depends on the project. If it's a really big project, then everybody works together. Also, when we work together, it's really close to each other. And, when we are doing projects, we have to keep secret, don't talk about anything.

Q   *I see. A very individual working relationship.*

Yes.

Q   *Is it connected to pay? Performance-related pay?*

Yes. Performance-related pay. When I was in the other company, every month the company would go to Tsukuji together, have dinner together, drink together and the younger ones have to serve the beer, and that's also part of the work. Actually it's not part of the work, but it is like part of the work.

Q   *I understand. But now, you don't have to do that here?*

Just, like some party together. But it is not work people, only for enjoyment.

Q   *And so, is there a bonus system, how is it arranged?*

There is a bonus. If I thought of my previous company, they gave me a bonus, but especially for the young people, it's reduced. That was one of the reasons I quit my previous job. When they would give me a bonus, they would say, 'I have not deserved a bonus'. [Laughter]. But I think that I was told by other people that they were told the same thing. So, that's pretty common right now, particularly as the economic situation is really bad.

Q   *So, can you tell me what it was like when you decided to leave the previous company? It must be hard – the labour market in Japan is different from Western labour markets. Did you know you had another job to go to? Tell me the story of how you left, if that's OK?*

Yes. My previous company was good for me, really different kinds of experience. Because, it was a really small company, I almost had to manage everything by myself. So, also, if you don't work for a company for one year, the next company won't take you. You're a quitter! So, I decided to stay there for at least a year. Soon after, around nine months after I started working in that company I started to look for a job. One reason is because of the company situation. The company was in the red for two years. Another reason is that the boss of the company was not reasonable. One day he would say one thing and the next day say another. Change the policy of the company, yes, but don't change one day then the next day! It was hard for me to follow the policy and it was not good for the customers! Because I have to say to a customer one week one thing and then another the next day.

Q   *So, what happened? One day you decided, 'I want to go'?*

No, I looked for a job, looked for a good position. [...] I was looking for other options at the same time and I found a good job, and I can speak a little bit of English, so I wanted to make use of my English as much as possible. And also my Japanese language. Also, I wanted to do something that is not routine. If I do the same thing every day, paperwork, computer, I won't enjoy it. At least I have communication [i.e. translation] skills, so I am looking for something that matches. Then I happened to find this position.

Q   *Can I ask you a bit about [JUSBank]. Do you think there is potential for you to develop and to stay a long time and move up the company?*

In that company, probably no. Because most of the people who are in a good position are native English speakers. Usually, not all. And also, [JUSBank] is a long-running and prestigious company, so you have to have a good back-ground. I don't know that I have it. And also, maybe, only one possibility is I can make a lot of money, make a successful deal. That's one opportunity. So, if I do that, it's possible.

Q   *I think, these days, in large Japanese companies, we've been told that they are reducing their graduate intake every year for the past ten years. Surely it must be hard for people leaving university at age twenty-two, twenty-three. What is it like for people leaving university now in Japan?*

This year it will be better, but many of my friends are still not working regularly, not full-time. This year we become thirty, but many of my friends are changing jobs, not satisfied with their jobs, still part-time or looking for a better position. The economic situation is bad. [...] So, I know that the young university graduates are struggling. They try hard, but they know that they cannot achieve their goal.

Q   *In your opinion, are young Japanese people interested in old-fashioned companies and the lifetime employment system? Do they want to leave university and work for Honda or Hitachi, become a salaryman and work there all their lives? Is that still an option?*

Actually, lifetime employment is good, because you are ensured that you are paid. But young people know that it is not possible.

Q   *Why is it not possible, is it too hard to get these jobs, too competitive?*
One thing is that many big companies are changing to not-lifetime. So, previously I'm sure that the contract said you are ensured lifetime, but I'm sure the current agreement will not say that. So, young people are not stupid!

The opinions of these two younger employees of JUSBank were more downbeat and critical than those of the *kachō*s and *buchō*s in the other companies. They were also more jaundiced about their own career prospects and those of their peers (which may be more of an age-related effect), but the image was created of an older generation which has benefited from the high-growth and bubble phases of the Japanese economy but had been reluctant to enable the younger generation also to benefit following the restructuring of hierarchies. The two younger interviewees were also much more strident than older managers in other firms in their view that lifetime employment has come to an end. Unfortunately we have only scratched the surface of this story, and there is a need for more research into the views of white-collar staff over different generations in Japan. However, our brief investigation into younger staff at a US-owned firm in Japan has broadly backed up the general argument about increased pressure on managerial labour, and suggests that further disruptions to traditional Japanese white-collar hierarchies and employment systems may take place. It also lends support to the critical interpretation of Japanese workplaces as being marred by sexism, bullying and authoritarian behaviour. Finally, it also suggests that Japanese institutions and administrative heritage have had little impact on the way in which this US investment bank has chosen to operate in Tokyo, although again we would need much more research evidence if we were to come to firm conclusions about this.

Conclusions

We will now briefly evaluate what we have found in our investigations of middle managers in Japan. Our evidence, despite some obvious differences relating to the long-term focus on employee development in Japan, was highly congruent with US and UK experiences – cost-cutting, de-layering, slower promotions, increased responsibility and more pressure and workload for middle managers. Of course, there is always the risk that Japanese employees will be less willing to divulge information, and will instead paint a simplistic, *tatemae*[13] picture. For example, the repeated references to the ageing workforce of Japan as an explanation for why firms have to change their employment structures were not always convincing. Cutting layers to speed up promotion was another classic *tatemae* explanation of de-layering. The *honne* view would be that promotion was actually taking longer after restructuring and in some cases not at all. This position was rarely volunteered to us (except by the two younger employees interviewed outside of company time and off company premises), although after a bit of pressing the *kachō*s and *buchō*s from the large Japanese firms did admit that their youngest *kachō*s were still around the same age as before. The need to develop 'engineering-only' career tracks did appear to be a more genuine attempt to tackle the problem of poor motivation, given the decline of upward mobility among *kachō*s or *kakarichō*s. On the other hand, we were not able to pursue more detailed investigations of this 'new' employment feature, and we were unable to determine whether people placed on these tracks benefit in any way, or whether they are simply trapped there. Bearing in mind the strong tendency for Japanese managers to ostracise 'difficult' characters, the new track could very well be a way of sidelining white-collar staff who are regarded as less cooperative than others and who do not take on the masses of extra responsibility and workload that people management entails.

When it came to work hours our middle managers were more open. Although the 'official line' often emerged – which referred to annualised working hours – when we asked managers more directly about their own personal hours, they were generally happy to discuss it in a more *honne* fashion (except in one interview in JElectronics when a younger *kachō* simply refused to tell us how many hours per week he worked, possibly because his superior was also in the room!). However, our data did contain important insights into the harsh working lives of middle managers in Japan, and the motivations for restructuring.

Although our analysis suggests that radical change has not occurred in Japanese firms, the combined impact of several smaller changes has brought about similar impacts on middle managers' working lives to those of their counterparts working in the UK and the USA. Jacoby

---

[13] For explanation of *tatemae* and *honne* please see footnote 1 on page 39 in Chapter 2.

(2005: 156) argues that 'there is evidence that a powerful new concern with minimising costs has taken hold in Japan, although as yet it has not changed fundamental business strategies'. Witt (2006) is also sceptical about the extent of change in Japan. While these analysts are correct to point out that the rhetoric and reality of financialisation have not penetrated nearly as far in Japan as they have in the USA and the UK, this is no real cause for celebration. Japanese organisations have always been tough and uncompromising working environments, and although many white-collar staff have enjoyed a range of robust and enduring entitlements since the war, these have always come at a huge cost to family life. The signs of this study, however, are that these costs are increasing as firms continue to exert cost-cutting pressures amid tougher international competition.

The effects of restructuring on middle managers were essentially similar to those of the USA and the UK. The varieties of capitalism literature (Hall and Soskice 2001; Whitley *et al.* 2003), while containing some very important insights into national economic differences, have not always described or explained this well, as the focus tends to be on the meso, institutional level, rather than that of the occupational and organisational experience of everyday employees. Although we would not dispute the nature of institutional embeddedness, or in the present case that restructuring pressures are refracted through a distinctly Japanese prism, we would argue that the end results of restructuring on employees are essentially similar, regardless of institutional context. Ultimately the economic pressures of global competition are transmitted from the macro and meso levels of the economy to everyday workforce experience at the micro level. Today's high-pressure corporations provide little scope for employee resistance to work intensification. In Japan the scope for resistance is even less than in the USA and the UK. The varieties of capitalism literature, therefore, while providing a useful counterweight to the often specious arguments of mainstream globalisation theorists, fails to adequately describe and account for the motive force of capitalism and its incessant demand for greater output and cost control. These intense pressures can seriously threaten employees' livelihoods and well-being, and this concern, in our view, is more relevant than endless academic debates over variation or convergence in business systems. Japan is indeed unlikely to converge with American employment, financial or innovation systems, and Japan will always maintain certain management and organisational traditions; however, global pressures for restructuring have very similar impacts on the realities of white-collar working life across the OECD nations, and this appears to be far more important.

In the years immediately preceding the 2008 global downturn, Japan's general macroeconomic climate and the performance of many of its firms had improved, but this had come at a major cost to employees. The working hours of Japanese middle managers are extremely long and the performance pressures are uncompromising. One area of solace for over-worked middle managers is that seniority-based pay and lifetime employment have largely remained in place, and we found few complaints over job security. If Japanese firms were able to combine this long-termism with a reduction of authoritarianism and an increase in hires among whom to share the massive workloads then Japanese workplaces may become less harsh. Hypothetically this may even lead to improved performance as the operational straightjacket placed on Japanese employees becomes loosened. However, it is debatable as to just what percentage of any improvement in Japan's economy could be attributed to firm restructuring, for as Froud *et al.* (2000: 771) argue, much depends on the macro context, with decisions around corporate change and the results of change being rooted in much larger economic domains, such as the location of plant, availability of investment capital, changing customer fashions, etc.

To reiterate, the Japanese story of firm restructuring does not fit well with the Lazonick and O'Sullivan (2000) 'downsize and distribute' explanation. Shareholder value logic is still relatively marginal to Japanese corporate life and, as Froud *et al.* argue (2006), remains a loose rhetoric which means different things to different stakeholders. Although Japanese firms do need to please capital markets more than they used to, the key reason for restructuring lies in management's desire to keep the firm competitive in highly uncompromising markets. The end results are therefore similar to those of corporate experience in the West; that is, fewer jobs and entitlements, greater cost control and the extension of responsibilities and working time for surviving staff. Although the Japanese response to economic slowdown has been more measured and less harsh than in the USA or the UK, Japan's firms are also 'doing more with less', just like their Anglo-Saxon counterparts. Baumol *et al.*'s 'dirty little secret' of downsizing (2003) applies just as much to Japan as to the United States. In all three countries the root cause of change is cost pressures. Even the optimistic account of the UK by White *et al.* (2004: 178) admits this openly. Despite the widespread calls from market analysts for Japanese firms to throw lifetime employment and seniority-based employment aside, they now appear wise not to have done this. The technical performance of Japanese companies remains hugely impressive, and this is still based on the long-term commitment model of employment, which for decades has been one of the bases of their competitive strength. Moreover, top executives in Japan are still not paid excessive bonuses/share options as there is not the same market for corporate control or executive talent as exists in the UK and the USA. Japanese workplaces exact extremely heavy demands on staff, but at least there is a strong degree of loyalty shown by the company in return for these sacrifices. This is something that many of the US or UK firms in our study could learn from.

On the other hand, tougher times mean a harsher climate for middle managers and other staff. Not everyone can cope with this new environment, and in Japan the end result for those who have been the most seriously affected can be tragic. The widespread use of bullying, intimidation and humiliation as management tools in Japan has had horrific consequences (and the extremely high suicide rate in Japan is testimony to this). Given traditional gender roles which put huge pressure on married men to provide for the family, and the culture of shame at large in society, the unpleasant personal results of job loss associated with corporate restructuring can be far worse in Japan than in Western contexts. There is also another element that we touched on in the automotive case studies above but which requires greater research – the use of *keiretsu* firms as a buffer to protect permanent employment in the parent company. We know much less about the smaller firms in Japan, where plant closures and compulsory redundancies are said to be far more common than in the household-name firms with their thousands of employees.

Our case studies confirm that, despite restructuring, several traditional and harsh features of Japanese corporate life remain in place. Heavy-handed authoritarianism, extremely slow promotion for younger staff, severe hierarchical mentalities, arbitrary management decisions, weak unions, mistreatment of workers and the restriction of female employees all remain serious problems that Japanese companies appear unwilling to address. Younger staff, especially younger female members, argue powerfully that their talents are being wasted in conservative companies.

6 | *Fighting back? Addressing the human costs of management restructuring*

We do need to know how to cooperate with The Organization but, more than ever, so do we need to know how to resist it.

(Whyte, 1960: 17)

Our interviews with middle managers in large firms across three countries contained a range of interpretations of the changing nature of white-collar working life. Yet despite clear differences between firm type, industry sector and the institutional frameworks of the three societies, we were struck by the similarity of so much of their economic and corporate experiences. While it would be wrong to assert that the changes wrought on large organisations since the 1990s have been universally unfavourable to salaried managers, there is very strong evidence to suggest that the working lives of mid-level managerial employees are considerably more pressured and possibly more insecure than they once were. The payoffs received by some, in terms of higher salaries and bonuses, wider responsibilities and more interesting and rewarding work, may to a certain extent have offset these losses, but the overall feeling of being overwhelmed in work while the traditional promotional ladder has been largely removed was a major and widespread finding. Our findings mostly support the words of Burke and Cooper (2000: 12), in that 'middle managers are angry, depressed and tired'.

Presenting the initial findings of our work at conferences and seminars while writing this book we were frequently asked about the sustainability of these practices. Can employers continue to enforce cutbacks and raise expectations in this manner? Can the working tasks of middle managers be continually and progressively expanded? What are the risks, in terms of alienating or 'burning out' staff? Within this context of a changing macroeconomic climate, this concluding chapter draws together the various strands in the book and connects the findings more closely with our understanding of the contemporary middle management labour process. In so doing, it analyses the successes and failures of company reform measures, discusses whether senior managers had any alternatives to the change processes they carried out, and considers whether there is scope for middle managers to resist the harshest effects of the new organisational ideology. We begin our conclusion by considering in more detail the impact of stress and overwork, problems which were common among the middle managers in our study.

The human costs of change: Overwork, stress and anxiety

We have observed many instances at a micro level of how corporate restructuring can cause overwork, stress and anxiety. The macro figures are equally disturbing. The UK's Health and Safety Executive estimates that the annual total cost to the economy from work-related ill-health is between 7.6 and 11.6 billion UK pounds.[1] A survey of members of the UK's Chartered Management Institute claims that managers typically work forty unpaid days a year, and around 70 per cent of the 1,500 managers surveyed claimed that the sheer volume of work and long hours mean they spend less time exercising and keeping fit.[2] Other figures from the HSE[3] suggest that stress, depression, or anxiety (almost a third of all causes of work absence) are to blame for the loss of around 10 million working days per year. Indeed over half a million people in Britain suffer from stress, anxiety or depression (Health and Safety Executive 2005: 9).

Although there is a decline in the number of days lost in the more recent figures, given our micro-level observations we would not suggest that this marks a major improvement; organisations do not appear to be ameliorating successfully the potentially harmful effects of restructuring. Such is the scale of psychological illness in Britain that work by the economist Richard Layard at the London School of Economics has

---

[1] UK Health and Safety Executive (2004) *Interim update of the 'Costs to Britain of Workplace Accidents and Work-Related Ill-Health'*, Sudbury, HSE Books, available at: www.hse.gov.uk/statistics/pdf/costs.pdf
[2] 'Pay trends pointers show mixed fortunes', *The Daily Telegraph*, 21 February 2008.
[3] UK Health and Safety Executive website: www.hse.gov.uk/statistics/tables/swit1.htm

argued for a radical new approach to this problem, involving allocating far greater levels of funding in the National Health Service to expand its capacity for psychological treatment (Layard *et al.* 2006; see also Glyn 2006: 178–80). Layard's report argues that the huge costs associated with expanding the capacity of the NHS in treatment and prevention of psychological distress would be rapidly offset by a reduction in days lost to stress, depression and anxiety.

Work-related anxieties can spill over into the home, contributing to family conflicts, especially in dual-career households when parents, for example, may clash over who is making the greater sacrifices at work in order to care for the children, or who is cutting back on family time to survive in uncompromising workplaces. Career parents can feel that family demands have made them less able to deliver effectively at work; for example, submitting reports late or to a poor standard, skipping and rescheduling meetings, and still not seeing enough of their children (Bunting 2004; Hochschild 2003; Wajcman 1998).

In 1999, the US Bureau of Labor Statistics claimed that white-collar workers account for the majority of cases of occupational stress.[4] In a detailed survey published in the same year, on occupational stress and ill-health in the USA, the National Institute for Occupational Safety and Health (NIOSH), reported that 40 per cent of US workers describe their jobs as 'very or extremely stressful'.[5] Moreover, NIOSH presented findings that suggest cases of stress- and anxiety-related illnesses, result-ing in time away from work, rose significantly, from 4,409 in 1998 to 5,659 in 2001. The NIOSH report suggested that stress and anxiety-related illness are 'much more severe than the average injury or illness', with an average case involving as many as twenty-five days away from work.[6] Indeed, measuring the impact of anxiety and depression in terms of working days lost does not explain the real social damage that such afflictions cause to sufferers and their colleagues and families.

---

[4] US Department of Labor, *Monthly Labour Review*, 14 October 1999: http://stats.bls.gov/opub/ted/1999/oct/wk2/art03.htm
[5] US National Institute for Occupational Safety and Health, Publication No. 99–101 (1999): *STRESS … at Work*: www.cdc.gov/niosh/stresswk.html
[6] US National Institute for Occupational Safety and Health, Publication No. 2004–146 (2004): *Worker Health Chartbook 2004*, Chapter 2: *Fatal and Nonfatal Injuries, and Selected Illnesses and Conditions*: www2a.cdc.gov/NIOSH-Chartbook/ch2/ch2-1.asp#anxiety

In Japan, the starkest result of organisational restructuring can be seen in the high rates of suicide, at around 30,000 per year (McCann *et al.* 2004: 41). Lamar (2000) reported that there has been a sharp increase recently in suicides relating to financial problems, and that middle-aged men are the social group at the highest risk. Lamar (2000: 528) noted that: 'Police officials said this was because they were most vulnerable to corporate restructuring.' Although suicide is, of course, at the very extreme end of the range of impacts of restructuring, evidence of anxiety brought on by organisational change programmes was common in our interviews. This is hardly surprising given the tough demands made on contemporary white-collar managers following change measures. This is not to say, however, that organisational change need be so painful (Burke and Cooper 2000: 13). We suggest instead that senior management could and should address the issues of overwork and stress, and the personal damage that restructuring can cause.

Although it has some obvious limitations (see Chapter 2), Bravermanian labour process theory, we argue, is well suited to explain the increasing pressure and intensity in white-collar managerial work. It is hard to see a reversal of these developments unless a major rethink takes place at top management level. Organisational reforms involving flattening hierarchies, devolving authority or even democratising the workplace – which ought to be a welcome change from the culture of fear that persisted in many traditional workplaces (Starkey and McKinlay 1994) – have actually brought about a schism between middle and senior management in terms of work and its reward. As we argue below, this schism has dangerous implications for the breakdown of collegiality and goodwill among white-collar workers. Many of our respondents bemoaned the lack of fairness in their organisations: they felt isolated from other managerial levels and were unhappy about the absence of recognition for work and personal sacrifice. These grievances can have serious repercussions for the performance of firms, and we suggest below that senior management would be well advised to consider ways in which to rebalance the organisation in such a way that middle managers' working lives are not so pressured and intensified.

A serious problem that our research identified was the sidelining of those who had taken time out from work, especially when the cause of absence has been stress-related illness. There still appears to be a stigma attached to admitting that work pressure might be unbearable. This unforgiving, 'macho' culture appears to be alive and well in contemporary organisations. We would suggest that its influence is harmful and short-sighted, as it can threaten employees' health, well-being and dignity, in return for uncertain gains to the organisation. Constantly driving employees forward under duress may not be a sensible way to motivate staff in the long term, and can easily result in staff feeling alienated from, and resentful towards, senior management and the complex, often unrealistic, goals of the organisation. Although it is tempting for academic observers to offer suggestions as to how companies might be run in a more sensible, humane fashion (for example, Cascio 2002a), our broader analysis of the economic and ideological drivers behind this overwork culture unfortunately lead us to pessimistic conclusions as to the likelihood of genuine change in middle managers' favour. It is to an exploration of these drivers that we now turn.

The modern corporation: Increased pressure, heightened tension

Earlier chapters discussed the extensive debates over changes to organisational form. Now might be a good time to take stock of where we have come in our analysis. Our data suggests that organisational change has been considerable in the three countries studied, although it has not always been radical. We argue that change is best understood as a reflection of the general intensification of labour processes, an intensification that flows from the broader rationalisation pressures of contemporary capitalism. Of course, organisational change is nothing new. As Kumar notes (2005: 33–52), many 'post-industrial society' analysts and their forebears predicted the end of hierarchical organisational forms as early as the 1950s, including anticipating the contraction of middle management. The bureaucratic pyramid does have limitations, but its time is far from over. Firms remain very hierarchical (including successful ones) in our sample, but company performance depends on a very wide range of factors, not simply on organisational form, as some reformist authors would suggest. As we have argued elsewhere (McCann *et al*. 2008: 347):

[S]hareholder value is an important, but not the sole, indicator of firm performance. Organisational success and the choice of which production units to restructure depends crucially on the competitiveness of products and services as well as more mundane issues such as the location of physical resources.

Mainstream business change analysts repeatedly overstate the importance of appropriate organisational design for delivering performance. Regular efforts are made to change organisational forms but, by themselves, such alterations cannot lead to 'step-changes' of performance for giant firms in crowded, mature industry sectors with mediocre financial returns (Froud *et al.* 2006: 95–8). Baumol *et al.* (2003: 265–7) conclude their book with a similar observation. They claim that organisational forms are less important than product markets, and that downsizings (and upsizings) are closely related to downturns (and upturns) in product sales. However, this rather sanguine view of the impact of change leads them towards a rather conservative conclusion that probably understates the traumas associated with organisational restructuring. While Baumol *et al.* and Froud *et al.* are quite right to argue that downsizing has not been nearly as extensive as is popularly thought, their books mostly examine macro-level financial, employment and strategy issues. We have attempted, instead, to look *inside* the firms – at the micro-level beliefs, experiences and interpretations of managers themselves. This internal, personal view has illuminated a far wider set of problems than those allowed for by Baumol and colleagues, notably in regard to issues of insecurity, anxiety and stress.

Our fundamental argument is this: our observations of thirty large organisations across three countries suggest there have been widespread moves towards flatter, less hierarchical, but more complex organisational systems with more group work and more responsibility for surviving middle managers. But these changes have been limited in their ability to induce major performance enhancements. Despite claims made in the more mainstream literature, these changes by no means amount to a paradigm shift towards a 'Knowledge Intensive Economy' or the 'Network Enterprise'. Instead, what we find is a concerted intensification of managerial labour within flatter, yet still bureaucratic, firms. The ever-expanding demands placed on white-collar employees are part of a much longer-term trend of the rationalisation of labour in the face of tougher performance pressures emanating from the growing ferocity of international competition and the slower growth of mature OECD economies. As such, our view is highly compatible with the broad thesis of Braverman, but applied to managerial, as opposed to blue-collar and craft, occupations. While Braverman's de-skilling thesis clearly does not apply to middle managers – indeed, the contrary is more accurate – his wider observations regarding the rationalisation pressures exerted on large organisations by the driving down of costs associated with large firms in late capitalism, are strongly supported by the evidence of this study. Other neo-Marxist writers point to similar conclusions, but applied to staff further down the working hierarchies (Thompson 2003; Jenkins 2007). Indeed, the travails of middle managers are intimately connected with those of front-line supervisors and workers – organisational pressures to work harder, smarter and on a wider range of tasks permeate many levels of employment. Beynon *et al.* (2002: 234, 250–1) suggest that the added costs brought on by the necessity of increasing the skill levels of some staff (which would include middle managers) can be offset by employing larger numbers of lower-cost and/or contract workers (the so-called 'Babbage principle'). In tandem, shifting higher-skilled work onto lower-paid staff is another widespread tactic for realising this broad employment-cost rationalisation strategy (Beynon 2002: 234, 250–1).

The changes carried out in our case organisations have led to increased work pressures on middle managers in return for greater responsibilities, higher-skilled roles and, in some cases, increased pay. Contrary to the widespread view of middle managers as a barrier to change that must be eradicated (middle managers as timeservers, penpushers, plodders or men in grey suits) we were generally impressed by the career stories of surviving middle managers, who mostly appeared highly motivated and able individuals trying to cope with a barrage of change measures and increased performance monitoring from above, alongside substantial pressures from below.

This depressing picture raises many important questions not only for our analysis but also for corporate management practice in general. Two in particular stand out. Firstly, does it have to be this way – or is there a contemporary argument for 'organisational choice' (Trist *et al.* 1962)? Secondly, rationalisation of costs and pressuring of labour has been ongoing for many decades – can this continue indefinitely? We attempt to answer these questions in the remainder of this section.

First of all, it is tempting to argue that firms could, to use a popular phrase from the lexicon of corporate social responsibility, 'do well by doing good'. Although intense global competitive pressures are certainly real, nothing is inevitable. Companies' response to pressure does not have to mean squeezing staff. Some of the modifications made to labour process theory (e.g. by Burawoy 1979; Edwards 1979) have involved a more sophisticated and thus less mechanical, direct and deterministic account of how valorisation is translated into work intensification and degradation. Rather than applying constantly upgraded performance targets and appraisals, increased performance might come instead from easing the workloads and pressure for important and valuable staff. Organisations are in danger of wasting their middle management talent by pushing too hard. Many employees have internalised the argument that there is no alternative, given the gravity of international competitive pressures. This uncritical acceptance of the status quo needs challenging. To improve the condition of middle management working life what is needed is not more design-tinkering, such as career coaches and culture-change programmes, or carrot-dangling, such as performance-related bonuses. Instead a more fruitful way forward is for senior managers to confront the long-hours culture, effect genuine increases in autonomy and bring about an *increased sharing of workload* by hiring more mid-level managers.

Some analysts claim that the best-run firms actually do treat their workers with more dignity, and gain competitive advantage from doing so. A popular example would be the budget carrier Southwest Airlines, which (supposedly) manages to run cheap flights without cutting employment costs down to the bone, and has also delivered excellent stock-market returns in the process (Pfeffer 1995/2005: 96–7). Bunting (2004: 94–101, 294–5) and Hochschild (2003: 281) note some laudable firm policies elsewhere, including flexible working (at BT), provision of subsidised daycare (Polaroid and Honeywell), crèches, and even dry-cleaning services (at Microsoft). However, they suggest that flexible working policies are either unavailable or have very limited take-up at middle management level, because management jobs are demanding, full-time positions. Managers taking up family-friendly policies and limiting their work time would instantly have their commitment questioned (Wajcman 1998: 81). Critical voices such as Bunting and Hochschild question the extent to which work-life balance policies genuinely assist working families, or whether they serve to further the corporate interest; making it easier for employees to work, rather than making it easier for them to pursue family activities or commitments. Many HR departments have developed 'well-being' programmes, encouraging staff to take part in relaxation techniques or exercise. But managerial employees are often too overloaded with work to take part in them.

These critical authors are right to question the true meaning of firms' work-life balance policies. There needs to be more substance for these policies to be effective, and they need to be buttressed by family-friendly reforms in government policy (Hochschild 2003: 280–3). But given the massive financial pressures on firms and governments, these are unlikely to happen. Top management holds all the cards. It shapes the company in its own image: demanding and aspirational (Wajcman 1998: 32–3). Executives are least likely to genuinely recognise the problem of overwork, as they often embody this uncompromising culture (Bunting 2004), and can be reluctant to trust those further down the hierarchy (Milkman 1998: 38). Competitive capitalism depends in part on repeated restructurings which tend to create relentless pressures on firms to deliver value. Where would the pressure for pro-family and pro-employee changes of policy come from, bearing in mind top management's generally robust view of the necessity for constantly driving up effort and quality in order to stay afloat in an increasingly competitive environment? If company X eases the pressure on staff, it believes it will disadvantage itself in the face of company Y which continues to push hard. In our companies we saw little concrete evidence of the kind of high-value, employee-favouring HR policies that Pfeffer (1995/2005) describes. Yet most of these companies described themselves as good employers. Indeed, several middle managers in the sample also claimed that their firms were good employers. But large firms depend on their middle managers to regularly work well beyond their formal hours of employment. Most of the middle managers we spoke to were prepared to keep putting in more effort and commitment, and they genuinely wanted their companies to be a success. Yet still there were widespread complaints about overwork, stress and anxiety, lack of family time and low morale. They kept giving, in the hope that eventually the pressure might ease.

Of course, some companies are more employee friendly than others. But all are affected by the serious financial and ideological pressures which entail that fair treatment and dignity of employees fall far down the list of corporate priorities. Even in Japan, where the ruthless demands of financialised capitalism have not penetrated as far as in the USA or the UK, still there are enormous personal pressures on middle managers. The relative absence of financialisation, and the persistence of Japanese-style corporate governance, does not translate into a lack of restructuring pressure in Japanese firms.

But does globalisation and financialisation really tie the hands of top management? We heard the argument countless times that this high-pressure environment is simply unavoidable given the severity of competition. Other analysts, on the other hand, have made the point that 'the uncompromising demands of international capitalism' argument is basically an excuse:

When managers, including CEOs, justify their actions by pleading powerlessness in the face of external forces, it is to the dehumanisation of practice that they resort. When they claim that competition or capital markets are relentless in their demands, and that individual companies and managers have no scope for choices, it is on the strength of the false premise of determinism that they free themselves from any sense of moral or ethical responsibility for their actions. (Ghoshal 2005: 79)

While listening to our middle managers' stories, we began to suspect that releasing some of the pressure, rather than constantly increasing it, could lead to a healthier workforce and, possibly, stronger organisational performance.[7] Success in world markets is not all about brute force, cost control and relentless effort. Other forms of work, notably creativity and fresh thinking, could be sources of competitive strength. It is perhaps disingenuous of top managers to claim that cost pressures are forcing them to make employment cuts, when they themselves are the beneficiaries of inflated salaries, bonuses and stock options. If the 'market dictates' that these emoluments (7.9 per cent of corporate profits in giant US firms according to Glyn 2006: 58) are necessary to attract and retain the best top management talent, then why does the market also dictate that hiring must be reduced, costs and headcounts must be cut, and more effort wrought out of surviving staff?[8]

Putting aside the moral argument, there could be 'business case' reasons for broader equality in the organisation. On 2004 figures[9], the average UK chief executive received a salary of £2.5 million, and he or

[7] Our study cannot answer the question of whether reducing the workload of individual middle managers by hiring more staff can lead to better performance thereby offsetting the cost of new hires. This is an aspirational assumption that would need testing in future research.

[8] One particular restructuring announcement, at the IT firm Logica, perfectly captured this double-standard. It outlined plans to stay competitive by shedding UK jobs to root out inefficiencies and cut costs (while increasing the size of its offshore workforce in India, Morocco and the Philippines to 8,000), yet also proposed increases in executive compensation. 'Logica aims to shed jobs and boost bonuses', *The Guardian*, 23 April 2008.

[9] 'Chief executives' pay rises to £2.5 m average', *The Guardian*, 4 August 2005.

she can receive far more in stock options. A middle manager's cost to the organisation, on the other hand, might be at best £100,000 per year including salary, bonus, pension and associated costs. Are we to assume that a chief executive is equivalent to twenty-five middle managers on his or her basic salary, and many more when stock options are included? Can it really be true that, for example, Wal-Mart's CEO is worth 600 front-line staff? Would the firm somehow be rudderless without his 'vision' and 'values'? Businesses and their advocates would refer to market value and the competition for executive talent. But are top executive leaders really superheroes that organisations cannot cope without? The performance of many top companies would suggest otherwise. Yet there are few signs of a reversal of the policy as major US and UK companies continue to roll out 'talent management programmes' geared to rewarding and retaining the fortunate few who have somehow managed to leap up the hierarchy while other middle managers work on with little prospect of promotion. Systems such as these systematically undervalue those further down the hierarchy who often make equally major sacrifices and contributions, and are likely to feel resentful of the message this sends.

On the other hand, we have seen how Japan still does not share this market for corporate control and competition for executive talent (see Dore 2000: 71–132). Japanese firms have typically hung onto staff, and the escalator of financial rewards in Japan was considerably flatter than in the Anglo-Saxon model. However, they also possessed an authoritarian culture whereby the hierarchy of priorities put the organisation and one's bosses first, and worker dignity much further down. Gender inequality also remains entrenched in Japanese organisations (see Mehri 2006). The new organisational ideology that has come to dominate managerial thinking in large firms in recent years is a mixture of US and Japanese influences. From the USA comes the supposed primacy of shareholder interests, the retreat of internal labour markets, union avoidance tactics, a 'can-do' performance culture, employee share-ownership plans and the market for top management 'talent' resulting in massive income inequalities. From Japan comes the devotion to high performance, long hours and putting the company first. In many ways the new organisational ideology represents the merging of the worst of both worlds, at least for those in the middle and lower ranks.

We are not expecting an end to the 'company first' ethos in Japan, the USA or the UK, or to a fundamental rethinking of corporate governance priorities in Western countries away from so-called 'shareholder value' and towards other stakeholders in the firm, notably employees (Ghoshal 2005: 81). We are saying that, with this in mind, middle managers themselves need to fight back against this culture of ratcheted work demands for limited returns to career development and security. But what avenues for resistance do they have? This is the topic of the next section.

Resisting the new organisational ideology

Whyte's classic text, *The Organization Man*, was highly critical of large organisations and the servile nature of hierarchical employment. He argued that the processes of organisational socialisation and indoctrination needed to be resisted in order for 'man' to throw off the shackles of 'organisation'. This idea has stood the test of time, but perhaps not in the way Whyte might have envisaged. He is probably correct about the indoctrinating forces of organisation, which have certainly survived into the twenty-first century. But organisations today simultaneously exert socialising and individualising pressures on their staff. The individualisation of employment in organisational life has meant a reduction of its social bonds, and a decline of communitarianism. The concept that people can achieve more as part of a team than as individuals did not appear regularly in our interviews. We would suggest that it is not the community that should be resisted, as Whyte promotes, but the de-socialisation of the firm that employees should attempt to oppose. By this we mean open discussion about the upward trends of executive pay and collective support and resistance to the culture of overwork. This would also mean middle managers personally resisting the 'inevitable' long-hours culture, and encouraging and supporting colleagues to do the same. Classic Marxist interpretations (Baran and Sweezy 1966: 324– 53) often indulge in speculative and nostalgic calls for world revolution or protracted crisis in capitalism. We do not subscribe to this view. Like capitalism, the giant organisation probably cannot be undone. But it can be adapted; made more humane, just as trade unionists have argued for many years. However, this can only come about through conflict and struggle. Firms will only change if they see a real value in doing so, or if they are somehow forced to change by government policy, union resistance or, perhaps more likely, by litigation from overworked managers and their families (Bunting 2004: 299). We have already shown how hard it is for senior management to change traditional organizational structures into new forms. The chances of employees or their advocacy groups humanising the organisation would be even harder.

Can unions be the place to organise this kind of resistance? Being an active union member is difficult for managers – it entails putting one's head above the parapet, and managerial workloads are so intense that it can be extremely hard to get the time to pursue union matters. White-collar staff also tend to have ambivalent relationships with unions: they are either not covered by collective bargaining agreements and working time arrangements, or are forced to resign from the union or become inert members once they are promoted to managerial levels. As such, it is usually harder for them to seek recourse through the unions, despite concerted efforts to launch campaigns around working time in recent years (Bunting 2004: 284–90). Union membership and union power has, of course, also been in long-run decline. In Japan, unions are extremely weak. But trade unions are one possible area of resistance and support, at least in the UK and the USA, where they are independent of firms.

Nevertheless, although employees describe increasingly large workloads, significant numbers are actively buying-in to the overwork culture. Recent academic work and media sources describe this as 'work addiction' (Burke 2006, Burke and Cooper 2008) or even 'binge working',[10] and the impacts of both on the well-being of employees and their families can be very unpleasant. Workaholic behaviours are not motivated solely by unmanageable workloads. Despite all the anxiety, overwork and stress, most of the middle managers we interviewed claimed to enjoy their work. Some even spoke of an 'amazing' family environment that they had become immersed in (see USRecruit, Chapter 3). Hochschild (2003) famously described the tendency for many staff to actually prefer being at work to home, because work is a place with structure, a semblance of rationality and challenge. Home, for many, does not have these features. While there are clearly positive points to be taken from opportunities for personal challenge at work, the downside is that work pressures can be ratcheted very easily in this kind of high-commitment environment (Bunting 2004). Redundancy (or its

[10] 'Binge working is harming family life', *Evening Standard*, 16 March 2005.

threat) in these circumstances can be more traumatic, as it means a loss of professional identity and exclusion from valued work-based friendship networks. All that a person has worked so hard to establish can be swept away in a moment. There are real dangers associated with staff over-committing to organisations which cannot promise to reciprocate with job security, financial rewards and recognition for personal sacrifice.

Moreover, financial rewards for hard work are becoming distributed inequitably. The growth in top management remuneration seldom reflects genuine increases in firm performance and returns to shareholders. Inequalities between top management and the rest of the workforce are growing rapidly. The widely espoused model of corporate governance, spearheaded by US corporations, can result in major differentials in income. Traditionally Japan did not follow this route – its version of corporate hierarchy depended almost exclusively on internal, or 'insider', governance, with large boards of directors populated by company men who had scaled tall internal career ladders. This system tended to tie employees to the firm for the duration of their career, and contributed to lower inequalities in income. Moreover, the defensive cross-shareholdings of Japanese firms insulated them from takeover or speculation. As a result, Japan has never really had a 'market for corporate control' (O'Sullivan 2000) and, by extension, no market for executive talent.

On 1999 figures, the ratio of the average Japanese company president's pay to that of the average graduate starting on the white-collar management track was a comparatively modest 11:1. In the UK it was 18:1, rising to 27:1 in the USA (Dore 2000: 24). For blue collars, the figures are even more extreme. Glyn (2006: 58) reports that in:

[T]he largest 500 US companies, the ratio of CEO pay to production worker earnings rose from 30 in 1970 to 570 in 2000. [...]. This contrasts with ratios in the range of 10–25 in Japan and Europe. CEO compensation [...] averaged 7.9 per cent of corporate profits in a large sample of US companies.

Although the UK shares the Anglo-Saxon corporate system with the USA, and therefore inequalities of pay are also heading in a North American direction, British board remuneration has always been a fraction of that of the States. The average UK chief executive's salary in 2004 was £2.5 million.[11] This is dwarfed by the figure for the USA,

---

[11] 'Chief executives' pay rises to £2.5 m average', *The Guardian*, 4 August 2005.

where CEOs received on average \$10.5 million in 2004.[12] It is not just the absolute numbers that cause concern, but also the trends. US CEO pay regularly climbs by 12–20 per cent per year as blue-collar and lower white-collar salary rises barely keep touch with inflation (Fraser 2001: 43, 186–91).[13] In 2005, directors' pay in the UK's FTSE 100 index leapt 28 per cent, while average earnings climbed just 3.7 per cent.[14] Such data also contrasts markedly with the below-inflation rise of 2.3 per cent received by the average UK middle manager in 2007.[15]

Widespread criticism of top management aggrandisement has had little or no impact on the trends, even when firms have come under government scrutiny for indulging in practices associated with stock-option pay, such as granting options at backdated, lower prices, or 'springloading'.[16] Bebchuk and Freid (2006) argue that the mainstream interpretation of executive pay as set by 'arm's-length contracting' is wide of the mark, and that the generous packages for senior management are actually the result of managerial power plays. 'It [executive pay] has distorted pay arrangements, diluted managers' incentives to enhance firm value, and even provided perverse incentives to take actions that reduce long-term firm value' (2006: 6). Froud *et al.* (2006: 54–64) aptly describe top management remuneration as 'value-skimming'

---

[12] 'US executive pay goes off the scale', *The Guardian*, 4 August 2005; 'Gap between directors and workers widens', *The Guardian*, 8 October 2004.

[13] 'TUC website puts bosses' pay packages on record', *The Guardian*, 5 August 2006; 'Boardroom pay bonanza goes on', *The Guardian*, 27 August 2004.

[14] 'Gap between the richest and poorest workers widens', *The Guardian*, 3 October 2006.

[15] 'Pay trends pointers show mixed fortunes', *The Daily Telegraph*, 21 February 2008.

[16] 'Springloading' is the ethically questionable practice whereby stock options for execs are awarded just before a stock-exchange announcement is made that is likely to trigger a boost in the share price. This is designed to contrive events so that the value of options is almost certain to rise regardless of the performance of the company or its executives. A similar trick is to backdate stock options, by assigning stock options to dates when the company's share price was lower, thereby artificially increasing the size of the award. 'Academic rocks corporate America by revealing boardroom reward ploys', *The Guardian*, 10 July 2006; 'Watchdog warns listed companies of crackdown on stock options malpractice', *The Guardian*, 26 September 2006. Steve Jobs, CEO and founder of Apple Computer, is one high-profile figure to come under scrutiny in recent years, and Apple is just one of dozens of firms which have been forced to restate their earnings after the disclosure of share options malpractice. 'Apple's Jobs "knew of share-option back-dating"', *The Times*, 29 December 2006.

rather than a tool for realising shareholder value. Outside of academia, dozens of protest websites attest to the groundswell of ill-feeling surrounding this issue, such as the TUC[17], AFL-CIO[18] and other independent pressure groups.[19]

Although there are very few English-language discussions of this issue in Japan, there are some strong signs that Japanese corporate governance is slowly moving in this direction (Taft and Singh 2003). Dore (2000, 2002, 2004) demonstrates that significant governance alterations have taken place, enabled by changes to the law (see also Jackson 2002: 122). Many analysts are actually frustrated with how slowly this change has taken place, arguing that the Japanese economy still lacks risk capital and is underequitised (Kosai 2002). Nevertheless, these changes are widely regarded as significant in Japan, and have not occurred without protest from shareholders and unions. Although the structure of the Japanese economy remains substantially divergent from that of the USA or the UK, attempts at emulation of the Anglo-Saxon model have been ongoing since the 1990s (see Chapter 5). According to Dore (2000: 74): 'More performance-related rewards [...] is the new way of showing how you *hito o taisetsu ni suru* [respect people] – respect, that is, not the needs they have in common with others, but their unequal contributions.'

One of our central concerns is that recent changes in corporate shape and philosophy have actually focused far too closely on the individual, resulting in the atomisation and isolation of staffers and the destruction of workplace collegiality. The corporation has proceeded so far down the road of higher debt gearing, riskier accumulation, financialisation, downsizing, delayering and individualisation that it has lost sight of the needs that people have in common, the needs that reformist-minded analysts are so keen to eradicate from Japanese organisations.

It is not just inequalities in income that generate discussion – gender and ethnic inequalities continue to be serious issues in large organisations, with women and minority workers still under-represented at senior management levels.[20] Female managers have a particularly hard

---

[17] www.worksmart.org.uk/company/
[18] www.aflcio.org/corporatewatch/paywatch/pay/index.cfm
[19] Such as the US pressure group Council of International and Public Affairs' 'Too Much' website: www.cipa-apex.org/toomuch/
[20] 'Women join the millionaires at last', *The Guardian*, 5 August 2005.

time under these intense conditions, as household responsibilities in dual-income homes still generally fall onto women (Hochschild 2003; Wajcman 1998). While financial inequality is severe in the USA, when it comes to gender relations, Japan is the worst offender. Although there has been substantial growth in the number of women in middle and senior corporate management in the USA and the UK since the 1980s (Helfat *et al.* 2006), research on the position of women in Japanese corporate hierarchies paints a far worse picture (Ogasawara 1998; Graham 2003; Mehri 2006).

Whereas there is reasonably widespread discussion of gender inequalities in the management and organisation studies literature, conversations on ethnic issues are disconcertingly thin on the ground. Our observations on these issues were, unfortunately, very limited, as our respondents in the USA and the UK were comprised overwhelmingly of white middle-class men. In Japan we spoke to just two women, one of whom worked in a US investment bank having grown frustrated with the sexism of her previous workplace, a venerable Japanese financial firm. We suggest that amid the significant restructurings of large organisations, issues of gender and ethnic inequalities remain major concerns. Although downsizing, business process re-engineering, hierarchy flattening and downward devolution of decision-making have all taken place to a greater or lesser extent, the traditional features of large workplaces – bureaucracy, power, inequality and authoritarianism – were still alive and well. This picture closely resembles the Marxist conception of the monopoly capitalist giant corporation (Baran and Sweezy 1966: 27–61), even though there has been such major macroeconomic change over the last forty years.

Some of the managers interviewed appeared able to adapt and survive in this environment. Others were not so able to do this. Staff with family responsibilities (the burden of which still tends to fall on women more than men) will struggle to be promoted if they cannot put in the very long hours expected. Our results mirror those of other authors reporting work overload in the UK and elsewhere (such as Bunting 2004; Eastman 1998; Fraser 2001; Green 2001; Worrall and Cooper 2001; Burke and Cooper 2008). The volume of work that middle managers are expected to complete means that their work hours, stress and responsibility levels have all increased following organisational restructuring measures. Although it is true that middle managers are given a large degree of formal autonomy in many areas (including setting their own hours), the volume of work necessitates very long working days, or the work simply won't be completed. It is therefore hard to envisage major personal resistance to the new organisational era.

Furthermore, it remains hard to change organisational traditions. UKUtilities, for example, remained male-dominated and the culture change has had limited impact in this respect. All of the companies retained some strongly bureaucratic management systems (see Hales 1999). On a more positive note, several of the middle managers across the organisations noted some recent changes away from directly author-itarian managerial cultures. This next section evaluates the extent to which change might come from firms themselves, perhaps as they begin to realise that there are potential organisational penalties from mistreat-ment of middle management staff.

The limits of 'responsible restructuring'

Firms themselves are increasingly adopting new internal tactics to combat the effects of stress and anxiety at work, partly as a genuine attempt to tackle stress, and partly to counter the signs of individual and collective resistance from white-collar employees. A recent trend is the emergence of career coaching or executive coaching. This can be very useful to manage-rial employees in that it provides them with a sympathetic, impartial person with whom to discuss daily stresses and strains. But much of the coaching culture, like other HR interventions, is really about inducing better work performance in the interests of senior management and profit-ability, by training employees to improve their 'time management' or work on their 'emotional intelligence' so that they can be better 'team players'.

Will workplace humanisation come from the firms themselves, per-haps through their HR departments? We saw limited evidence of this. Senior HR managers claimed to be concerned with the overloading of staff, but seemed unable to deal with the problem. Work-life balance policies can simply be a process by which organisations broaden the interface through which employees can experience the working world. They are not a solution to the problem of stress and overwork. New working arrangements are similar to the ways in which companies increasingly interact with their customers online. Companies adopt work-life balance style language when they market to their customers these new online systems. They claim to recognise that their customers lead busy lives, and offer the possibility of paying bills online in the middle of the night. Homeworking, broadband internet at home, mobile phones, Blackberrys, PDAs and laptops are all useful systems, but they have the unfortunate effect of tying people even closer to their work. The real solution is to *take work away from people*. This will mean bucking the trend of doing more with less, via cost-cutting, redundancies and early retirements. Instead it would involve *increased hiring* in order to share the workload more reasonably. Arguably, restructuring need not be a zero-sum game between executive management and staff. If large firms spent more on hiring and retaining staff, the pay-offs to workplace health and productivity could conceivably outweigh the costs.[21]

An interesting trend to emerge in the literature has evolved around the question of how well (or badly) restructuring has been carried out, and how the harshest effects of change can be ameliorated by sophisticated and sensitive HR practices. Downsizing need not necessarily result in depression for staff and poor returns to investors, but this can be almost guaranteed to happen if some basic tenets of how best to treat staff are ignored. Ignorance or avoidance of these measures was common in the USA, particularly in the early years of restructuring. Wayne Cascio is probably the main figure in this school of thought. He argues that firms' first reaction to a downturn is to cut costs and make layoffs, and that these policies are often carried out in panic-stricken fashion with little regard for the impact these changes can have on the company's longer-term future. Skills are lost and resentment builds up among survivors who are asked to do the work of those who have left. Moreover, the financial performance of the firms is frequently no better after restructuring (Cascio 1998, 2002a, 2002b).

Burke and Nelson (1997: 327) are also scornful of those firms in which downsizing was 'done badly'. They note how 'surviving managers find themselves working in new and less friendly environments,

---

[21] Further research is needed as regards the potential payoffs to firms of a *reversal* of the trends towards downsizing and work intensification. There is widespread research evidence to suggest that overwork and stress are serious problems in firms in the UK, the USA and Japan. A recent survey from a mainstream HR consultancy (Garrow *et al*. 2007: 6) states that 'there are indications that the ongoing squeeze on resources and roles is becoming counter-productive. [...]. Organizations are likely to reap greater benefits from building some slack back into the system in terms of resource, rather than waiting until the 'pips squeak' and intellectual and other capital is lost.'

stretched thin, managing more people and jobs, working longer'. They offer a three-step programme for minimising the traumas associated with restructuring, starting with '1. Initiation: planning the revitalisation efforts [...] 2. Implementation: smoothing the transition [...] 3. Institutionalisation: healing and refocusing' (1997: 328–9). While this 'responsible restructuring' viewpoint has certain merits, it tends to place too much emphasis on narrow, technical, managerialist solutions to the problem, such as Noer's four-step psychological intervention programme for reducing survivor sickness (Noer 1993). Responsible restructuring sounds very similar to the supposed 'cutting and caring' that took place at USElectronics. While perhaps not meaning to, this literature sometimes repeats the managerialist line that there is really no alternative to the harsh facts of competitive life. Burke and Nelson (1997: 327) suggest that '[e]mployees need to develop a more autonomous, less dependent link with the organisation'. Noer also suggests that the severity of organisational change was so intense, that well-intentioned efforts by firms to continue to offer long-term paternalistic careers are misguided, because they simply cannot make such commitments, and will eventually be forced to break them. 'If organisations insist in offering internal career planning, they are simply misleading their employees and setting up inevitable crises' (Noer 1998: 219).

These studies do not provide a clear understanding of the wider picture. We would argue that even in firms where 'responsible restructuring' has been attempted, the overall effects on middle managers are very similar – longer working hours, heavier workloads and pressure, but on the other hand, possibly more interesting and engaging work. Personal psychological interventions, or a deliberate diminution in one's level of attachment to a firm might be moderately helpful to certain individuals, but they will not put an end to the trends that create these personal ill-effects in the first place. Cascio's (2002a) analysis of the weak financial performance of downsizing firms is also contentious. He argues that downsizing is partly responsible for declines in share price and profitability. This is likely to be true in part. But he does not outline why firms downsize in the first place: surely a major explanation is that these firms are already suffering from poor performance and downsizing simply reflects and exacerbates these existing effects (see Baumol *et al.* 2003)? While we agree that financially successful firms also indulge in downsizing (Cascio 2002a: 28), his analysis is weak on the wider economic drivers of international capital that encourage top management to squeeze staff costs. Downsizing isn't simply a poor choice taken by those at the top. While senior management always has some leeway in how it goes about change (as we have seen in Japan), broader economic forces such as financialisation and product market weakness are extremely hard for large firms to resist in ways other than restructuring and cost rationalisation. These changes, even when implemented 'responsibly', rarely lead to gains for employees. Instead, our evidence indicates that the impacts of restructuring usually range from difficult to traumatic for middle managers and other employees.

The 'responsible restructuring' literature (such as Cascio and Noer), therefore, while accurate on the potential and actual costs of change, is perhaps too optimistic about how these costs can be 'managed out', thereby moving the literature in a very managerialist direction, reminiscent of such publications as Cameron *et al.* (1991: 58), which is generally enthusiastic about downsizing – provided it is 'managed effectively'. A similar problem exists for the literature that defends middle managers as effective and important players (Huy 2001; Balogun 2003). It tends to reduce the highly complex, political, economic and moral issues of organisational restructuring to a narrow one of technical competence, as if better-informed and more open senior management can take away the pain just by acting more 'responsibly'. For example, Huy tells a story of when middle managers at Hewlett-Packard were 'consulted early and often about strategic and operational questions' during a reorganisation of a troubled business unit. 'The end result was one of the speediest turnarounds ever of an HP division' (Huy 2001: 76). At best, the 'responsible restructuring' position does provide a much more balanced, empirically realistic and humane alternative to the mainstream 'business case for change' literature. However, it also potentially advocates the establishment of corporate environments in which middle managers lay the seeds of their own destruction, or effectively carry out senior executives' dirty work: 'At the telecom company I studied, middle managers' focus on continuity contributed to a relatively smooth downsizing of 13,000 positions' (Huy 2001: 78).

The underlying philosophies of the 'high-road', 'high-commitment', or responsibility theories are hard to disagree with. However, in many of our case studies, humane and sophisticated policies were rarely adhered to by senior management. More problematically, when they did install high-performance systems or restructure 'responsibly', the 'win-win' scenario of gains for employees and the firm rarely materialised (see the many critiques of HPWS, such as Godard 2004; Jenkins 2007). Staff were 'consulted early and often' about change in many of the cases, but this was of little comfort. Instead, the imperatives of financial pressures dominate the proceedings, leading, all too often, to an 'ends justifies the means' attitude about the human impact of organisational change. This has been expressed to us with some vivid imagery, sometimes, and worryingly, from HR professionals themselves, including 'if you can't stand the heat, get out of the kitchen' (Japanese electronics firm) or, most charmingly, 'you either shit on the pot or get off' (UK bank). It is a major concern how this kind of authoritarian culture has come to dominate a wide range of management practices. This is what we mean by 'normalised intensity' (McCann *et al.* 2008) and that its prevalence in contemporary firms across different societies is becoming difficult to resist. Moreover, we agree with the responsible restructuring literature in that the ends of normalised intensity do not always justify the means – poorly motivated, stressed and overworked employees tend not to perform well, and in situations of increased workload and wider responsibilities, the quality of the middle manager's work can suffer.

Our view is that the issues of downsizing and restructuring are much too socially and economically important to be reduced to one of simply 'how best to manage' change. Restructuring is so ubiquitous, and usually has such unpleasant effects for employees that it deserves a much wider, more sociological, understanding. Our approach has been to provide sociological observation of the impacts of restructuring, 'warts and all', and to provide a 'real-world' account of the lives of middle managers in these tougher times. In general, what we found, while not universally negative, has some concerning implications for middle managers' working lives. If one looks deeper than the issue of 'how best to manage' downsizing, it becomes clear that restructuring is an inherent feature of capitalism's unremitting search for greater profitability. Top management's appetite for efficiency gains is insatiable, even when the gains rarely materialise (Braverman 1974/1998; Baran and Sweezy 1966). That is why restructuring is so ubiquitous, even if the results of change are often moderate or even negative (see Froud *et al.* 2000b). Incessant drives for increased profitability lie at the very heart of contemporary capitalism, and it would be wrong to erase this from the picture, as so much of the HR or 'responsible restructuring' literature does. Instead, there is a need for a more sober analysis of the real prospects for revival and renewal of the quality of middle managers' working lives, based on a broader understanding of the struggle for employee dignity. That is the focus for the final section of this book.

Restoring the dignity of managerial work

The spectre of economic determinism hangs over our analysis. It would be simplistic to argue that increased international competitive pressures necessarily and mechanistically result in organisational change and work intensification. Firms, and people, have the ability to act in other ways, to take different causes of action. Are there genuine alternatives to this scenario of constant pressure and work degradation? Can organisations develop more humane policies for their workers, and can middle managers resist the impacts of restructuring? Can secure employment, collegiality and worker dignity be defended in some way? In our interpretation, changes to modes of working that accrue in the favour of middle management appear unlikely to come from the direction of senior management, even if some firms are more enlightened than others. Most of the corporations in our sample had been profitable for some time, indicating that pressures for change are not purely economic: there are broader justifications for restructuring and work intensification, including more ephemeral sources, such as 'world best practice'. Although there are wide variations on this theme in practice, there are some generic, universal ideas of what being a 'great' company entails. Elsewhere we have described this as the 'new organisational ideology' (McCann *et al.* 2004). Across a range of large corporations there appeared to be certain shared concepts about what the current phase requires from organisations and staff. The firm must be lean, intolerant of waste, flexible and responsive to a range of stakeholders. Its managerial staff must show high commitment, work long hours and give total dedication. They must have the 'right' attitude, meaning an inexhaustible supply of energy and effort, openness to regular change measures and an acceptance that employment security is not a given. They must take on a very wide range of responsibilities, demonstrating creativity and initiative (but without rocking the boat so much as to upset certain sources of traditional power). They are either non-unionised, or inert union members. The white-collar 'model citizen' that emerges from this scenario appears to be an equally dominant idea across the three countries studied, even when corporate governance systems and broader economic structures differ.

Like the 'off the shelf' management systems employed in so many of our case studies, the language of the urgent need for restructuring is used everywhere, even when a firm is highly profitable. This raises the issue of whether restructuring can really be 'read-off' from increased international competition. How much restructuring is really necessary? Although some of our case corporations were struggling economically (notably USAuto) during the period of our research, the majority were highly profitable. USRecruit had a profit margin of around 18 per cent, and made a gross profit of $3.8 billion at year-end 2007. In the same year USUtilities reported $2.1 billion gross profit at an astonishing profit margin of 51.6 per cent. In first-quarter 2006, JAutoGroup made a net profit of ¥525 billion (approximately $5.1 billion), and JSteel made ¥258 billion ($2.47 billion). UKSteel reported end of 2006 tax year profits of £313 million; UKDrinksPLC made nearly £2.1 billion in 2007.[22] Yet all these firms and their senior executives claimed to be under constant pressure to cut costs, and this message was repeated by employees lower down the hierarchy. Evidently, these corporations were profitable, but not profitable enough. As Ghoshal notes, continually citing competition or pleading poverty absolves management from responsibilities to its workers. Throwing up one's hands and saying 'it's beyond my control' is a morally questionable practice. The same argument has been well made by Hirst and Thompson (1999: 4) about politicians who state of globalisation, 'we can't intervene, market forces are too powerful'. This needs to be challenged, as too many stakeholders in firms have adopted this seductive view uncritically, legitimising the 'there is no alternative' position even further. How big do the profits have to be for the pressure on staff to finally ease?

The extension and intensification of white-collar work poses serious implications for staff well-being and performance, and senior managers would be reckless to ignore some of the symptoms we observed. It does not appear that the pressures on corporations will ease in the near future. In fact, given some important changes in the geo-economy, in particular the rapid growth of China, competitive pressures are likely to

---

[22] Financial numbers from company reports, FAME database and Japan Company Handbook 2006.

increase. If this is the case, CEOs, HR managers and boards of directors must give more thought to the issue of managing the volumes of work and levels of pressure that experienced and valued staff are exposed to. Culture change programmes and career coaching by themselves are not going to be enough to genuinely ameliorate middle management overwork and stress. Although this runs counter to the fashionable mantra of lean thinking and cost-cutting, firms should consider hiring greater numbers of white-collar staff in order to ease the burdens on overstretched employees. If firms can justify paying millions of dollars in compensation to CEOs while still clinging to the ideology of shareholder value, they can certainly afford to hire and train more middle managers to deal with the overwork facing so many staff. This in turn might help to redress the depressing situation of job loss and job insecurity that is the reality for middle managers and others who staff the large firms in the USA, the UK and Japan.

Another issue that senior HR and top executives might consider paying attention to is the task of rebuilding collegiality. Many of our middle manager respondents felt somewhat isolated and unsupported. There was much emphasis on competing, rather than cooperating, with colleagues. Mainstream HR literature suggests that people working together can achieve more than the sum of their parts (Pfeffer 1995/ 2005). This kind of collegiate thinking has been criticised in some circles as the Japanese model fell into disrepute. However, these ideas are worth defending, and the shift towards individualisation of pay and conditions should at least be questioned, rather than tacitly accepted or promoted. In conditions where pressure and conflict are common in large workplaces, and where staff juggle with heavy workloads, managers somehow need to show empathy and understanding (Hochschild 2003). Senior management need to find ways to take the pressure off middle management staff. Although most pressure emanates from the huge workloads middle managers are grappling with, considerable amounts are also derived from interpersonal conflict as collegiality is eroded against a backdrop of the individualistic, 'model citizen' white-collar worker. It is under these pressured conditions that other unpleasant features arise, notably bullying and intimidation (Mehri 2006; Starkey and McKinlay 1994). The risks of psychological damage creep up steadily in environments like this. Moreover, when everyone is rushing the quality of work almost inevitably suffers as mistakes are made and lower standard work is submitted. How can one take pride in doing a good job when work tasks are expedited under so much time pressure? It is not just that managing one's workload can be difficult, but completing *good* work can be even more demanding under conditions of normalised intensity. This is another area where taking the pressure off mid-level staff could clearly benefit senior managers, if only such a policy were attempted.

Senior managers ought to turn their attention in a genuine fashion to the growing crisis of the 'time bind' (Bunting 2004). Much has been written in recent years of excessive working hours and intensive work demands, with many analysts suggesting that overwork is a major concern (Burke and Cooper 2008). Others, however, consider complaints about overwork to be exaggerated, citing statistics that suggest, when one takes into account the growing part-time proportion of the workforce, average working hours are at historic lows in many OECD nations (Bonney 2005). Many have also suggested that job insecurity is not nearly as serious as is often claimed (Fevre 2007). We take the point that it is very easy to mistakenly describe contemporary workplaces as miserable dystopias of overwork and precarious employment. However, in terms of the specific sample of middle-level managers in our large corporations, overwork was a critical issue. Job security, while a considerably less serious problem, was also a concern for many of our respondents.

At heart, middle managers' concerns focused on the steady increases in pressure that they have experienced over the years. Many respondents suggested that these pressures were not solely felt by middle managers, but felt in different ways by staff up and down the hierarchy, including top executives, whose working hours have increased even since the high levels reported in Mintzberg's (1973) famous study (see Tengblad 2006 for figures on the USA; and Robinson and Shimizu 2006 for Japan). At the time of Mintzberg's research, senior executives worked between forty and fifty-three hours per week, whereas today, for example, CEOs regularly put in as much as sixty to eighty hours per week (Tengblad 2006: 1446). This sets the tone for 'what is required' by contemporary work organisations. Further down the hierarchy, middle managers often stated that everyone was working harder, down to front-line supervisors and workers, and they did not want to give the impression that they were somehow uniquely affected by work intensification. Sadly, there was a widespread feeling that tougher workplace demands were simply the new reality, and that the intensification of

work and extension of the working day and week were largely inevitable. This was true in each of the three countries that formed the basis
for our study. Japanese firms appeared able to extract almost total
dominance over their male workers' time, particularly as salarymen's
wives typically did not work. With increasing female labour force
participation across all developed societies, this scenario is changing.
However, mainstream analyses of highly competitive work environments, which laud the high-commitment management systems of
Japanese workplaces such as Toyota and Sony, tend to skate over
work-life issues (see, for example, Liker and Morgan 2006: 17–8).
Clearly the issue of working hours connects closely to that of gender
inequality. While we acknowledge some of the points made by Fevre
(2007) and Bonney (2005) in their scepticism about job insecurity and
long hours, based on our study we would instead suggest that there is an
urgent need for firms' colonisation of middle managers' time to be
properly addressed and limited (see Green 2006).

Unfortunately, given the long-run decline in the influence of the HR
function relative to accounting and finance in both Anglo-Saxon and
Japanese contexts (Jacoby 2005), this also appears unlikely. A serious
approach to addressing the politics of the time bind (see Bunting 2004:
271–325) might liberate staff from the straightjacket of work intensity
and encourage a rethink of authoritarian workplace practices. To
reiterate, one of our central findings was the enormous commitment
and personal sacrifice made by highly skilled white-collar workforces.
The managers we interviewed were far from the popular stereotype of
an overprotected and irrelevant cadre of bureaucrats. Intensive work
pressures, lengthening working time and growing stress levels must be
tackled if firms are to realise the input of these skilled, experienced and
committed middle managers. It is an open question as to whether senior
management has the ability or will to genuinely address these serious
problems.

While Hochschild was certainly convincing in her argument about
the propensity of some employees to 'escape into work' – because work
can offer the regularity, recognition and logic that families often cannot – we suggest that if present trends continue people will question the
point of offering so many sacrifices to the organisation for such little
relative return, and might be tempted to retreat back into the family.
Wages and bonuses may have grown for some middle managers (mostly
in US and UK companies) but financial income is not a substitute for

genuine well-being. It is this lack of collegiality, absence of respect and lack of dignity that is particularly concerning for managerial employees.

Conclusions

Our study has uncovered substantial evidence of unpleasant and difficult working conditions for mid-level managers across three of the richest and most advanced countries in the world. These findings have emerged from large organisations, some of which are world-renowned for their influence and achievements. The general description of working life in these organisations is downbeat, and there have been several occasions where we were disappointed by what we heard. These descriptions included: the accounts of employees at a US car plant who had few positive things to say about their working lives (Chapter 3); the story of a bank manager in the UK who was so disgusted with how things were developing that he decided to quit corporate life for good (Chapter 4); and accounts by younger employees in Japan that authoritarian and sexist management was alive and well (Chapter 5).

It could be better than this. As we have tried to demonstrate in this chapter, while there are obvious pressures that the international system places on firms in terms of competition, cost control and technological developments, economic and technological determinism do not have to dominate the agenda. People in senior leadership positions in large organisations should think clearly about the necessity of the demands they are making on themselves and their staff. Not all organisations, public or private sector, can be 'world class' – they can't all move (as the corporate mantra suggests) from 'good to great' (Collins 2001). Corporations should learn to live within their means and not continually push employees so hard. Is international competition really so severe that it precludes consideration of a genuine duty of care to employees? This is a short-sighted position to take, but across all our case corporations, at all levels of the organisation, managers were taking it, presumably because they have not been exposed to other ways of thinking.

But will such a change of thinking ever be initiated and carried through? Fraser (2001: 228) concludes her generally depressing book on white-collar workers in the USA on an optimistic note:

With the weakening of the stock market [...] the 'sweatshop' corporation no longer seems invincible. In the new millennium, white-collar Americans have begun voting with their feet and their pocketbooks. [...] Many people told me proudly that they kept the phone numbers of a couple of head-hunters [...] or regularly visited employment websites. Some kept hidden files documenting their managers' errors so that they would have ammunition to fight back with. [...] Meanwhile, men and women I never would have imagined working for a small company or start-up contemplated making the switch. [...] With the evolution of the Internet, the involvement of white-collar unions, and, perhaps most importantly, the support of major players in the investment community, white-collar workers were no longer isolated targets or helpless victims of a harsh new work world. Change seems possible, even inevitable.

While elements of this view appear encouraging, it still points mostly to individual tactics as a way of surviving. We have seen precious little evidence in our study to suggest or expect any major, organised resistance to overwork pressures. The conclusion is that genuine change would have to come from the stratum which seems to believe it has the least to gain from changing organisational situations more in middle managers' favour – senior executives at the summit of corporate pyramids. Although unions and other stakeholders can play a role in protecting staff and preventing abuses, a concerted effort by top management is needed to kick-start any possible improvement in the quality of working life. Middle managers, like all staff, need to experience more genuine support and collegiality from those above and around them. Senior managers need to recog-nise and build upon the devotion, experience and goodwill of white-collar managers before these values get lost in resentment and exhaus-tion. It is up to senior managers to attempt to bring this change about. It remains to be seen, however, whether they are willing or able to effect the kind of rethinking of working practices that is so despe-rately needed in modern corporations. If our neo-Bravermanian ana-lysis of the effects of fundamental capitalist rationalisation on the structuring of large firms is correct then such a rethinking is, regret-tably, unlikely.

Unlike some earlier Marxist commentators (e.g. Baran and Sweezy 1966; Mandel 1971), we make no predictions about capitalism's crisis, collapse or overthrow. We take no pleasure from our downbeat obser-vations of the economic performance of large corporations. Although the growing income inequality in contemporary capitalism is, for us, deplorable, economic growth and stability, wealth and job creation can be essential platforms for the development of successful, democratic and civilised societies. Given that work in large organisations is such a prominent activity of human life, it is vital that the quality, dignity and meaning of work at all levels improve if that life is to be made more livable.

Appendix

Table 1. *Turnover and headcount of main American case organisations at start of research.*

Company Name	2003 Turnover (US$)	2003 Headcount (Approx)
USAuto	164 billion	300,000
USBank1	8.3 billion	6,500
USBank2	2.8 billion	2,200
USCity	N/A	12,000
USElectronics	27 billion	85,000
USEngineering	7 billion	27,000
USHospital	2.8 million (not-for-profit company)	6,000
USRecruit	14.9 billion	1,000 at head office (approximately 4 million temporaries worldwide)
USSteel	6 billion	10,600
USUtilities	4 billion	96,260

Table 2. *Turnover and headcount of main British case organisations at start of research.*

Company Name	2003 Turnover (UKP)	2003 Headcount (Approx)
UKAuto	7.4 billion	17,000
UKDrinksConglomerate	9.4 billion	38,955
– of which UKDrinks	–756 million	–310
UKEngineering	0.9 billion	15,450
UKHospital	270 million	3,700
UKInsurance	3.2 billion	5,104
UKCity	N/A	16,500
UKSteel	7.2 billion	25,000
UKUtilities	2.0 billion	15,674

Table 3. *Turnover and headcount of main Japanese case organisations at start of research.*

Company Name	2003 Turnover (Million Yen)	2003 Headcount (Approx)
JAutoGroup	6,828,588	38,000
JAutoComps	619,191	6,300
JCity	N/A	10,500
JElectronics	35,219	3,200
JEngineering	226,143	9,000
JSteel	2,749,306	45,000

References

Abegglen, J. C. (1958), *The Japanese Factory. Aspects of its Social Organisation*. Glencoe, IL: Free Press.

Abegglen, J. C. and G. Stalk Jr. (1988), *Kaisha: The Japanese Corporation*. New York: Basic Books.

Ackroyd, S. (2002), *The Organization of Business: Applying Organizational Theory to Contemporary Change*. Oxford University Press.

Adler, P. S. (1992), 'The 'Learning' Bureaucracy: New United Motor Manufacturing, Inc.' in B. M. Staw and L. L. Cummings (eds.), *Research on Industrial Behaviour*. Greenwich, CT: JAI Press.

Adler, P. S. (2007), 'The Future of Critical Management Studies: A Paleo-Marxist Critique of Labour Process Theory', *Organization Studies* 28: 1313–45.

Amable, B. (2003), *The Diversity of Modern Capitalism*. Oxford University Press.

Appelbaum, E. and R. Batt (1994), *The New American Workplace: Transforming Work Systems in the United States*. Ithaca: Cornell University Press.

Appelbaum, E., T. Bailey, P. Berg and A. L. Kalleberg (2000), *Manufacturing Advantage: Why High-Performance Work Systems Pay Off*. Ithaca: Cornell University Press.

Armstrong, P. (1989), 'Management, Labour Process, and Agency', *Work, Employment and Society* 3: 307–22.

Arthur, M. B. and D. Rousseau (1996), *Boundaryless Careers: A New Employment Principle for a New Organisational Era*. New York: Oxford University Press.

Ashkenas, R., D. Ulrich, T. Jick and S. Kerr (1995), *The Boundaryless Organization*. San Francisco: Jossey-Bass.

Augar, P. (2000), *The Death of Gentlemanly Capitalism: The Rise and Fall of London's Investment Banks*. London: Penguin.

Bacon, N., P. Blyton and J. Morris (1995), 'Among the Ashes: Trade Union Strategies in the UK and German Steel Industries', *British Journal of Industrial Relations* 34: 25–50.

Bakan, J. (2005), *The Corporation: The Pathological Pursuit of Profit and Power*. London: Constable.

Balogun, J. (2003), 'From Blaming the Middle to Harnessing its Potential: Creating Change Intermediaries', *British Journal of Management* 14: 69–83.

Baran, P. A. and P. M. Sweezy (1966), *Monopoly Capitalism: An Essay on the American Economic and Social Order*. London: Penguin.

Barley, S. and G. Kunda (2004), *Gurus, Hired Guns and Warm Bodies: Itinerant Experts in a Knowledge Economy*. New Jersey: Princeton University Press.

Barley, S. R. and G. Kunda (2006), 'Contracting: A New Form of Professional Practice', *Academy of Management Perspectives*, 20: 45–66.

Bartlett, C. and S. Ghoshal (1998), *Managing Across Borders: The Transnational Solution*. Boston: Harvard Business School Press, 2nd edition.

Baumol, W. J., A. S. Blinder and E. N. Wolff (2003), *Downsizing in America: Reality, Causes, Consequences*. New York: Russell Sage Foundation.

Bebchuk, L. A. and J. M. Fried (2006), 'Pay Without Performance: Overview of the Issues', *Academy of Management Perspectives* 20: 5–24.

Berle, A. A. and G. C. Means (1933), *The Modern Corporation and Private Property*. NewYork: Macmillan.

Best, M. H. (1990), *The New Competition: Institutions of Industrial Restructuring*. Cambridge: Polity.

Best, M. H. (2001), *The New Competitive Advantage: The Renewal of American Industry*. Cambridge University Press.

Beynon, H. (1986), *Working for Ford*. Harmondsworth: Penguin.

Beynon, H., D. Grimshaw, J. Rubery and K. Ward (2002), *Managing Employment Change: The New Realities of Work*. Oxford University Press.

Blau, P. M. and M. W. Meyer (1987), *Bureaucracy in Modern Society*. New York: Random House, 3rd edition.

Bonney, N. (2005), 'Overworked Britons? Part-time Work and Work-life Balance', *Work, Employment and Society* 19: 391–401.

Braverman, H. (1974/1998), *Labor and Monopoly Capital: The Degradation of Work in the Twentieth Century*, London: Monthly Review Press.

Brown, P., A. Green and H. Lauder (2001), *High Skills: Globalization, Competitiveness and Skill Formation*. Oxford University Press.

Brunsson, N. (2006), *Mechanisms of Hope: Maintaining the Dream of the Rational Organization*. Copenhagen Business School Press.

Bunting, M. (2004), *Willing Slaves: How the Overwork Culture is Ruling Our Lives*. London: Harper Collins.

Burawoy, M. (1979), *Manufacturing Consent: Changes in the Labor Process under Monopoly Capitalism*. University of Chicago Press.

Burchill, B. J., D. Day, M. Hudson, D. Lapido, R. Mankelow, J. P. Nolan, H. Reed, I. C. Wichert and F. Wilkinson (1999), *Job Insecurity and Work Intensification*. York: Joseph Rowntree Foundation.

Burke, R. J. (ed.) (2006), *Research Companion to Working Time and Work Addiction*. Cheltenham: Edward Elgar.

Burke, R. J. and C. L. Cooper (2000), 'The New Organizational Reality: Transition and Renewal', in R. J. Burke and C. L Cooper (eds.), *The Organization in Crisis: Downsizing, Restructuring, and Revitalization*. Oxford: Blackwell.

Burke, R. J. and C. L. Cooper (2008), *The Long Hours Culture: Causes, Consequences and Choices*. London: Emerald.

Burke, R. J. and D. L. Nelson (1997), 'Downsizing and Restructuring: Lessons from the Firing Line for Revitalizing Organizations', *Leadership & Organization Development Journal* 18: 325–34.

Burns, T. and G. M. Stalker (1961/1994), *The Management of Innovation*. London: Tavistock Publications.

Cameron, K. S., S. J. Freeman and A. K. Mishra (1991), 'Best Practices in White-Collar Downsizing: Managing Contradictions', *Academy of Management Executive* 5: 57–73.

Cascio, W. F. (1993), 'Downsizing: What Do We Know? What Have We Learned?' *Academy of Management Executive* 7: 95–104.

Cascio, W. F. (1998), 'Learning from Outcomes: Financial Experiences of 311 Firms that have Downsized', in M. K. Gowing, J. D. Kraft and J. C. Quick (eds.), *The New Organizational Reality: Downsizing, Restructuring and Revitalization*. Washington, DC: American Psychological Association.

Cascio, W. F. (2002a), *Responsible Restructuring: Creative and Profitable Alternatives to Layoffs*. San Francisco: Berrett-Koehler.

Cascio, W. F. (2002b), 'Strategies for Responsible Restructuring', *Academy of Management Executive* 16: 80–91.

Cascio, W. F. (2006), 'Decency Means More than "Always Low Prices": A Comparison of CostCo to Wal-Mart's Sam's Club', *Academy of Management Perspectives* 20: 26–37.

Castells, M. (2000), *The Rise of the Network Society*. Oxford: Blackwell, 2nd edition.

Chandler, A. (1977), *The Visible Hand: The Managerial Revolution in American Business*. Cambridge, MA: Harvard University Press.

Collins, J. (2001), *Good to Great: Why Some Companies Make the Leap – and Others Don't*. New York: Harper Business.

Cornfield, D. B., K. E. Campbell and H. J. McCammon (eds.) (2001), *Working in Restructured Workplaces*. London: Sage.

Danford, A. (1998), 'Work Organisations in Japanese Firms in South Wales: A Break from Taylorism?' in P. Thompson and C. Warhurst (eds.), *Workplaces of the Future*. London: Macmillan Business.

Delbridge, R. (1998), *Life on the Line in Contemporary Manufacturing: The Workplace Experience of Lean Production and the 'Japanese' Model.* Oxford University Press.

DiMaggio, P. J. and W. W. Powell (eds.) (1991), *The New Institutionalism in Organizational Analysis.* University of Chicago Press.

Doogan, K. (2001), 'Insecurity and Long-Term Employment', *Work, Employment and Society* 15: 419–41.

Dore, R. (1973), *British Factory, Japanese Factory, The Origins of Diversity in Industrial Relations.* London: Allen and Unwin.

Dore, R. (1987), *Taking Japan Seriously.* London: Athlone.

Dore, R. (1996), 'The End of Jobs for Life? Corporate Employment Systems: Japan and Elsewhere', LSE Centre for Economic Performance Occasional Paper no 11. available at: http://cep.lse.ac.uk/pubs/download/occasional/OP011.pdf

Dore, R. (2000), *Stock Market Capitalism: Welfare Capitalism: Japan and Germany versus the Anglo-Saxons.* Oxford University Press.

Dore, R. (2002), 'Stock Market Capitalism and its Diffusion', *New Political Economy* 7: 115–21.

Dore, R. (2004), 'The Americanization of Japanese Corporate Companies: How Far Has it Come, How Far Will it Go?' Paper presented to Centre for Japanese Studies, Cardiff, October.

Downs, A. (1995), *Corporate Executions: The Ugly Truth About Layoffs – How Corporate Greed is Shattering Lives, Companies and Communities.* New York: Amacom.

Drucker, P. (1947), *Big Business: A Study of Political Problems of American Capitalism.* London: W. Heinemann.

Dudley, K. M. (1994), *End of the Line: Lost Jobs, New Lives in Postindustrial America.* University of Chicago Press.

du Gay, P. (2000), *In Praise of Bureaucracy: Weber, Organization, Ethics.* London: Sage.

Dutton, J. E. and S. J. Ashford (1993), 'Selling Issues to Top Management', *Academy of Management Review* 18: 397–428.

Dutton, J. E., S. J. Ashford, R. M. O'Neill, E. Hayes and E. E. Weirba (1997), 'Reading the Wind: How Middle Managers Assess the Context for Selling Issues to Top Managers', *Strategic Management Journal* 18: 407–25.

Earley, J. S. (1956), 'Marginal Policies of "Excellently Managed" Companies', *The American Economic Review* 46 (1): 44–70.

Eastman, W. (1998), 'Working for Position: Women, Men, and Managerial Work Hours', *Industrial Relations* 37: 51–66.

Edwards, R. (1979), *Contested Terrain: The Transformation of the Workplace in the Twentieth Century.* London: Heinemann.

Erturk, I., J. Froud, S. Johal and K. Williams (2004), 'Pay for Corporate Performance or Pay as Social Division? Rethinking the Problem of Top Management Pay in Giant Corporations', *Competition & Change* 9: 49–74.

Fevre, R. (2007), 'Employment Security and Social Theory: The Power of Nightmares', *Work, Employment and Society* 21: 517–35.

Fine, L. M. (2004), *The Story of Reo Joe: Work, Kin and Community in Autotown, USA*. Philadelphia: Temple University Press.

Fisher, S. R. and M. A. White (2000), 'Downsizing in a Learning Organization: Are There Hidden Costs?' *Academy of Management Review* 25 (1): 244–51.

Fishman, C. (2006), 'The Wal-Mart Effect and a Decent Society: Who Knew Shopping was so Important?' *Academy of Management Perspectives* 20: 6–25.

Fraser, J. A. (2001), *White-Collar Sweat-Shop: The Deterioration of Work and its Rewards in Corporate America*. New York: W. W. Norton.

Friedman, A. (1977), *Industry and Labour: Class Struggle at Work and Monopoly Capitalism*. London: Macmillan.

Froud, J., S. Haslam, S. Johal and K. Williams (2000a), 'Shareholder Value and Financialization: Consultancy Promises, Management Moves', *Economy and Society* 29: 80–110.

Froud, J., C. Haslam, S. Johal and K. Williams (2000b), 'Restructuring for Shareholder Value and its Implications for Labour', *Cambridge Journal of Economics* 24 (6): 771–97.

Froud, J., S. Johal, A. Leaver and K. Williams (2006), *Financialization and Strategy: Narrative and Numbers*. Abingdon: Routledge.

Froud, J. and K. Williams (2007), 'Private Equity and the Culture of Value Extraction', *New Political Economy* 12 (3): 405–20.

Galbraith, J. K. (1967), *The New Industrial State*. Boston: Houghton Mifflin.

Garrow, V. and E. Stirling (2007), *The Management Agenda 2007*. Horsham: Roffey Park.

Gedajlovic, E., T. Yoshikawa and M. Hashimoto (2005), 'Ownership Structure, Investment Behaviour and Firm Performance in Japanese Manufacturing Industries', *Organisation Studies* 26 (7): 35.

Gerlach, M. L. (1992), *Alliance Capitalism: The Social Organization of Japanese Business*. Berkeley: University of California Press.

Gershon, P. (2004), *Releasing Resources to the Front Line, Independent Review of Public Sector Efficiency*. London: HM Treasury, available at: www.hm-treasury.gov.uk/media//879E2/efficiency_review120704.pdf

Ghoshal, S. (2005), 'Bad Management Theories are Destroying Good Management Practices', *Academy of Management Learning & Education* 4: 75–91.

Giddens, A. (2000), *The Runaway World: How Globalisation is Reshaping our Lives*. London: Profile.

Gifford, J., J. Hennessey, D. Boury and A. Sinclair (2009), *The Management Agenda 2009*. Horsham: Roffey Park.

Glyn, A. (2006), *Capitalism Unleashed: Finance, Globalization and Welfare*. Oxford University Press.

Godard, J. (2004), 'A Critical Assessment of the High Performance Paradigm', *British Journal of Industrial Relations* 42 (2): 348–78.

Golding, T. (2003), *The City: Inside the Great Expectation Machine*. London: FT Prentice Hall.

Gordon, D. M. (1996), *Fat and Mean: The Corporate Squeeze of Working Americans and the Myth of Corporate "Downsizing"*. New York: Free Press.

Gowing, M. K., J. D. Kraft and J. C. Quick (eds.) (1998), *The New Organizational Reality: Downsizing, Restructuring, and Revitalization*. Washington, DC: American Psychological Association.

Graham, F. (2003), *Inside the Japanese Company*. London: RoutledgeCurzon.

Graham, F. (2005), *A Japanese Company in Crisis: Ideology, Strategy, and Narrative*. Abingdon: RoutledgeCurzon.

Graham, L. (1995), *On the Line at Subaru-Isuzu*. Ithaca: Cornell University Press.

Green, F. (2001), 'It's Been a Hard Day's Night: The Concentration and Intensification of Work in Late Twentieth-Century Britain', *British Journal of Industrial Relations* 39: 53–80.

Green, F. (2006), *Demanding Work: The Paradox of Job Quality in the Affluent Economy*. New Jersey: Princeton University Press.

Grimshaw, D., K. Ward, J. Rubery and H. Beynon (2001), 'Organisations and the Transformation of the Internal Labour Market', *Work, Employment and Society* 15: 25–54.

Hales, C. (1999), 'Bureaucracy-lite and Continuities in Managerial Work', *British Journal of Management* 13: 51–66.

Hall, P. A. and D. Soskice (eds.) (2001), *Varieties of Capitalism: The Institutional Foundations of Comparative Advantage*. Oxford University Press.

Hammer, M. and J. Champy (1993), *Re-engineering the Corporation: A Manifesto for Business Revolution*. New York: HarperCollins.

Hamper, B. (1992), *Rivethead: Tales from the Assembly Line*. New York: Warner Books.

Handel, M. (ed.) (2003), *Sociology of Organizations: Classical, Contemporary and Critical Readings*. London: Sage.

Hasegawa, H. and G. D. Hook (eds.) (1997), *Japanese Business Management: Restructuring for Low Growth and Globalization*. London: Routledge.

Hassard, J. (1993), *Sociology and Organizational Theory*. Cambridge University Press.

Hassard, J., L. McCann and J. Morris (2007), 'At the Sharp End of New Organizational Ideologies: Ethnography and the Study of Multinationals', *Ethnography* 8 (3): 324–44.

Hatano, T. (1995/2005), 'Executive Commentary on Jeffrey Pfeffer's article "Producing Sustainable Competitive Advantage Through the Effective Management of People"', *Academy of Management Executive* 9: 69–71; and reprinted in *Academic of Management Executive* 19: 106–7.

Health and Safety Executive (2004), *Interim update of the "Costs to Britain of Workplace Accidents and Work-Related Ill-Health"*. Sudbury, HSE Books, available at: www.hse.gov.uk/statistics/pdf/costs.pdf

Health and Safety Executive (2005), *Health and Safety Statistics 2004/5*, Sudbury, HSE Books, available at: www.hse.gov.uk/statistics/overall/hssh0405.pdf

Heckscher, C. (1996), *White Collar Blues*. New York: Basic Books.

Heckscher, C. and A. Donnellon (eds.) (1994), *The Post-Bureaucratic Organisation: New Perspectives on Organisational Change*. London: Sage.

Helfat, C. E., D. Harris and P. J. Wolfson (2006), 'Women and Men in the Top Executive Ranks of US Corporations', *Academy of Management Perspectives* 20 (4): 42–64.

Hirst, P. and Thompson, G. (1999), *Globalization in Question*. Cambridge: Polity, 2nd edition.

Hirst, P. and J. Zeitlin (eds.) (1990), *Reversing Industrial Decline*. Oxford: Blackwell.

Hite, L. M. (2007), 'Hispanic Women Managers and Professionals: Reflections on Life and Work', *Gender, Work and Organization* 14: 20–36.

Hochschild, A. R. (1997), *The Time Bind: When Work Becomes Home and Home Becomes Work*. New York: Metropolitan Books.

Hochschild, A. R. (2003), *The Second Shift*. London: Penguin, 2nd edition.

Hutton, W. (1995), *The State We're In: Why Britain is in Crisis and How to Overcome It*. London: Jonathan Cape.

Huy, Q. N. (2001), 'In Praise of Middle Managers', *Harvard Business Review* 79: 72–9.

Iida, T. and J. Morris (2008), 'Farewell to the Salaryman? The Changing Roles and Work of Middle Managers in Japan', *International Journal of Human Resource Management* 19: 1074–89.

Ikeda, M. (1998), 'Globalization's Impact on the Subcontract System', in H. Hasegawa and G. Hook (eds.), *Japanese Business Mangement*. London: Routledge.

Inagami, T. (2001), 'From Industrial Relations to Investor Relations? Persistence and Change in Japanese Corpoate Governance, Employment Practices and Industrial Relations', *Social Science Japan Journal* 4: 225–41.

Jackall, R. (1988), *Moral Mazes: Inside the World of Corporate Managers*. Oxford University Press.

Jackson, G. (2002), 'Financial Markets and the Corporation', *New Political Economy* 7: 121–24.

Jacoby, S. M. (1997), *Employing Bureaucracy: Managers, Unions and the Transformation of Work in American Industry 1900–1945*. New York: Columbia University Press.

Jacoby, S. M. (2005), *The Embedded Corporation: Corporate Governance and Employment Relations in Japan and the United States*. Princeton University Press.

Jacoby, S. M., E. M. Nason and S. Kazuro (2005), 'Corporate Organization in Japan and the United States – Is there Evidence of Convergence?' *Social Science Japan Journal* 8: 43–68.

Jaikumar, R. (1986), 'Postindustrial Manufacturing', *Harvard Business Review* 64 (6), 69–76.

Jenkins, J. (2007), 'Gambling Partners? The Risky Outcomes of Workplace Partnerships', *Work, Employment and Society* 21: 635–52.

Kamata, S. (1973), *Japan in the Passing Lane: An Insider's Account of Life in a Japanese Auto Factory*. London: Allen & Unwin.

Kanter, R. M. (1977), *Men and Women of the Corporation*. New York: Basic Books.

Kanter, R. M. (1989a), *When Giants Learn to Dance: Mastering the Challenges of Strategy, Management and Careers in the 1990s*. London: Simon and Shuster.

Kanter, R. M. (1989b), 'The New Managerial Work', *Harvard Business Review* 67 (6): 85–92.

Kaplan, R. S. and D. P. Norton (1996), *The Balanced Scorecard: Translating Strategy into Action*. Boston: Harvard Business School Press.

Katz, R. (1998), *Japan: The System that Soured*. London: M. E. Sharpe.

Kaysen, C. (1957), 'The Social Significance of the Modern Corporation', *American Economic Review* 47 (2): 311–19.

Kenney, M. and R. Florida (1993), *Beyond Mass Production: The Japanese System and its Transfer to the US*. Oxford University Press.

Kersley, B., S. Oxenbridge, G. Dix, H. Bewley, A. Bryson, J. Forth and C. Alpin (2006), *Inside the Workplace: Findings from the 2004 Workplace Employee Relations Survey*. London: Routledge.

Korczynski, M. (2001), *Human Resource Management in Service Work*. Basingstoke: Palgrave.

Kosai, Y. (2002), 'A Reformist's View of Japanese Reform', *New Political Economy* 7: 124–5.

Kumar, K. (2005), *From Post-Industrial to Post-Modern Society*. Oxford: Blackwell, 2nd edition.

Kwan, C. H. (2002), 'Japan is Cursed by Gresham's Law: Let Darwin's Law Rule', *Miyakodayori* **43**, available at: www.rieti.go.jp/en/miyakodayori/043.html?mode=print

Lamar, J. (2000), 'Suicides in Japan Reach a Record High', *British Medical Journal* 321: 528.

Layard, R. *et al.* (2006), *The Depression Report: A New Deal for Depression and Anxiety Disorders*. London School of Economics, Centre for Economic Performance, available at: http://cep.lse.ac.uk/textonly/research/mentalhealth/DEPRESSION_REPORT_LAYARD.pdf

Lazonick, W. and M. O'Sullivan (2000), 'Maximising Shareholder Value: A New Ideology for Corporate Governance?' *Economy and Society* 29: 13–35.

Leavitt, H. (2007), 'Big Organizations are Unhealthy Environments for Human Beings', *Academy of Management Learning & Education* 62 (2): 253–63.

Liker, J. K. and J. M. Morgan (2006), 'The Toyota Way in Services: The Case of Lean Product Development', *Academy of Management Perspectives* 20: 5–20.

Littler, C. D. and G. Salaman (1982), 'Bravermania and Beyond: Recent Theories of the Labour Process', *Sociology* 16: 251–69.

Littler, C. R. (1982), *The Development of the Labour Process in Capitalist Societies*. London: Heinemann Education.

Littler, C. R. (2006), '*A Signalling Theory of Strategy*'. Paper presented to Academy of Management Annual Conference, Atlanta, Georgia.

Littler, C. R. and P. Innes (2004), 'The Paradox of Managerial Downsizing', *Organization Studies* 25: 1159–84.

Lowe, J., J. Morris and B. Wilkinson (2002), 'British Factory, Japanese Factory and Mexican Factory: An International Comparison of Front Line Management and Supervision', *Journal of Management Studies* 37: 541–62.

Mandel, E. (1971/1999), *Late Capitalism*. London: Verso.

March, J. G. and H. A. Simon (1958), *Organizations*. New York: Wiley.

Marchington, M., D. Grimshaw and J. Rubery (eds.) (2004), *Fragmenting Work: Blurring Organizational Boundaries and Disordering Hierarchies*. Oxford University Press.

Matanle, P. (2003), *Japanese Capitalism and Modernity in a Global Era: Re-fabricating Lifetime Employment Relations*. New York: Oxford University Press.

Maxton, G. P. and J. Wormald (2004), *Time for a Model Change: Re-engineering the Global Automotive Industry*. Cambridge University Press.

McCann, L., J. Hassard and J. Morris (2004), 'Middle Managers, the New Organizational Ideology, and Corporate Restructuring: Comparing

Japanese and Anglo-American Management Structures', *Competition & Change* 8: 27–44.

McCann, L., J. Morris and J. Hassard (2008), 'Normalized Intensity: The New Labour Process of Middle Management', *Journal of Management Studies* 45: 343–71.

McCraw, T. K. and R. S. Tedlow (1997), 'Henry Ford, Alfred Sloan, and the Three Phases of Marketing', in T. K McCraw (ed.) *Creating Modern Capitalism: How Entrepreneurs, Companies, and Countries Triumphed in Three Industrial Revolutions*. Cambridge, MA: Harvard University Press.

McGovern, P., V. Hope-Hadley and P. Stiles (1998), 'The Managerial Career after Downsizing: Case Studies from the Leading Edge', *Work, Employment and Society* 12: 457–77.

McKinlay, A. (2005), 'Knowledge Management', in S. Ackroyd, R. Batt., P. Thompson and P. Tolbert (eds.) *Oxford Handbook of Work and Organization*. Oxford University Press.

McLean, B., and P. Elkind (2004), *The Smartest Guys in the Room: The Amazing Rise and Scandalous Fall of Enron*. New York: Viking.

Mehri, D. (2005), *Notes from Toyota-Land: An American Engineer in Japan*. Ithaca: Cornell University Press.

Mehri, D. (2006), 'The Darker Side of Lean', *Academy of Management Perspectives* 20: 21–42.

Meiksins, P. (1994), 'Labor and Monopoly Capital for the 1990s: A Review and Critique of the Labor Process Debate', *Monthly Review* 46: 45–59.

Milkman, R. (1997), *Farewell to the Factory: Auto Workers in the Late Twentieth Century*. Berkeley: University of California Press.

Milkman, R. (1998), 'The New American Workplace: High Road or Low Road?' in P. Thompson and C. Warhurst (eds.), *Workplaces of the Future*. London: Macmillan Business.

Mills, C. W. (1953), *White Collar: The American Middle Classes*. Oxford University Press.

Mintzberg, H. (1973), *The Nature of Managerial Work*. New York: Harper and Row.

Moore, M. (1997), *Downsize This!* London: Boxtree.

Morris, J., M. Munday and B. Wilkinson (1993), *Working for the Japanese*. London: Athlone.

Morris, J., B. Wilkinson and J. Gamble (2008), 'Strategic International Human Resource Management or the "Bottom Line"? The Cases of Electronics and Garments Commodity Chains in China', *International Journal of Human Resource Management*, in press.

Mouer, R. and H. Kawanishi (2005), *A Sociology of Work in Japan*. Cambridge University Press.

Noer, D. (1993), *Healing the Wounds: Overcoming the Trauma of Layoffs and Revitalizing Downsizing Organizations*. San Francisco: Jossey-Bass.

Noer, D. (1998), 'Survivor Sickness: What it is and What to do About it', in M. K. Gowing, J. D. Kraft and J. Quick (eds.) *The New Organizational Reality: Downsizing, Restructuring, and Revitalization*. American Psychological Association Press, Washington, DC.

O'Doherty, D. and H. Willmott (2001), 'Debating Labour Process Theory: The Issue of Subjectivity and the Relevance of Poststructuralism', *Sociology* 36: 457–76.

Ogasawara, Y. (1998), *Office Ladies and Salaried Men*. Berkeley: University of California Press.

Ohmae, K. (1994), *The Borderless World: Power and Strategy in the Interlinked World*. London: HarperCollins.

O'Sullivan, M. (2000), *Contests for Corporate Control*. Oxford University Press.

Osborne, D. and T. Gaebler (1992), *Reinventing Government*. Wokingham: Addison Wesley.

Osterman, P. (ed.) (1996), *Broken Ladders: Managerial Careers in the New Economy*, Oxford University Press.

Osterman, P., L. Kochan, R. M. Locke and M. Piore (2001), *Working in America: A Blueprint for a New Labour Market*. Cambridge, MA: MIT Press.

Penn, R. and H. Scattergood (1985), 'Deskilling or Enskilling?: and Empirical Investigation of Recent Theories of the Labour Process', *British Journal of Sociology* 36: 611–30.

Peters, T. (1992), *Liberation Management*. New York: Macmillan.

Peters, T. and R. M. Waterman (1987), *In Search of Excellence*. New York: Harper and Row.

Pfeffer, J. (1995/2005), 'Producing Sustainable Competitive Advantage Through the Effective Management of People', *Academy of Management Executive* 9: 55–69; and reprinted in *Academy of Management Perspectives* 19: 95–106.

Pfeffer, J. (1998), 'Six Dangerous Myths About Pay', *Harvard Business Review*, May-June 1998: 108–119.

Porter, M. E. (1990), *The Competitive Advantage of Nations*. Basingstoke: Macmillan.

Porter, M. E., M. Takeuchi and M. Sakakibara (2000), *Can Japan Compete?* London: Macmillan.

Porter, M. E. and C. H. M. Ketels (2003), *UK Competitiveness: Moving to the Next Stage*. London: ESRC.

Porter, M. E., K. Schwab and A. Lopez-Claros (2005), *The Global Competitiveness Report*. Basingstoke: Macmillan.

Rapoport, R., L. Bailyn, J. K. Fletcher and B. H. Pruitt (2002), *Beyond Work-Family Balance*. San Francisco: Jossey-Bass.

Ray, L. J. and A. Sayer (eds.) (1999), *Culture and Economy after the Cultural Turn*. London: Sage.

Rayner, C., H. Hoel and C. Cooper (2001), *Workplace Bullying: What do we Know? Who is to Blame? And What can we Do?* London: Taylor & Francis.

Reed, M. (2005), 'Reflections on the "Realist Turn" in Organization and Management Studies', *Journal of Management Studies* 42: 1621–44.

Reich, R. (1991), *The Work of Nations: Preparing Ourselves for 21st Century Capitalism*. London: Simon & Shuster.

Reis, C. (2004), *Men Working as Managers in a European Multinational Company*. Mering, Germany: Rainer Hampp Verlag.

Robinson, P. and N. Shimizu (2006), 'Japanese Corporate Restructuring: CEO Priorities as a Window on Environmental and Organizational Change', *Academy of Management Perspectives* 20: 44–75.

Rohlen, T. P. (1974), *For Harmony and Strength: Japanese White-Collar Organization in Anthropological Perspective*. Berkeley, CA: University of California Press.

Roth, L. M. (2007), 'Women on Wall Street: Despite Diversity Measures, Wall Street Remains Vulnerable to Sex Discrimination Charges', *Academy of Management Perspectives* 21: 24–35.

Rubery, J. and D. Grimshaw (2002), *The Organization of Employment*. Basingstoke: Palgrave.

Sako, M. (2006), *Shifting Boundaries of the Firm: Japanese Company – Japanese Labour*. Oxford University Press.

Sallaz, J. (2004), 'Manufacturing Concessions: Attritionary Outsourcing at General Motors' Lordstown, USA Assembly Plant', *Work, Employment and Society* 18: 687–708.

Schor, J. B. (1992), *The Overworked American: The Unexpected Decline of Leisure*. New York: Basic Books.

Sennett, R. (1998), *The Corrosion of Character: The Personal Consequences of Work in the New Capitalism*. London: W. W. Norton.

Sewell, G. (2005), 'Nice Work? Rethinking Managerial Control in an Era of Knowledge Work', *Organization* 12: 685–704.

Shiller, R. J. (2008), *Sub-prime Solutions: How Today's Global Financial Crisis Happened, and What to Do About it*. Princeton University Press.

Sims, D. (2003), 'Between the Millstones: A Narrative Account of the Vulnerability of Middle Managers' Storying', *Human Relations* 56 (10): 1195–1211.

Sklair, L. (2001), *The Transnational Capitalist Class*. Oxford: Blackwell.

Smith, V. (1990), *Managing in the Corporate Interest*. Berkeley: University of California Press.

Smith, R. C. and I. Walter (2006), *Governing the Modern Corporation, Capital Markets, Corporate Control, and Economic Performance*. Oxford University Press.

Starkey, K. and A. McKinlay (1994), 'Managing for Ford', *Sociology* 28: 975–90.

Stinchcombe, A. (1974), *Creating Efficient Industrial Administrations*. New York: Academic Press.

Sveningsson, S. and M. Alvesson (2003), 'Managing Managerial Identities: Organizational Fragmentation, Discourse, and Identity Struggle', *Human Relations* 56: 1163–93.

Taft, D. and G. Singh (2003), 'Executive Compensation: A Comparison of the United States and Japan', *Compensation and Benefits Review* 35, 3.

Taylor, F. W. (1911), *The Principles of Scientific Management*. New York: Harper & Brothers.

Tengblad, S. (2006), 'Is there a 'New Managerial Work'? A Comparison with Henry Mintzberg's Classic Study 30 Years Later', *Journal of Management Studies* 43: 1437–61.

Teulings, A. W. M. (1986), 'Managerial Labour Process in Organised Capitalism: The Power of Corporate Management and the Powerlessness of the Manager', in D. Knights and H. Willmott (eds.), *Managing the Labour Process*. Aldershot: Gower.

Thomas, R. and D. Dunkerley (1999), 'Careering Downwards? Middle Managers' Experiences in the Downsized Organization', *British Journal of Management* 10: 157–69.

Thomas, R. and A. Linstead (2002), 'Losing the Plot? Middle Managers and Identity', *Organization* 9: 71–93.

Thompson, P. (2003), 'Disconnected Capitalism: or why Employers Can't Keep Their Side of the Bargain', *Work, Employment and Society* 17: 359–78.

Thompson, P. and S. Ackroyd (1995), 'All Quiet on the Workplace Front? A Critique of Recent Trends in British Industrial Sociology', *Sociology* 29: 615–33.

Thompson, P. and S. Ackroyd (2005), 'A Little Knowledge is Still a Dangerous Thing: Some Comments on the Indeterminacy of Graham Sewell', *Organization* 12: 705–10.

Tinker, T. (2002), 'Spectres of Marx and Braverman in the Twilight of Postmodernist Labour Process Research', *Work, Employment and Society* 16: 251–81.

Trist, E. L., G. W. Higgin, H. Murray and A. B. Pollack (1963), *Organizational Choice: Capabilities of Groups at the Coal Face Under Changing Technologies, The Loss, Re-discovery & Transformation of a Work Tradition*. London: Tavistock.

Vitols, S. (2001), 'The Origins of Bank-Based and Market-Based Financial Systems: Germany, Japan and the United States', in W. Streeck and K. Yamamura (eds.) (2001), *The Origins of Non-Liberal Capitalism: Germany and Japan in Comparison*. Ithaca: Cornell University Press.

Vogel, E. F. (1980), *Japan as Number One*. New York: HarperCollins.

Wajcman, J. (1998), *Managing Like a Man: Women and Men in Corporate Management*. Cambridge: Polity.

Walker, G. (2006), 'Review of Jim Collins' (2001) *Good to Great*', *Academy of Management Perspectives* 20: 120–1.

Watanabe, S. (2000), 'The Japan Model and the Future of Employment and Wage Systems', *International Labour Review* 139 (3): 307–33.

Watts, J. H. (2009), 'Allowed into a Man's World – Meanings of Work-Life Balance: Perspectives of Women Civil Engineers as 'Minority' Workers in Construction', *Gender, Work and Organization* 16 (10), 37–57.

Werther, W. B. Jr. (2003), 'Enron: The Forgotten Middle', *Organization* 10 (3): 568–71.

White, M., S. Hill, C. Mills and D. Smeaton (2004), *Managing to Change? British Workplaces and the Future of Work*. London: Palgrave.

Whitley, R. (1999), *Divergent Capitalisms: The Social Structuring and Change of Business Systems*. Oxford University Press.

Whitley, R., G. Morgan, W. Kelly and D. Sharpe (2003), 'The Changing Japanese Multinational: Application, Adaptation and Learning in Car Manufacturing and Financial Services', *Journal of Management Studies* 40, 3: 643–72.

Whyte, W. H. (1960), *The Organization Man*. London: Penguin.

Williams, K. (2000), 'From Shareholder Value to Present-Day Capitalism', *Economy and Society* 29, 1: 1–12.

Williams, K., C. Haslam, S. Johal and J. Williams (1994), *Cars: Analysis, History, Cases*. Providence, RI: Berghahn Books.

Witt, M. A. (2006), *Changing Japanese Capitalism: Societal Coordination and Institutional Adjustment*. Cambridge University Press.

Womack, J. P., D. T. Jones and D. Roos (1990/2007), *The Machine that Changed the World: How Lean Production Revolutionized the Global Car Wars*. London: Simon & Shuster.

Worrall, L., F. K. Campbell and C. L. Cooper (2000), 'The New Reality for UK Managers: Perpetual Change and Employment Instability', *Work, Employment and Society* 14, 4: 647–68.

Worrall, L. and C. L. Cooper (2001), *The Quality of Working Life: 2000 Survey of Managers' Changing Experiences*. London: Institute of Management.

Zucchino, D. (2004), *Thunder Run: The Armored Strike to Capture Baghdad*. New York: Atlantic Monthly Press.

Index